Production Standards
for Profit Planning

Books by Spencer A. Tucker

SUCCESSFUL MANAGERIAL CONTROL BY RATIO-ANALYSIS
McGraw-Hill Book Company, New York, 1961

COST-ESTIMATING AND PRICING WITH MACHINE-HOUR RATES
Prentice-Hall, Inc., Englewood Cliffs, New Jersey, 1962

THE BREAK-EVEN SYSTEM: A Tool for Profit Planning
Prentice-Hall, Inc., Englewood Cliffs, New Jersey, 1963

PRICING FOR HIGHER PROFIT: CRITERIA, METHODS, APPLICATIONS
McGraw-Hill Book Company, New York, 1966

THE COMPLETE MACHINE-HOUR RATE SYSTEM FOR COST-ESTIMATING AND PRICING
Prentice-Hall, Inc., Englewood Cliffs, New Jersey, 1975

CREATIVE PRICING FOR THE PRINTING AND ALLIED INDUSTRIES
North American Publishing Company, Philadelphia, Pennsylvania, 1975

HANDBOOK OF BUSINESS FORMULAS AND CONTROLS
McGraw-Hill Book Company, New York, 1979

PROFIT PLANNING DECISIONS WITH THE BREAK-EVEN SYSTEM
Thomond Press, New York 1980

Foreign Translations

Japanese Translation of SUCCESSFUL MANAGERIAL CONTROL BY RATIO-ANALYSIS
Charles E. Tuttle Company, Tokyo, 1964

CONTROL DE GESTION (METHODO DE LOS RATIOS)
Editorial Hispano Europea, Barcelona, 1968

L'ÉVALUATION DES COÛTS ET LA DÉTERMINATION DES PRIX PAR LA MÉTHODE THM
Enterprise Moderne D'Edition, Paris, 1965

BREAK-EVEN ANALYSE: DIE PRAKTISCHE METHODE DER GEWINN-PLANUNG
Verlag Moderne Industrie, Munich, 1966

EL SISTEMA DEL EQUILIBRIO: INSTRUMENTO PARA LA PLANIFICACION DE LAS UTILIDADES
Herrero Hermanos Sucs., Mexico City, 1966

WINST EN WINSTPLANNING
Samson Uitgeverji BV., Alphen Aan Den Rijn, Holland, 1968

POLITICA DE PRECIOS
Ediciones Deusto, Bilbao, Spain, 1971

German Translation of SUCCESSFUL MANAGERIAL CONTROL BY RATIO-ANALYSIS
Verband Für Arbeitsstudien REFA E.V., Darmstadt, Germany, 1966

Production Standards for Profit Planning

Spencer A. Tucker, Ph.D., P.E., C.P.P.

President, Martin & Tucker, Inc., Management Consultants
Managing Director, Profit Planning & Management Institute

Thomas H. Lennon, P.E., C.P.P.

Vice President, Martin & Tucker, Inc., Management Consultants
Senior Lecturer, Profit Planning & Management Institute

VNR VAN NOSTRAND REINHOLD COMPANY
NEW YORK   CINCINNATI   TORONTO   LONDON   MELBOURNE

Library of Congress Catalog Card Number: 81-14743
ISBN: 0-442-88016-2

Manufactured in the United States of America

Published by Van Nostrand Reinhold Company
135 West 50th Street, New York, N.Y. 10020

Van Nostrand Reinhold Limited
1410 Birchmount Road
Scarborough, Ontario M1P 2E7, Canada

Van Nostrand Reinhold Australia Pty. Ltd.
17 Queen Street
Mitcham, Victoria 3132, Australia

Van Nostrand Reinhold Company Limited
Molly Millars Lane
Wokingham, Berkshire, England

15 14 13 12 11 10 9 8 7 6 5 4 3 2 1

Library of Congress Cataloging in Publication Data

Tucker, Spencer A.
    Production standards for profit planning.

    Includes index.
    1. Production standards. I. Lennon, Thomas H.
II. Title.
T60.3.T83   1982   658.5'4   81-14743
ISBN 0-442-88016-2   AACR2

For Our Grandchildren
and
the Memory of Natalie

Contents

Preface

The basis for developing and presenting anything new is need. The new approach given in this book is to prove the direct impact that production standards have on company profits.

Making a profit is not a novel idea. It is after all the reason you are in business. Therefore, it is the responsibility of management to exploit every opportunity to insure a satisfactory return on the company's total capital employed.

Modern profit planning as the new business science, affords an opportunity to every company for creating a program to determine the sources of profit potential, while providing the necessary disciplines for controlling everyday activities. During the next decade, with more and more indeterminate problems besetting managements, profit planning will emerge as the single most important technique.

Cost is the base from which profits are measured. One-half of the cost equation is time—operational time of production facilities used to make the product. As such, time expressed as production standards is the most crucial and irreplaceable element in establishing the vital link between goods produced and the company's "bottom line."

This book was written with these purposes in mind:

To demonstrate the indispensable need for production standards in all areas of a company's economy.

To acquaint the profit planner, or anyone else involved in any aspect of company operations, with the basic ingredients of production standards.

To provide the user with a step-by-step approach to observe the impact on profits caused by varying qualities of standards setting.

To provide a simple, easily understood plan so that the profit planner or others can intelligently approach work measurement and thus police the manufacturing cost structure as a basis for price evaluation and other critical economic decisions.

To orient the reader to the language of timestudy and production standards; to know how standards are developed and constructed and to be able to question the developers intelligently.

As the first book of its kind ever written, it will also serve as a handbook and study guide for those candidates sitting for the professional designation, "Certified Profit Planner" (CPP) written examination.

With this knowledge in hand, the reader will be able to:

Analyze production and cost reports quickly and identify variances from standard.

Review the structure of production standards, based on the job and operational variables to test their equity.

Anticipate areas of potential departures from plan and thus be able to take action to avoid variances.

Identify in advance new product areas to determine their future production impact on profits.

Make profitable decisions for upgrading the manufacturing process to insure satisfactory performances and increase the potential for profit.

Purify the data by which decisions are to be made in the areas of:

Waste control

Cost estimating and pricing

Productivity and performance measurements

Make-or-buy

Scheduling and machine loading

Justifying capital expenditures

Alternate facility selection

To demonstrate the need for and techniques for using operational parameters in the development of proper production standards, the authors have included more than 40 actual standards taken from a wide cross section of industry.

It is *not* the intent of the authors to attempt to make industrial engineers or professional timestudy observers out of the reader. Nor do we expect the reader to set standards. We do want the reader to realize and know the effect that poor standards will have on the company's profits and the misleading effects that such standards will have in all areas of decision making.

New York, NY   S.A.T. and T.H.L.

Acknowledgments

The authors wish to thank Mr. Mori Spiegel and other staff members of
Martin & Tucker, Inc. for their valuable advice, suggestions, and
constructive comments in the preparation of the material. Special thanks is
given to Mr. Michael M. Tucker who reviewed and corrected formula
logic. Finally, our thanks are extended to Philip Schafer for his editorial
contribution.

S.A.T. and T.H.L.

List of Exhibits

Production Standards
for Profit Planning

1

How Long Will It Take and What Will It Cost?

No rational economic decision can be made in any manufacturing enterprise without the use of direct costs. Conventional or traditional forms of costing, principally whole or "full" absorption costing, obscure the identity and sources of company profit. This can lead to decisions that reduce rather than improve profit.

Direct costs are irreplaceable for the measurement of product costs, divisional and company profit, the economical use of facilities, and for providing rational management information. These elements are discussed in separate chapters.

In a manufacturing company, the standard cost of a production operation involves both the hourly cost of the process—known as the *machine-hour rate* (MHR)[1] (or the work center rate) and the amount of time to process the product through each of these work centers—known as *production standards* (PS). Thus, if an operation costs $20 per hour to run and it takes 15 minutes (0.25 hour) for the product to pass through that operation, the production cost is $20 × 0.25, or $5. Assuming that the direct hourly cost (MHR) is correct, then the resulting cost calculation is *solely* a function of the accuracy of the time value of 0.25 hour. Obviously, to the extent that the amount of time is misstated, the "cost" will appear to be above or below $5. In price evaluation, which leads to accept/reject decisions in the marketing area, this often overlooked factor of time equity will affect directly the company's entire profit structure. In effect, poor time values inadvertently prompt management to push the wrong product or order and reject profitable ones, and cause poor judgment in other areas of decision making.

---

[1]See Spencer A. Tucker, *The Complete Machine-Hour Rate System for Cost-Estimating and Pricing*, Englewood Cliffs, New Jersey: Prentice-Hall, Inc., 1975.

Time and Work

If you're paying someone to work, then time is money. The previous example of an operational time of 0.25 hour is an expression of working time; i.e., it takes 0.25 hour for the worker and/or worker and machine, to do that operation. The statement of time is an expression of work, and the amount of work determines the cost.

Work Measurement and Standard Time

To determine the time required to perform work, several procedures can be used, as will be discussed in later chapters. All involve various techniques and skills—work measurement tools. Work measurement can be defined as a technique for determining the amount of time required to perform a task or produce a unit of output. In determining this time, the timestudy engineer has to compare the working pace or speed observed during the operation, with the concept of what is believed to be "normal" for doing the job. Rating the worker or evaluating the machine speed and adding various time allowances (to be treated later) to this *normalized* time, result in a "standard time."

If the method by which a task is performed keeps changing, prompted either by management or the worker, then the original standard time cannot be applied consistently. Therefore, a time value can be considered a standard time *only* when related to a *standard method* of *production*; hence, the term *production standard* (PS).

Profit Planning

Profit planning, economic measurements, and the decision-making process require sound and reliable direct costs. The production cost segment of total direct costs requires sound and reliable production standards. If the PS are wrong by 20%, the resulting production costs will be wrong by exactly the same percentage. If the time values used are inaccurately low, the total cost will be understated resulting in less-than-expected profit, and vice versa.

Proper PS are required to make every economic evaluation in the firm, e.g., cost estimating, target pricing and price decisions, productivity measurements, waste reduction, facility profitability, make-or-buy determinations, scheduling and machine loading, justifying capital expenditures, evaluating economy of machine repairs and replacement, selecting the least costly method of processing the product (alternate facility selection), performance control, variance analysis and cost control, and production, sales and management incentive compensation plans. These are discussed and demonstrated in later chapters.

Production Standards and Industry Practices

Where do production standards come from? In the experience of the authors, company management states "We have them." And they make this response regardless of the form in which the "standards" exist, irrespective of their formality and consistency, or how they came into being. Thus, PS are perhaps supervisor's estimates, salespeople's guesses, management's judgments, historical performances, and so forth. But somehow, management seems to believe that it has the correct (and safe?) time values. It seems to us that this could simply be an exercise in ignoring the critical importance of PS.

In addition, they believe that developing PS can be "expensive and time consuming.'' We respond with ''lost profit contribution due to poor estimating can be more expensive and will directly affect the bottom line.'' A typical and damaging rationale is ''inaccuracy in time estimating will be compensated by higher volume!'' It is almost the same as saying that even though the company has booked marginal or loss-producing work (because of improper cost bases), they will make up for lost profits by booking more of the same!

2 Impact of Production Standards on Profit Planning

As stated earlier, direct costs are essential to all elements of profit planning. Production standards are exactly one-half of the cost equation. The basic cost equation for each operation involved in the production process is:

$$\text{Hourly Direct Cost of a Production Facility}$$
$$\text{Times the Standard Time to Process}$$
$$\text{the Product through that Facility.}$$

In simpler terms, direct production cost *per operation* used is:

MHR × PS

The accuracy of the hourly direct cost (MHR) figure does not insure the same accuracy in the operational cost. Likewise, accurate PS do not guarantee a correct operational cost. Both MHR and PS exert equal force on the final cost figure as shown on Exhibit 2–1.

Impact of PS on Cost Estimating

Cost estimating implies a predetermination of cost. This cost, which is expected to be incurred when the work is done, is then used as a basis for economic measurement and planning in the company. Therefore, cost estimating is a projection of costs, whether for job orders, products, parts, facility profitability, make-or-buy, etc.

In cost estimating for price evaluation (besides the obvious inclusion of materials and other direct-product/order costs), the total direct costs of an order or product must include the direct production costs that are expected to be incurred at every productive operation in the manufacturing process. The procedure calls for listing the sequence of operations required to produce the item and specifying for each the respective MHRs and standard times.

Exhibit 2–1
It Takes Two to Estimate

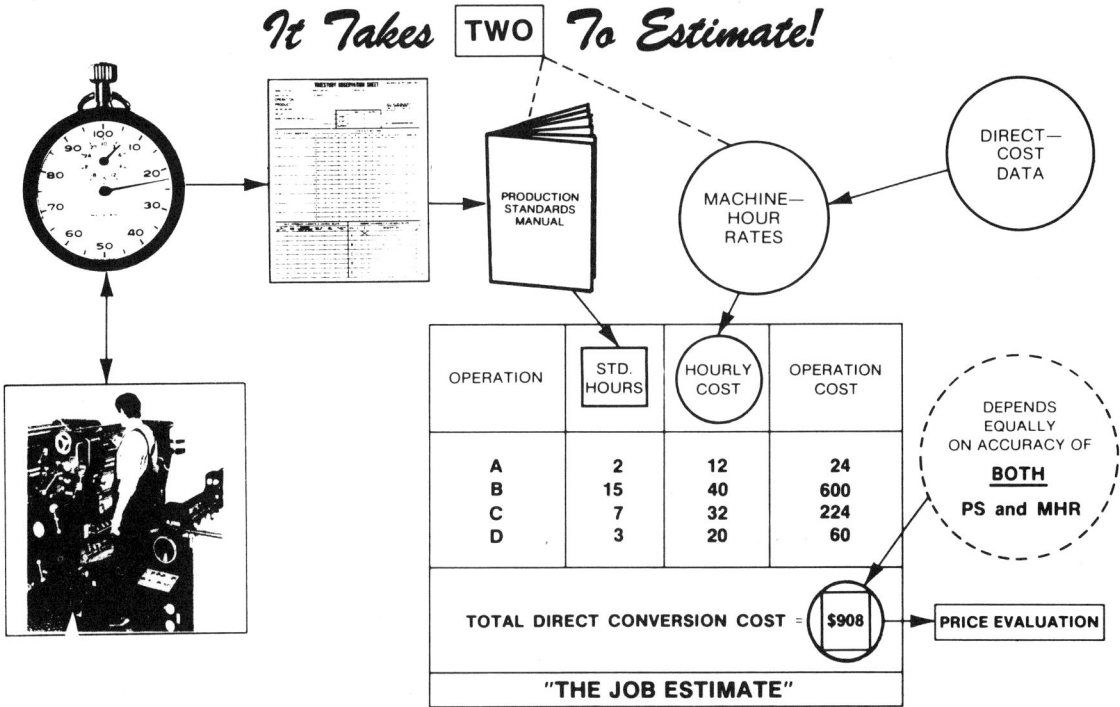

When these two factors are multiplied and totaled for all of the operations, the result is the total direct production cost, as shown in the following example:

	Quantity of Units Produced = 10,000				
	Production Standard		Hours		
Sequence of Operations	Standard Pieces per Hour	Standard Hours per M	Required for the Quantity	Direct MHR	Direct Production Cost
A	2,000	0.50	5.00	$23	$115
B	1,250	0.80	8.00	36	288
C	4,000	0.25	2.50	56	140
D	250	4.00	40.00	12	480
				Total	$1,023

If the above set of time values is found to be incorrect and 10% should be added to each PS, the correct total Direct Production Cost would be $1,125.30. The reader is urged to check this new cost figure by increasing by 10% the hours required for the quantity at each operation, thereby proving that whatever the error is in PS, that same error will be reflected in cost. It is obvious that where insufficient time is allowed, costs are understated and the company is misled in its profitability measurements. Where the reverse is true, the deception causes an overstatement of costs. In the former case, this can lead to booking unprofitable work; in the latter, losing what could have been profitable.

Engineered production standards are developed by people with professional skills in work measurement; therefore, they do not have any organizational bias. They favor no one and simply reflect objectively the work that is taking place. However, instead of these engineered PS, management sometimes shortcuts this professional necessity by using rules of thumb, supervisors' estimates, salespeople's estimates, historical data, trade association industry-wide statistics, or something else.

Varying Cost Estimates

In Exhibits 2–2 and 2–3, a cost estimate is prepared using supervisors' and salespeople's time estimates. As the reader will learn later, proper MHRs include a cost allowance for "subsidy" representing the difference between standard performance and the expected level of productivity. Where engineered standards are not available, an *estimate* for subsidy is included to call management's attention to the need for a more accurate subsidy figure once proper standards are available. For the purpose of these examples, however, we have not included a subsidy in these MHRs since we do not have a measurement of performance to compare these estimated "standards." This subject is treated later in the book.

Exhibit 2–2
"Allowed Hours"
Supplied by Supervisor,
Tending to be
Self-Protective[a]

Production Center	Estimated Run Speeds per Hour	Allowed Hours	Direct MHR	Direct Conversion Costs
Makeready				
Extruder-Lamin		5	$16.62	$ 83.10
8-Color Gravure		9	26.15	235.35
Run				
Extruder-Lamin	175 fpm	20	16.62	332.40
8-Color Gravure	300 fpm	11.67	26.15	305.17
Slit and Rewind	90 fpm	38.83	7.15	277.63
Wrap and Palletize		24	2.30	55.20

Direct Conversion Costs	$1288.85
Selling Price	$ 960.00
Profit Contribution	$ 328.85
PV Ratio	0.34

Comment
With this apparent loss figure, management is prompted to turn down the order. But is it really a bad order?

What would the direct conversion be if some one else gave management their opinion of "Allowed Hours"?

[a]See Exhibit 2.5 for summary.

Exhibit 2–2 shows an estimate based on allowed hours supplied by production supervisors—surely the type of information that is biased in their favor because they feel that they will be measured against these standards. As such, it is usually self-protective and causes an inflated cost.

Exhibit 2–3 is the same job estimated with the interested salespeople supplying the allowed hours. The bias here is caused by their drive for sales and commissions, which they feel could be increased if lower costs were used.

Exhibit 2–4 is still the same job estimated using engineered production standards.

It would be helpful to the reader to review the comments at the bottom of each of these exhibits.

Exhibit 2–5 is a summary of the resulting effect of different sources of PS.

Contribution and Price Evaluating

A review of terminology and concepts regarding Exhibits 2–2 through 2–5 is in order.

1. In certain industries, principally job shop or custom manufacturing, the term *conversion cost* is used. This term is synonymous with production cost.

**Exhibit 2–3
"Allowed Hours"
Supplied by the
Marketing People,
Tending to be Volume
and Commission
Motivated[a]**

Production Center	Estimated Run Speeds per Hour	Allowed Hours	Direct MHR	Direct Conversion Costs
Makeready				
Extruder-Lamin		2	$16.62	$ 33.24
8-Color Gravure		4	26.15	104.60
Run				
Extruder-Lamin	375 fpm	9.33	16.62	155.06
8-Color Gravure	750 fpm	4.67	26.15	122.12
Slit and Rewind	250 fpm	13.98	7.15	99.96
Wrap and Palletize		12	2.30	27.60

Direct Conversion Costs	$542.58
Selling Price	$960.00
Profit Contribution	$417.42
PV Ratio	0.435

Comment.
With this apparent profitable figure, management not only wants to book this order but books as many of these as possible to the limits of their critical machine capacity.

But is it a correct decision? Will the company really earn all of that estimated contribution?

[a]See Exhibit 2.5 for Summary.

**Exhibit 2–4
"Allowed Hours"
Computed by the
Estimator from an
Equitable Set of
Engineered Production
Standards**[a]

Production Center	Estimated Run Speeds per Hour	Standard Hours	Standard Direct MHR	Standard Direct Conversion Cost
Makeready				
Extruder-Lamin		3	$ 16.62	$ 49.86
8-Color Gravure		6	26.15	159.90
Run				
Extruder-Lamin	250 fpm	14	16.62	232.68
8-Color Gravure	500 fpm	7	26.15	183.05
Slit and Rewind	150 fpm	23.3	7.15	166.60
Wrap and Palletize		16	2.30	36.80

Direct Conversion Costs	$825.80
Selling Price	$960.00
Profit Contribution	$134.11
PV Ratio	0.14

Comment
With this proper contribution measurement, management can make correct ACCEPT/REJECT pricing decisions based on how profitably orders make use of the critical facilities—and balance this committed time against the contribution to be generated.

Management can also make other vital estimating/pricing decisions based upon these rational data.

[a]See Exhibit 2.5 for Summary.

2. *Profit contribution,* or just *contribution,* is the difference between selling price and direct costs. The amount left over from individual transactions pays for the fixed costs, with the remainder being profit—during a time period.
3. Profit-volume ratio (PV) is the ratio of contribution dollars to sales dollars, denoting the power of the revenue dollar to contribute. It is also a velocity ratio, as it shows the speed at which a sales dollar can pay for the period fixed costs. It is generally expressed as a decimal instead of a percentage.

In the pricing[1] arena, the rational way to accept or reject business is to (1) know the prevailing market price for an item (within a close range) and then (2) using the company's direct costs for that item, decide on the adequacy of the contribution that would result from accepting the order. Other considerations involving the return from employing the company's working capital and the time usage of critical facilities is beyond the scope of this book.[2]

---

[1]See Spencer A. Tucker, *Pricing for Higher Profit*, New York: McGraw-Hill Book Company, 1966.

[2]See Spencer A. Tucker, *Handbook of Business Formulas & Controls*, New York: McGraw-Hill Book Company, 1979.

Exhibit 2–5
The Impact of Equitable Time Values in Estimating and Pricing
(Materials and DOCs Not Included)

Production Center	Allowed Hours Supplied by			O.o.p. MHR	Direct Conversion Costs		
	Foremen (1)	*Salespeople (2)*	*Standards (3)*		*Foremen (1)*	*Salespeople (2)*	*Standards (3)*
Preparation							
a	5.00	2.00	3.00	$16.62	$ 83.10	$ 33.24	$ 49.86
b	9.00	4.00	6.00	26.15	235.35	104.60	159.90
Run							
a	20.00	9.33	14.00	16.62	332.40	155.06	232.68
b	11.67	4.67	7.00	26.15	305.17	122.12	183.05
c	38.83	13.98	23.30	7.15	277.63	99.96	166.60
d	24.00	12.00	16.00	2.30	55.20	27.60	36.80

(1) Foremen's estimate: Direct Conversion Cost	$1,288.65		
(2) Salespeople's estimate: Direct Conversion Cost		$542.58	
(3) Estimate from standards: Direct Conversion Cost			$825.80
Competitive SP	960.00	960.00	960.00
(1) Contribution from Foremen's estimate	(328.85)		
PV	(0.34)		
(2) Contribution from Salespeople's estimate		417.42	
PV		0.435	
(3) Contribution from Engineered standards			134.11
PV			0.140

Decision prompted by (1): Turn Down Order
Decision prompted by (2): Book the Order
Decision prompted by (3): Based on Rational Data
(1) Loses contribution
(2) Overcommits facilities
(3) Can correctly balance against facility time and alternate uses

Source of Allowed Hours

Using "loose" standards (overstated time values), represented by Exhibit 2–2, would mislead the company into rejecting that order. But Exhibit 2–4, using proper standards, shows that the company would be making $134.11 in contribution, perhaps at a time this inflow was most needed. On the other hand, using "tight" PS (understated time values), as shown in Exhibit 2–3, would mislead the company into believing that there would be a contribution of $417.42 available if they booked the order. In addition to the error on that particular order, this tight PS approach could prompt the company to book more work of this type and could displace on its facilities, higher contributing work.

MHR and PS

The development of MHR is largely from existing and/or estimated cost and financial data. To develop a rational set of MHR, direct costs must be *traceable* to and *specifically identifiable* with the production facilities they represent.

The skills needed to do this come from financial, cost, and production people. With cost data properly separated between direct and period (fixed) costs, MHR can be constructed in a relatively short time.

Production standards are another matter. Their construction usually requires more time and a greater degree of professionalism. Competent standards-setters must have complete technical knowledge of the operation under study, in terms of machine characteristics, capabilities and limits of the operators, behavior of materials, and a full familiarity with the item being processed. They must have enough experience and knowledge to enable them to immediately spot deviations from standard methods, recognize foreign work elements, understand the waste and spoilage probabilities, and so on. In short, experienced observers must have the analytical skills to identify all the *parameters* of the operation and to develop standards that will reflect these parameters.

In general, in the development of MHR, specific industry experience is not that crucial. In setting PS, however, industry knowledge and experience is critically needed.

Ironically, more attention is usually given to developing MHR than to PS despite their equal importance in pricing and other economic decisions. Hopefully, the reader will see how and why this focus is illogical as well as profit-draining.

Later chapters will also demonstrate the indispensable need for PS in other economic areas of the company.

3 Methods Study and Work Measurement

It is generally agreed that work measurement and timestudy was started around 1881 by Frederick W. Taylor with his observations of machine-shop operations at the Midvale Steel Company. Later on, Frank and Lillian Gilbreth did their microstudies of work. Some evidence points towards researchers as far back as the seventeen hundreds, but Taylor is the one who formalized the approaches and explained timestudy in the following manner.

1. Divide the work of a person performing any job into simple, elementary motions.
2. Pick out the useless movements and discard them.
3. Study the same elementary movements done by several skilled operators, and, with the aid of a stopwatch, select the quickest and best method of making each elementary movement known in the industry.
4. Describe, record, and index each elementary movement with its proper time, for easy retrieval.
5. Study and record the percentage of time that must be added to the actual working time of a good operator to cover unavoidable delays, interruptions, and so forth.
6. Study and record the percentage of time that must be added to cover the newness of a good worker to a job, the first few times that it is done.
7. Study and record the percentage of time that must be allowed for rest, and the intervals at which rest must be taken in order to offset physical fatigue.

This book will deal with each of these areas in some detail.

Taylor's real contribution to industry was his scientific method, his substitution of fact-finding for rules-of-thumb. His questioning attitude and his constant search for the facts earned him the respect that he still holds as a proponent of science in management. He was a pioneer in applying science to that phase of industry which ultimately affected the worker. He understood that he was dealing with a human problem as well as with materials and machines, and he approached the human side of his investigations with an understanding of its psychological aspects. Taylor was constantly concerned with the questions, ''Which is the best way to do this job?''; ''What should constitute a day's work?''; and other problems of a similar nature.

Since Taylor and the Gilbreths, others have made even more sophisticated investigations into methods improvement and work measurement. Prominent among these are Harold B. Maynard and Mitchell Fein. Fein has pioneered new approaches to work measurement and the sharing of the gains from higher productivity directly with the workers who generate them.

Finding the One Best Way

The best way to perform a specific task is determined by a systematic study of the methods, materials, tools, and equipment currently available. It is commonly defined as a study of the motions used in the performance of an operation for the purpose of eliminating all unnecessary motions and therefore, building up a sequence of the most useful motions for maximum efficiency. Other factors contributing to the ''best way'' include lighting, heating, ventilation, vibration, and noises that surround the job. These conditions should be adjusted to insure the greatest comfort to the worker with due consideration for output and greatest overall economy.

Finding the one ''best way'' must imply that it is the best way, *all factors considered*. What may be the best way in one case (or at one time or in one company), may not be the best way in another. Manual handling of parts can be replaced by automatic devices—but only if the cost and volume justifies it. Jigs and fixtures can often be modified to decrease the time required, but again the business conditions at the moment must economically justify it.

Alternate methods must also be considered. Obviously, it would not be ''best'' to pay the high setup cost of a multidrill to process only a small quantity of parts. Nor would it be advisable to aim for the low setup cost of a single-spindle drill press when a large quantity of parts is involved. A further example from the printing industry: 4-color jobs can be run once through a 4-color press with one expensive makeready, or twice through a 2-color press with two running costs and two inexpensive makereadies. The quantity to be processed determines which is the better way.

Methods Study

It is not practical to talk about production standards or work measurement unless we are fairly certain that the operational methods underlying the standard time have been studied and standardized. The observer or analyst must approach the job assuming that nothing about the operation is perfect, questioning everything about the job, e.g., the *way* the job is being done; the *materials* that are being used; the *tools* and *equipment;* the *working conditions;* and so on.

There is no substitute for the WHAT?, WHY?, WHO?, WHERE?, WHEN?, HOW? questions.

1. *What* is done? What is the purpose of the operation?
2. *Why* is the work done? What would happen if it were not done? Is every part of the job necessary?
3. *Who* does the work? Who could do it better? Can changes be made to permit a person with less skill and training to do the job?
4. *Where* is the work done? Could it be done somewhere else more economically?
5. *When* is the work done? Would it be better to do it at some other time?
6. *How* is the work done? This involves a study of the sequence of elements in the operation and the application of the principles of motion study as developed by the Gilbreths.

After all phases of the work or operation have been thoroughly questioned as above, there are usually the following possibilities for improvement:

1. Eliminate all unnecessary work.
2. Combine operations or elements.
3. Change the sequence of operations or elements.
4. Simplify the remaining required operations or elements.

A Methods Checklist   Industrial engineers generally make checklists of specific and detailed questions in various areas of investigation, as in the following sample.

1. *Materials*
   1.1. Can cheaper material be substituted?
   1.2. Is the material uniform and in proper condition when brought to the operator?
   1.3. Is the material of proper size, weight, and finish for most economical use?
   1.4. Is the material being utilized to the fullest extent?
   1.5. Can some use be found for scrap and rejected product?
   1.6. Can the number of storages of material and of product in process be reduced?
2. *Materials Handling*
   2.1. Can the number of times the material needs to be handled be reduced?
   2.2. Can the distance moved be shortened?
   2.3. Is the material received, moved, and stored in suitable containers, pallets, and so on. Are these kept clean?
   2.4. Are there delays in the delivery of materials to the operator?
   2.5. Can the operator be relieved of handling materials by the use of conveyors?
   2.6. Can backtracking be reduced or eliminated?
   2.7. Can material movement be eliminated or reduced by a change in the layout or by combining operations?
3. *Tools, Fixtures and Instruments*
   3.1. Are these devices the best for the operation?
   3.2. Are they in good condition?

3.3. Can these devices be provided or changed so that less skill is required to perform the operation?

3.4. Can engineering changes be made to simplify the design of these devices?

4. *Machine*

4.1. *Setup or Makeready*

4.1.1. Should the operator set up his own machine?

4.1.2. Can the number of setups be reduced by proper lot size?

4.1.3. Can job references, e.g., drawings, color swatches, and so forth, be obtained without delay?

4.1.4. Are there delays in making inspection of first units produced?

4.2. *Operation*

4.2.1. Can the operation be eliminated?

4.2.2. Can the work be done in multiple?

4.2.3. Can the machine speed be increased to optimum speed considering the cost of waste?

4.2.4. Can an automatic feed be used?

4.2.5. Can the operation be divided into two or more short operations?

4.2.6. Can two or more operations be combined into one?

4.2.7. Can the sequence of the operation be changed?

4.2.8. Can the amount of scrap and spoiled work be reduced?

4.2.9. Can the product or part be prepositioned for the next operation?

4.2.10. Can interruptions be reduced or eliminated?

4.2.11. Can an inspection be combined with an operation?

4.2.12. Is the machine in good condition?

5. *Operator*

5.1. Is the operator qualified mentally and physically to perform the operation?

5.2. Can unnecessary fatigue be eliminated by a change in tools, fixtures, layout or working conditions?

5.3. Is the base hourly pay rate correct for this type of work?

5.4. Is supervision satisfactory?

5.5. Can the operator's performance be improved by further instructions?

6. *Working Conditions*

6.1. Are the heat and ventilation conditions satisfactory for the job?

6.2. Are washrooms, lockers, rest rooms, and dressing facilities adequate?

6.3. Are there any unnecessary hazards involved in the operation?

6.4. Is provision made for the operator to work in either a sitting or standing position?

6.5. Are the length of the working day and the rest periods set for maximum economy?

6.6. Is good housekeeping maintained throughout the plant?

The above list of questions, by no means complete, shows some of the elements that enter into a thorough consideration of the task of finding the best way to do work.

Expressing the Time Standard

The Production Standards are expressed as time values—standard minutes (or hours) to perform a specified task or produce a quantity of units. They can also be inverted to express the output per minute (or hour). For example, a standard is 0.80 standard hours per hundred units. This is equivalent to $100/0.80 = 125$ units per hour. If 950 units are to be processed through that machine, the standard time would be $950 \times 0.80 = 7.60$ hours (or $950/125 = 7.60$ hours).

For a manually controlled activity, the PS is the time it takes for a qualified person to perform an operation safely and correctly when working at a normal pace and includes allowances for personal time, fatigue, and unavoidable delays.

For a machine-controlled operation, the standard is the machine time with allowances for unavoidable delays.

Standards are expressed somewhat differently for *incentive plans,* viz: a *standard-hour plan* uses the time standards for the calculations; and for machine-controlled operations, they may be increased by a percentage to provide a bonus-earning opportunity. (See Appendix for more discussion.) For *piece-work plans,* the time values are converted to "dollars or cents per unit of production."

Methods and Profit Planning

The best method should be used for every job. What does that mean? Who sets the method? How does the company recognize this "best" method? How does this involve profit planning?

In simplest terms, the analysis and improvement (if possible) of the operating methods should be an integral part of setting production standards. No professional industrial engineer will establish a PS without *defining* the observed method and *attempting to improve it.* Many PS, however, are established (and used for cost estimating) without any clear description of the method for which the standard is applied.

Methods analysis has two primary purposes and benefits: (1) it provides the opportunity to improve the methods (now, or sometime in the future when conditions permit) and (2) even in those cases where methods improvement does not seem practical, a documented description can assure that an operation will be performed consistently. It is hardly unusual to find that different people are doing the same job (or the same elements) in a different manner. But it is important to have the job "standardized" so that it can be performed each time in the same way. Without this assurance, it is difficult to develop meaningful cost estimates. If the job methods cannot be defined and predicted, the chance of significant variances becomes much greater, thereby making the contribution measurement and analysis for the job useless. For pricing decisions, this cost variance becomes dangerous.

Someone may ask, "Why worry about the method as long as the existing method is reflected in the cost estimate?" In other words, "If the method is poor, the cost will be in the estimate and management will realistically be acting on real costs." As stated in our prior discussion, unless methods are documented, there is a high probability of *unpredictable variances* due to unstandardized methods. In addition, a better method means lower cost, higher contribution, and a strengthening of the company's position in the market-place.

Setup and Makeready Methods

Preparatory operations should not be overlooked in reviewing methods. Often, because the more skilled people perform these operations, management is (or seems to be) reluctant to question how this work is being done. Occasionally, these workers consider it insulting to be measured or have their work analyzed; therefore, this approach has to be treated carefully. However, from a strictly business viewpoint, there is no good reason not to attempt to improve and document these methods. Obviously, the benefits are faster and less expensive setups with more consistent and better quality levels. A better setup invariably means a higher and more predictable running efficiency with better quality of output.

Summary

It is not the intention of this book to cover the detailed techniques used by industrial engineers in methods analysis. A good program will involve the supervisors and the workers since they are a source of valuable ideas. Methods include the machinery, materials, manual procedures used by the workers, and others. The latter include the sequence of steps, the assignment of duties to members of a crew, the hand tools available, material handling equipment used, and so forth. Any method can obviously be improved. The analysis must reflect economic advantages and this requires an engineering discipline. The amount of time spent on the analysis of any operation must relate to the potential benefits.

The "absolute best way" will never be achieved but the best method *available* can be identified. And, as management knows, there are *continual improvements* in materials, equipment, and so on, which make it mandatory to review existing methods (even the previously selected "best" ones) for possible improvements.

4 Basic Requirements for Developing Production Standards

People do not work at the same tempo for an entire day and, consequently, do not produce the same output hour after hour. Consistent output can only be produced by a machine that never runs out of material, goes at the same speed, doesn't have to stop for instructions, has no jamups, and never has to go to the rest room.

Human beings though, get tired, have to take care of their personal needs, have to absorb instructions, check quality, and so on. Regardless of how PS are established, they must recognize these factors in order to adequately measure the time needed at each production center to make the required quantity of good product. These measurements are made in terms of man-hours or machine-hours. There are many techniques used for developing PS (viz, timestudy, work sampling), which will be explored later in the book.

Direct observation is the most common procedure followed in establishing a time standard. Usually this means timestudy. Although all standards are not established this way, it is the basic procedure known and recognized and will form a backdrop for discussing the basic requirements.

There are a number of basic requirements that all standards must have. We will examine them one by one before beginning to discuss some of the more specific standards-setting techniques.

Parameters

Parameters are the variable factors, the characteristics of the job, that cause the time to vary. A great deal of effort must often be spent identifying these variables. It is probably the single most important factor needed to establish useful standards and costs.

There must be a cause-and-effect relationship before a factor can be considered a parameter. The basic question to ask is, "If the parameter changes can it affect the *unit* standard time required to produce a product on a particular machine?''

The speed of the machine will obviously affect the time, but it is a result of one or more parameters and not a parameter itself. The number of people in the crew may affect the time. Product specifications, such as: size, quality, thickness of material, color required, and so on, may also affect the setup and running time on a piece of equipment.

For example, consider an envelope folding machine that processes a variety of sizes, materials, paper weights, and so forth, as well as a number of different types of envelopes (with or without windows, printing, etc.). In some plants, an average speed and output per hour is used for a wide range of envelopes, but it can be off by as much as 30% or more on an individual job, causing the resulting conversion (production) cost to be off by the same amount.

As another example, consider a ''cold header'' machine (used to make bolts and other fasteners from coils). The diameter, type of metal, shape of the finished part, and so on, will substantially affect the running speed, the setup time, as well as the characteristic downtime. Using an average time standard for all products made on a particular heading machine can lead to disastrous misevaluations of the direct costs and contributions.

The quantity of product to be made might affect the unit standard time when a piece of equipment requires a ''run in'' period to get up to ''cruising'' speed. When a small quantity is run, the time spent at cruising speed becomes a smaller portion of the total time and hence, the unit time increases. In larger runs, the time required to get the machine up to standard speed is proportionally smaller and hence, the unit time is less. This is true in industries that convert and print paper, paperboard, and plastic film. In those cases, sheets may be fed initially at a speed of 3,000 per hour to make certain that the quality and color positioning is acceptable, and then be increased to 4,500 per hour—its standard cruising speed.

The size of the crew might affect the unit processing time. With a relatively small crew, the machine may have to be paced down to run slower so that the crew can keep up with the output. With a larger crew, the machine can be run faster without the limiting factor of fewer people. In either case, the standard unit time would vary, and therefore, the crew size becomes an important parameter.

The company should identify the variables (possible parameters) that may affect the time required to process a job, and it should do this for every production center. Then there will, at least, be a checklist to use in determining how many of these variables are significant and how many can be reflected in the standards in a practical way.

If there is no checklist, the subject has probably not been given enough thought, and the standards-setting process should be reviewed.

It is obviously impractical to specifically measure the effect of each operational variable. Some combining and perhaps averaging is normally required after an analysis to determine the effect on costing and the profit-planning process, as well as on the monitoring and control of costs.

Parameters can be reflected in tables or formulas and can be expressed as factors to increase or decrease the standard time. Examples of parameters will be given and discussed in Chapter 11. Correlations between the standard times and parameters must be tested. It should not be assumed that there is a correlation simply because the supervisor or operator thinks there is. Their comments should certainly be welcomed; they could be helpful in identifying parameters, but the correlation or significance of each must be tested before the standards can be accepted for cost purposes. Market forces should not affect the selection of parameters. For example, a specific type of material may affect prices but may not affect running speed and therefore should not be selected as a parameter.

At any rate, a PS should rarely be expressed as one number, as this would indicate that there were no parameters and that no matter how variable the conditions were, the same amount of time would be required each time the operation occurred.

Accuracy

Accuracy is something everyone always wants, but it is difficult to define and very few companies are sure they have enough of it. Accuracy must relate to the use of PS and must be adequate for the purpose. A general understanding by management will provide a policy framework for establishing and maintaining standards. Accuracy is a function of how carefully and thoroughly the data are obtained, analyzed, and used to construct the standards.

As mentioned earlier, management must understand the importance of *relative* accuracy, particularly in relation to the accuracy of the MHR. Since the PS is multiplied by the MHR in calculating production costs, the answer will not be any more accurate than either of these factors. As much as possible, accuracy must be built into the standard when it is initially developed, but very often a testing and refinement process is vital for a healthy standards and profit-planning program.

There are a variety of techniques used by experienced industrial engineers to determine what has to be done to achieve a specific level of accuracy. Some of these are very sophisticated, but some very simple ones suffice in many instances. Accuracy is not created or assured by more detail. Standards expressed to four decimal places (such as 0.0385) will not be any more accurate than one rounded off to 0.04 unless the development data justify the implication of the greater accuracy.

If an effort is going to be made to improve accuracy, it should be equitably divided between MHRs and PSs. The MHRs are usually updated and refined periodically to reflect changes in various costs. A logical question ensues: At that time, is equal attention given to production standards to update them for changes in methods, parameters, and so on?

The subsidy built into the MHR reflects the performance against the standards that are being used—another critical reason for reviewing both the MHR and PS.

Representative

Standards must be representative. This requirement is partly related to the two previous sections on Parameters and Accuracy, but deserves its own emphasis. Every standard represents an average of all the jobs it is designed to cover. Therefore, sufficient representative data from those jobs (or those types of jobs) have to be obtained.

Seasonal, product and other variances should be identified. For instance, if indoor temperature and humidity conditions vary with the seasons and if these factors affect the time to produce the work, a decision must be made whether it is best to have seasonal standards or a single year-round standard with some known degree of error. In the latter case, data must be obtained from each season. Although this may sound rather obvious, it is not unusual to find that a company had set standards during a summer period and never adjusted them for year-round conditions.

Standards for new production centers or new products should not be set on the basis of an assumed similarity to other operations. This could cause a problem for the next new product and worse, it can mushroom later when a standard is needed for some other product with a seeming similarity to the first. If the same standard is used again, there is a progressive deterioration and the time values are no longer representative. In some extreme situations, standards are used for a completely different cross section of operations—the original ones no longer in existence. By using this practice, the effect on contribution measurement is obvious.

Simple and Easily Understood

If your standards are not documented and understood by those who must use them, or who are measured against them, it is likely that they are in need of review and are not providing adequate profit-planning information.

The supervisors, estimator, profit planner, scheduler, and so on, do not need to understand all of the analytical work that went into the development of the standards, but they must have a sufficient general understanding to assure credibility. They must have confidence in their ability to measure costs and performances, and adequate tools for identifying, recognizing, and evaluating other economic factors.

The formats upon which the standards are prepared are important. Clear descriptions, graphs, tables, etc., will assure that they will be consistently applied. Every attempt should be made to express PS in quantitative and discrete terms. Qualitative terms, such as: "difficult," "regular," "small," "close," "precise," and so on, should not be used since these descriptions are subject to wide interpretation and judgmental error. The calculated costs will depend on which estimator happens to be providing the input.

Up-to-Date

Since profit-planning and control is for today and tomorrow, the standards must be current and must reflect existing conditions. The insidious creeping methods changes, which are not reflected in the current PS being used, are probably one of the single largest factors responsible for deteriorating standards. Even companies which make sure that standards are initially set properly often lack a definite policing program to assure updating. Lack of this element of standards administration can permit once proper standards to become inequitable.

Take the case of a change in crew size. This could have been done to improve the equipment utilization and the MHR changed accordingly. But was the PS checked and adjusted with the same care? A definite policy and log is recommended. The policy should state the frequency of audits (such as every 6 to 12 months). A methods-change log must be kept to identify every change that might affect the standards. When there are sufficient changes (on a cumulative basis), the log will trigger a review and update. Sometimes a policy is set up that refers to changes in PV measurements. It might state that when methods changes accumulate to the point where it causes a PV change of at least 0.01 at some "benchmark" selling price, an investigation should be made.

Changes in conditions should not be assumed to offset each other. In some situations, a company lazily assumes that if the MHR increases, the PS will decrease with a negligible effect on direct production cost. This is tantamount to playing Russian roulette in pricing and other economic decisions.

Complete When PS are complete, they will detail all the conversion costs required for the job at hand, after being multiplied by the MHRs. Operational standards must cover, not only the repetitive cycle times (i.e., running time), but setup or makeready times as well. Allowances must be included to cover all conditions that will affect the required time. Although these will be discussed in greater detail later on, it must be recognized that allowances are needed for every PS, and these should be stated and documented on every standards bulletin.

Good standards *coverage* assures the most complete identification of direct costs. Some so-called "indirect" operations, such as: packing, shipping, setup, receiving, warehousing, and so forth, can be recognized as production centers, but usually are not because no one has developed an approach to measuring them. We will demonstrate how these and other operations can be measured, using techniques that we will discuss later. Maximum PS coverage should be a management target. Do you know what your coverage is?

Organization and Responsibility If your company has an Industrial Engineering Department, it should have the responsibility of establishing and maintaining methods and standards. Consulting services are often used to assist or guide the Industrial Engineering Department, particularly when it is first being set up. Smaller companies do not have the need for full-time expertise in this area and often use outside consulting services for all their standards work. Since standards development requires a particular expertise (usually of a specific industry nature) and sufficient objectivity, many firms employ consultants periodically to audit their practices.

Since Production Standards are used for monitoring and controlling factory performance (as well as for estimating, etc.), the responsibility for their maintenance should not be a function reporting to production management. This function should report to the next higher level eliminating the possibility of production managers checking on themselves.

Known Performance Level The performance level represented in the PS should be identified clearly and should be thoroughly understood by all direct and service management personnel who are in any way related to them. In a later chapter, we will discuss expected performance levels in more detail, but in general, the PS should be established to reflect the 100% "fair day's work" level. This is an established concept and industrial engineers are trained to work with it. However, in some incentive plants standards are expressed at 120% to 130% levels for which operators receive bonus or incentive premium pay.

A subsidy should be included in the MHR so that the standard hour can be used as a common yardstick. Then the pure 100% standard can be used as a target for purposes of monitoring and controlling factory performance.

Since actual observed performances on manually controlled operations will range from less than 50% (in a nonmeasured environment) to 120% or more (under incentive conditions), an accomplishment or pace rating must be applied to the actual times to normalize them; i.e., to convert them to the time it would have taken had the operation been performed at 100% when it was observed. This rating is an essential ingredient of a sound standards development and maintenance system, and management should assure itself that any in-house Industrial Engineering efforts are employing this tool.

For machine-controlled operations, the optimum speeds must be identified; see Chapter 12.

5 Techniques for Developing and Using Production Standards

PART 1: Techniques for Developing PS

Basically, there are only two techniques for developing PS: direct observation and historical data. All other methods of obtaining data are derivatives of these.

In most situations, both of these methods must be used. Direct observation (timestudy, work sampling, production studies, ladders, etc.) is used to obtain information that is not available from historical records and to apply judgment on the effectiveness of the operation. Direct observation also often provides information needed for the selection of parameters.

On the other hand, in some situations, historical data (production and performance records) may be sufficient to establish standards. In almost all cases however, the historical data provide supplementary information about allowances, frequencies of certain operations, performances, and so forth. Historical data are also widely used for *backtesting*; i.e., the application of the developed standards to historical production records in order to test them and modify or refine them as needed.

As we discuss some of the specific techniques, we must remember that *both* personnel and machines must be measured. The production standards for the production center may be expressed as machine- or man-time. The amount (or nature) of the manual work may affect the machine cycle.

DIRECT OBSERVATION

Stopwatch Timestudy Timestudy with a stopwatch is the original and most widely recognized method. Basically, the operation is broken down into separate elements in order to make it easier to time and analyze the operation. There is a separate section in Chapter 8 on this important aspect of any observation technique. A simple stopwatch may be used and either snap back or continuous readings may be taken. The selection of one of these types of readings usually depends on the length of the elements. Some observers use more than one watch, enabling them to obtain elapsed times more accurately. Electrical timing devices also can be used to, not only record elapsed time, but develop averages, in addition to performing other computations in the process of calculating standard times. Also, motion picture and video tape equipment is becoming more widely used.

Speed Rating

The next important aspect of timestudy is the rating; i.e., the application of an accomplishment level to the manual elements of the operation. This may also be called speed rating, normalizing, or leveling. Since standards should reflect 100% performance (or 120%–130% in the case of some incentive plans), the actual time that is observed must be converted into equivalent time at 100%, if the work is not being done at that rate when the observation is taken. As a matter-of-fact, it is unlikely that all people will perform at exactly 100% when being studied. Therefore, it is clear that judgment and experience must be applied to adjust the observed time in order to set equitable PS.

Experience

In order to establish engineered PS through timestudy, a trained and experienced observer is required. The manner in which the study is made and the judgments that are required make it essential that adequate expertise be employed since the information developed will be used to help evaluate and run the company.

Sampling

Timestudies may run for long periods of time or be taken intermittently, depending on how many observations are needed. Work sampling is another observation method. It is based on the statistical evidence that if unbiased samples are taken, they will reveal the same distribution of time that would have been observed during a fuller timestudy. If 10% of the observations during a 480-minute shift indicate that the machine was down due to a malfunction, there is good reason to state (after a sufficient number of shifts are studied) that the machine was down, for this particular reason 10% of the time, or 48 minutes. Or, if manual work is studied, 5% of the observations may indicate that an operator was palletizing the material coming off a machine, indicating 5% of the entire day (24 minutes) was spent doing this. In this manner, information can be obtained on each element (or groups of elements) of the job. Accomplishment ratings can also be applied to work sampling observations thereby permitting the development of 100% standard time values.

Work sampling was initially (and still is) used for ratio-delay studies, a technique to determine how much of the time a machine or process was down for various reasons. Increasingly, it is being used as a much broader tool, permitting standards to be established where observations must be taken over a wide time period (because of variable conditions) in order to develop a representative and accurate standard. This technique also tends to be less tiring and permits observers to oversee and analyze the operation much more critically than they would be able to do if they were continuously taking conventional timestudies. On the other hand, a highly repetitive operation may not require a long period of observation and, therefore, a conventional timestudy would do just as well. A simple watch of some type is used in work sampling, but it is used to identify the observation times, not the elapsed times of the elements.

Often, work sampling easily permits observations to be made on more than one person or machine during the study; this sometimes is valuable because data are collected more quickly. The relationship between the activities of the various subjects is also easy to evaluate.

The accuracy and validity of the work sampling technique is proven, but studies must be carefully arranged to minimize bias. Establishing random observation times (if necessary) and observation rules can accomplish this. After the procedure has been set up, however, the advantage of this technique is that people, other than the industrial engineer, can often assist in taking the observations. They can assist in the collection of the data to provide credibility for the entire process. If supervisors, for instance, make some of the sampling studies, they learn something about the characteristics of the operation in the process and help lend credibility to the standards. Obviously, this occurs because of their participation in the data observation and collection. Then, with the unquestioning support of supervisors, the standards become a more powerful tool in the measurement and control of factory performance.

Incidentally, work sampling is extremely useful in measuring a variety of functions in the company; supervisors and office personnel are examples. Although PS may not be used for these functions in the calculation of cost estimates, they can be extremely valuable in analyzing and improving them (by reducing costs, improving effectiveness, and so on).

Work sampling is effectively employed to determine or verify performance that must be known in order to develop the proper subsidy in the MHR and to determine the Annual Chargeable Standard Hours (ACSH). Daily performance reports may measure the overall downtime (the difference between standard and actual time), but the nature or profile of the downtime should be known in order to consider improvement strategies. At this point, management can project an improved performance level for the upcoming period in which the cost estimates will be made and in which the company profit will be planned and monitored. Exhibit 5–1 is an example of a work sampling study.

This study was taken over a four-week period, initially on four people in the mold setup department, in order to identify delays and methods improvements that could affect the elapsed time of the average setup. A few of the findings and corrective strategies were as follows:

1. The ''test-set and adjust'' time was longer than the supervisor felt it should be for qualified setup people. An analysis indicated that training in this area would help.
2. The need for ''making and altering parts'' was reduced after this study indicated the potential benefits of preplanning and making sure that all parts were available (or made) beforehand.

Exhibit 5–1
Work Sampling: Mold Setup Department (4-Week Study)[a]

February 2 through February 29, 1981

Observation Time	Operator	Disconnect Lines	Remove Cavity-Core	Install Cavity-Core	Remove Mold	Install Mold	Connect Lines	Test-Set-Adjust	Get Parts	Parts to Storage	Correct Problem	Make or Alter Parts	Lost Time–Errors	Repairs	Work in Mold Area	Rest-Idle–Personal	Policy
7:35AM	A	X															
	B	X															
	C								X								
	D																
10:17AM	A		X														
	B											X					
	C															X	
	D																
10:53AM	A																
	B								X								
	C						X										
	D												X				
12:41PM	A		X														
	B															X	
	C															X	
	D															X	
2:12PM	A			X													
	B			X													
	C					X											
	D																
Percent of total observations during a 4-week period		3.2	2.8	4.9	2.3	3.7	9.8	17.4	7.1	1.2	6.1	8.3	3.2	6.2	15.7	7.3	10.8	= 100%

[a]Seven hour segment of 4-week study.

3. Much of the "work in the mold area" could have been done by someone assigned to the machine shop. After this was implemented, the elapsed time of the setups was reduced.

In short, this type of study brought into focus the areas that could (and did) benefit from management attention.

Exhibits 5–2 through 5–4 are other examples of work sampling studies.

The study shown in Exhibit 5–2 was taken over a period of several months by the supervisors in the shipping department on the ten people assigned to the four general functions shown in the "category" column (explained at the bottom of the sheet). The purpose of the study was to develop rough standards for use in manpower scheduling. The "number of containers" was the primary parameter, and therefore a count was made each day and related to the number of "work" observations.

The study also showed the time saved when the product was moved directly

Exhibit 5–2
Work Sampling: Shipping Department

Date 1/24/81 Tour 1 Time 8:18 AM Employee	Category	Search for Items or Storage Place	Rearranging Material in Storage Area	Move to and From Storage Area	Load Skids	Unload Skids	Paperwork	Tape or Stamp Loads	Clean Up Dock Or Warehouse	To or From Assigned Job	Picking Up or Dropping Empty Skids	Idle–Rest
Joan	3			X								
Cynthia	3	X										
Maria	3					X						
Sue	3					X						
Pat	4					X						
Mary	4					X						
Ida	2	X										
Antonia	1					X						
Connie	1					X						
Josephine	1					X						

Codes

1 = Warehouse
2 = Servicing assembly department
3 = Order picking
4 = Truck loading

from molding to shipping (without interim storage), leading to further deliberate synchronization of these two areas, wherever possible.

Other useful evaluations were also made (although not shown on this particular sample); viz, the paperwork was analyzed and simplified as it consumed a substantial amount of time.

The study in Exhibit 5–3 made over a period of several weeks to measure the relative amount of "makeready" and "run" time (the information needed to develop the MHR) and the types of "downtime" in order for proper allowances to be included in the Production Standards.

Exhibit 5–4 presents a summary of the data collected in Exhibit 5–3. This bar chart format visually conveys the quantitative significance of the information. For example, the setup consumes more time (during the average week or month) on the L. O. machine than on the others, and therefore, more precision is required in the development of those standards.

Exhibit 5–3
Work Sampling:
Envelope Folding
Department

Date 7/28/81
Shift 1

		Observation Time		
Machine	8:40 AM	9:52 AM	12:30 PM	2:17 PM
LO: #1	1	1	1	4
MO: #1	2b	2b	1	1
#2	1	1	3b	1
Hi-Speed: #1	1	3b	3a	3b
#2	3b	3b	1	1
#3	1	1	1	3b
WR: #1	4	4	4	4
#2	2a	2a	1	1
#3	1	4	2b	1
#4	4	4	4	4

Codes

1 = Machine operating

2a = Machine being setup–being worked on

2b = Machine being setup–not being worked on

2c = Job being setup–adjuster obtaining tools or materials

3a = Machine down (during run)–being worked on

3b = Machine down (during) run)–not being worked on

4 = Machine not manned (because of no order or no operator)

Exhibit 5–4
Summary of Ratio-Delay
Studies (Sampling)

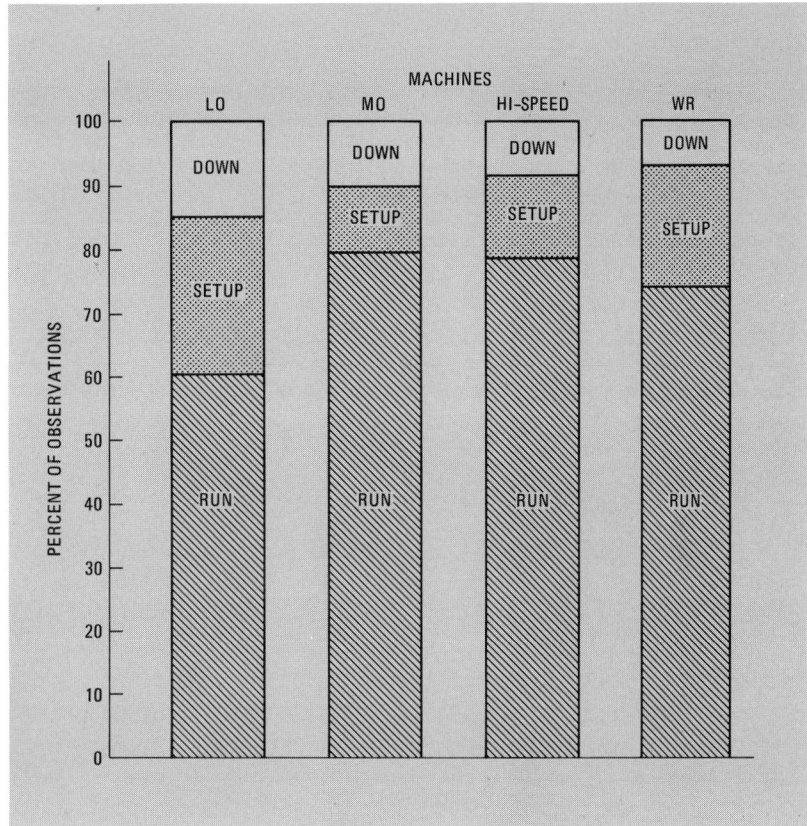

Production Studies Production studies are direct observations with the objective of identifying characteristics of the operations; e.g., the nature of the downtime, the quality level, the total scrap produced, the assistance needed from a setup person, and so forth. This information is supplemental to the establishment of PS. Also, a study of this type is often used to test a standard after it is developed and certainly before using it for estimating and profit-planning. Exhibit 5–5 shows a production study that was taken due to poor performance against the existing standards. Production studies, such as these, provided background data for discussions with the supervisors. With this type of job breakdown, differences in speed and delay patterns between various jobs provided more refined standards by identifying parameters that were not recognized in the original standards.

These studies are also employed when standards are originally set to identify how long it takes for the machine to reach cruising speed, the frequency of certain delay elements, and so on.

A "Ladder study" is one name applied to a technique in which personnel record and time their own activities. This can be done with a wrist watch or other suitable timing device. For example, an office clerk can record his or her activities within major categories (worked out with the Industrial Engineering Department in advance) and indicate how long it takes to perform each of these activities. This type of study obviously is not rated (leveled)

Techniques for Developing and Using Production Standards

Exhibit 5–5
Production Study

Operation <u>Print</u>
Equipment <u>2-Color Offset press</u>[a]
Operators <u>J.S. and B.M.</u>

Date <u>8/16/81</u>
Observer <u>ABC</u>

Start Time	Elapsed Minutes	Activity Description	Production Count		Speed/ Hour	Job Number	Quality Level
			This Run	Cumulative Total			
8:00AM	20	Makeready	—	—		1,421	
8:20	23	Run	2,800		6,000–8,000/hr		
8:53	16	Down— (material warped)			—		
9:09	18	Run	2,100	4,900	7,000		Light
9:27	3	Down			—		
9:30	16	Break			—		
9:46	9	Run	1,125	6,025	7,500		OK
9:55	23	Change Over (MR)				1,473	
10:18	12	Run	600	600	3,000		OK
10:30	22	Down-run (jams)	800	1,400	2,800		Marks
10:52	11	Down (interference)	—	—	—		
11:03	39	Run	2,100	3,500	3,300		
11:42	15	Ink problem—slow	480	3,980	2,000		
11:57		Stop for lunch Etc.					

[a]In this case only one machine was studied. A Production study can cover a department (without as much detail on each machine).

and will not be segmented into fine elements. But, it can provide some valuable information on jobs that are difficult to define and measure. Sometimes ladder studies are used merely to construct a list of activities that are to be further studied in detail by the industrial engineer. Exhibit 5–6 illustrates a ladder study in a production planning and control department.

This information can be used to identify a better sequence of work, to highlight activities that consume the greatest amount of time (and therefore would benefit most from methods improvements), to analyze communications problems, and so forth.

Notice that from 8:51 to 9:33 (42 minutes), the clerk was involved with a "material" problem. Because of these delays, he or she did not have time to perform any other function. Therefore, this information will help to factually evaluate the value of corrective strategies.

Even a crude operational breakdown, such as this, will help to determine whether this clerk's work is related to certain production centers, whether it varies with the number of orders processed, or the number of facility hours, and so on. This information is valuable in determining whether the expense should be included in MHRs or DOCs. Although it is unlikely that PS would be applied for this work (as a separate production center), the analysis of the

**Exhibit 5–6
Production Study
("Ladder Study") as
Reported by the Person
Doing the Job**

Job Title <u>Production Clerk</u>
Department <u>Production Planning and Control</u>
Date <u>8/23/81</u>
Responsibilities <u>As Described</u>

Start Time	Elapsed Minutes	Activity Description[a]
7:52	24	Review yesterday's data—(production and rejects)
8:16	35	Revise and post today's schedule
8:51	42	Discuss material problem with superintendent
9:33	17	Study new orders
9:50		Obtain production standard for new item
Not recorded	45	Draft tomorrow's schedule
10:35		Weekly meeting
		Etc.

Comment
When standard activity classifications can be identified beforehand, they can be preprinted on this form to minimize the time the person must spend writing in the descriptions.

Another form of Self-Study is work sampling, in which the person would record what he or she was doing only at random observation times. A random number generator can be used for this purpose.

[a]The breakdown in this case is determined by the clerk, but it should be reviewed (and modified, as necessary) on subsequent studies.

time spent on these activities is an essential step in the construction of total direct cost.

This type of "self-study" may also be used by managerial and professional personnel to evaluate their activities and to provide a basis for staffing.

Production studies are very helpful in determining how certain costs should be reflected in the cost estimate. For instance, some administrative functions are related to the number of orders processed and should therefore, be applied as a DOC (Direct-Order Charge) in the form of a "transaction" cost. Other administrative jobs may be related to the number of people on the payroll and can therefore, be applied on the AB (Allocable Budget)—a step in MHR construction—in proportion to the number of people in each production center. The production study can provide the identifying information needed to establish these cost schedules.

HISTORICAL DATA

Historical data are normally available through some type of production or performance reporting system. The formats and contents of these reports vary widely and great care must be taken to properly define the information that is expressed. If no "direct observation" is possible (or delayed because of other conflicting Industrial Engineering activity), historical data can be used to establish *temporary* standards. Rating (leveling) can be supplied through sampling techniques and then applied to the historical data. For example, a few sampling studies could determine that a department's performance was about 85%. As a result, the historical average data could be pegged at 85% and future fluctuations above and below that level could indicate the range of performance. An analysis would then show how many times, and under what conditions, the performances reached or exceeded 100%.

Although direct rating is not possible after the fact, analysis of historical data can often provide an estimate of a standard. Some sophisticated mathematical techniques are also available, e.g., linear programming and multiple regression analysis. These are not covered in this book but your Industrial Engineering function should be able to employ them when necessary.

Historical data may pertain to personnel, as well as machines, and records must be clearly defined to make sure that all of the time is accounted for. This can be done in reconciliation with payroll records. If some of the machine time is not recorded because of certain types of downtime, it may not be possible to determine the running performance, the proper allowances for downtime, and so on. In a great many companies, we find that these records are not complete and require careful analysis by someone with professional expertise to extract usable data.

Historical data are also invaluable for testing the PS. *Backtesting* provides an instant reference point. Whenever standards are installed, the company should know what the recent past performance has been against these standards. When analyzing these performances, both the average level as well as the fluctuation patterns should be reviewed. Thus, when the standards are used for estimating, variances can be anticipated.

PART II: Using Standard Data for PS

Standards can be either purchased or developed inside the company. The term "standard data" refers only to the format in which the standards are presented and not the methods used to develop them. It is important to note that all standard data were originally developed through direct observation, historical data, or a combination of both.

A few of the standard data systems that can be purchased are:

1. Micromotion data, such as: MTM (Methods Time Measurement) or WF (Work Factor). These have been developed by engineering or consulting companies and are useful in measuring and analyzing manual motions. Methods improvements, particularly of highly repetitive operations, are often identified through the use of these micromotion tools. MTM and WF are systems of basic manual time values and do not relate to any specific industry.
2. Standard elemental data which relate to nonmanufacturing operations, such

as office and clerical operations, maintenance work, and so forth. Various textbooks contain these data.

3. Standard elemental data for specific industries using highly technical operations and calling for considerable skilled judgment. Among these are: high-quality printing, watchmaking, and tool and die making. In other industry applications, one can find standard data for construction work that covers, for example, the operations of installing pipe and concrete. These data are sometimes supplied by trade associations to their members. In other cases, some consulting firms develop specialized industry data.

4. Trade association data for its own industry. These are largely average experience information obtained from its members but may not be uniform or objective. Usually, these standards either lack parameters or present them in subjective categories. The description of the various conditions of machinery and the methods in use is minimal. The data represent a composite average of the firms in the industry and have little value as standards for an individual firm. They are possibly useful as a guide to compare with speeds with those "suggested" by the manufacturers of the equipment.

Good standard data must have all the characteristics that internally developed PS would have. That is, the data must include allowances, must reflect a known performance level, must be developed using logical parameters, and so forth. It is essential that the data be completely described. Some standard data do not include allowances; some do. Some machine data reflect optimum rather than average conditions. Normally, it is a good idea to test any data obtained from the outside in order to determine the performance when used under normal plant activities and thereby indicate any modifications needed so it may be used as a meaningful yardstick.

Standard data can also be developed inside the company. Most industrial engineers will organize and arrange the standards in order to provide data to measure other similar or identical operations. This implies that a makeready (change-over), for instance, may be broken down into basic elements, such as: clean various parts of the machine, make adjustments, and move the next roll or skid load of material, because in the future, these elements can be assembled in any required combination without studying another job.

One of the advantages of standard elemental data is that a new job can be measured before it is actually performed, assuming of course that the basic characteristics can be identified. In this manner, cost analyses can be made before the job is run. Of course, all standards used for cost estimating are, in a real sense, standard data because they are used to measure the cost and planned contribution before the job is priced and booked. PS used for estimating are usually combinations of elemental standard data. Exhibits 5–7 through 5–9 are examples of internally developed standard data.

These standards were developed to cover a variety of material handling operations under specific conditions. They were used to construct standards for shipping department operations, as well as to develop the "external" work standards for machine operators who had to move the work to and from their machines.

Exhibit 5–7
Example of Standard Data: Material Handling Operations in a Shipping Department (in Normal Minutes; P, F, and D Must be Added)

Distance between Points in Feet	Move Load on Truck		Move Load on Skid with Jack		Get Empty Truck		Drag Empty Skid or Pallet	
	One Way	RT^a	One Way	RT^a	One Way	RT^a	One Way	RT^a
0	.150	.150	.450	.450	.150	.150	.100	.100
1	.156	.161	.456	.461	.155	.159	.106	.110
2	.162	.172	.462	.472	.160	.168	.112	.120
3	.168	.183	.468	.483	.165	.177	.118	.130
4	.174	.194	.474	.494	.170	.186	.124	.140
5	.180	.205	.480	.505	.175	.195	.130	.150
6	.186	.216	.486	.516	.180	.204	.136	.160
7	.192	.227	.492	.527	.185	.213	.142	.170
8	.198	.238	.498	.538	.190	.222	.148	.180
9	.204	.249	.504	.549	.195	.231	.154	.190
10	.210	.260	.510	.560	.200	.240	.160	.200
12	.222	.282	.522	.582	.210	.258	.172	.220
14	.234	.304	.534	.604	.220	.276	.184	.240
16	.246	.326	.546	.626	.230	.294	.196	.260
18	.258	.348	.558	.648	.240	.312	.208	.280
20	.270	.370	.570	.670	.250	.330	.220	.300
22	.282	.392	.582	.692	.260	.348	.232	.320
24	.294	.414	.594	.714	.270	.366	.244	.340
26	.306	.436	.606	.736	.280	.384	.256	.360
28	.318	.458	.618	.758	.290	.402	.268	.380
30	.330	.480	.630	.780	.300	.420	.280	.400
32	.342	.502	.642	.802	.310	.438	.292	.420
34	.354	.524	.654	.824	.320	.456	.304	.440
36	.366	.546	.666	.846	.330	.474	.316	.460
38	.378	.568	.678	.868	.340	.492	.328	.480
40	.390	.590	.690	.890	.350	.510	.340	.500
42	.402	.612	.702	.912	.360	.528	.352	.520
44	.414	.634	.714	.934	.370	.546	.364	.540
46	.426	.656	.726	.956	.380	.564	.376	.560
48	.438	.678	.738	.978	.390	.582	.388	.580
50	.450	.700	.750	1.000	.400	.600	.400	.600
55	.480	.755	.780	1.055	.425	.645	.430	.650
60	.510	.810	.810	1.110	.450	.690	.460	.700
65	.540	.865	.840	1.165	.475	.735	.490	.750
70	.570	.920	.870	1.220	.500	.780	.520	.800
75	.600	.975	.900	1.275	.525	.825	.550	.850

^{a}RT = round trip.

**Exhibit 5–8
Example of Standard
Data: Material Handling
Operations in a Packing
Department (in Normal
Minutes; P, F, and D
Must be Added)**[a]

Distance between Points, in Feet	Drag or Push Boxes					
	8–20#		100#		200#	
	One Way	RT[b]	One Way	RT[b]	One Way	RT[b]
0	.100	.100	.100	.100	.100	.100
1	.105	.109	.106	.110	.107	.111
2	.110	.118	.112	.120	.114	.122
3	.115	.127	.118	.130	.121	.133
4	.120	.136	.124	.140	.128	.144
5	.125	.145	.130	.150	.135	.155
6	.130	.154	.136	.160	.142	.166
7	.135	.163	.142	.170	.149	.177
8	.140	.172	.145	.180	.156	.188
9	.145	.181	.154	.190	.163	.199
10	.150	.190	.160	.200	.170	.210
12	.160	.208	.172	.220	.184	.232
14	.170	.226	.184	.240	.198	.254
16	.180	.244	.196	.260	.212	.276
18	.190	.262	.208	.280	.226	.298
20	.200	.280	.220	.300	.240	.320
22	.210	.298	.232	.320	.254	.342
24	.220	.316	.244	.340	.268	.364
26	.230	.334	.256	.360	.282	.386
28	.240	.352	.268	.380	.296	.408
30	.250	.370	.280	.400	.310	.430
32	.260	.388	.292	.420	.324	.452
34	.270	.406	.304	.440	.338	.474
36	.280	.424	.316	.460	.352	.496
38	.290	.442	.328	.480	.366	.518
40	.300	.460	.340	.500	.380	.540
42	.310	.478	.352	.520	.394	.562
44	.320	.496	.364	.540	.408	.584
46	.330	.514	.376	.560	.422	.606
48	.340	.532	.388	.580	.436	.628
50	.350	.550	.400	.600	.450	.650
52	.360	.568	.412	.620	.464	.672
54	.370	.586	.424	.640	.478	.694
56	.380	.604	.436	.660	.492	.716
58	.390	.622	.448	.680	.506	.738
60	.400	.640	.460	.700	.520	.760

[a]Use 50% of values for roller conveyor. [b]RT = round trip.

**Exhibit 5–9
Standard Data, Machine
Example: Pickup and
Position Pieces to the
Machine (One at a
Time)**

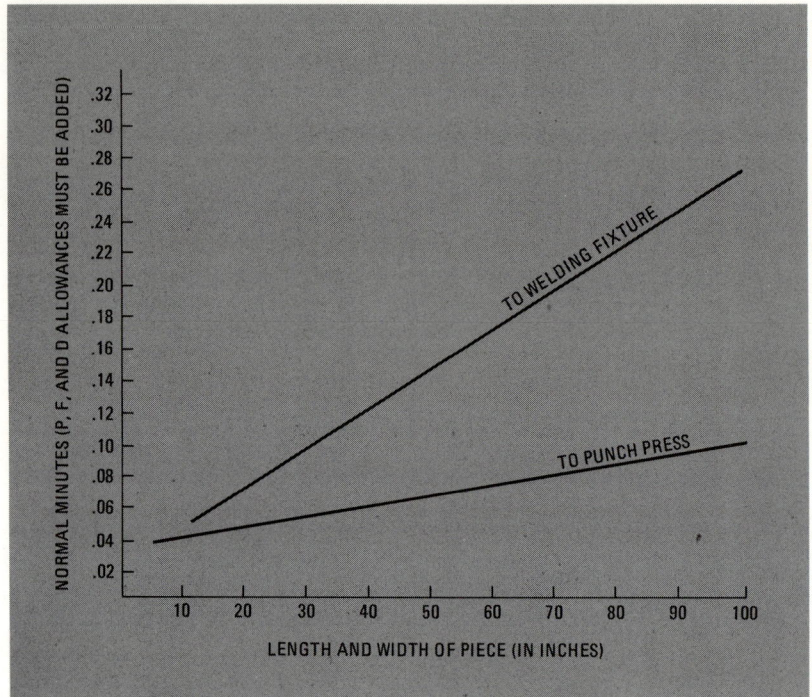

Exhibit 5–8 was developed along with Exhibit 5–7 to cover the movement of individual boxes.

Exhibit 5–9 illustrates (in graph form) data for moving individual pieces to a punch press or welding fixture. Note that the single parameter (length + width, in inches) was appropriate for these objects, but these data should not be applied to different objects or used in a different environment without testing.

6 Direct Observational Tools

As previously stated, there are several methods for measuring work through direct observation. One is the stopwatch timestudy. Other more sophisticated techniques include micromotion and memomotion by means of motion-picture films. These techniques are used for the analysis of both manual and machine operation. The ultimate purpose, besides setting standards is operational methods improvement, workplace layout, and work simplification. There are other techniques, such as production study and work sampling, but in this chapter we shall concentrate on the stopwatch timestudy because many of the same basic principles apply to other techniques.

Timestudy Devices and Equipment

Timestudy is used to determine the time required by a qualified person working at a normal pace to do a specific task. Implied also in this definition is that the person has time for personal needs and rest (so that a normal pace can be sustained for a full shift). It should be noted that while motion study is largely analytical, timestudy is mostly the measurement of work. The result of a timestudy is the time in minutes or hours that a person suited to the job and trained in the specific method will need to perform the job if he or she works at a normal tempo.

The equipment needed for timestudy consists of timing devices and auxiliary equipment. The most prevalently used timing device is a decimal-minute stopwatch. In recent years, a hand-held decimal-minute digital-displayed timing device has become available. However, we shall confine ourselves to the stopwatch. Auxiliary equipment consists of an observation board, tachometer, and perhaps a miniature calculator.

Stopwatches   The decimal-minute stopwatch, shown in Exhibit 6–1, has a dial divided into 100 equal spaces (instead of the conventional 60 spaces, representing the 60-second minute), each of which measure 0.01 minute, the hand making one complete revolution per minute. A smaller dial is divided into 30 spaces, each of which represents 1 minute, the smaller hand making one complete revolution in 30 minutes. The hands of the watch are controlled in different ways depending on the style of the watch used. Exhibit 6–1 shows a watch where the starting and stopping mechanism is controlled by the slide (A). Pressing the top of the stem (B) returns the hand to zero. But some watches may start again when the pressure on the stem is released. Some stems operate by the first pressure which starts the hand and a second pressure to stop it at any place on the dial. Timestudy engineers use different watch styles by preference or by specific requirements of the timing task. Certain watches have two large hands (split type), one which runs continuously and the other for snap-back or time-out use.

The 60-second stopwatch, shown in Exhibit 6–2 and generally used at sports events, by psychologists, and others, is not suitable for a time-study of an operation being broken down into small elements. It may be used for production studies where the elapsed time intervals are large. The dial is broken down into 60 spaces, each of which measures 1 second, with the hand making one complete revolution per minute. Taking elemental readings with such a watch would give an accuracy of 1 part in 60, whereas, the decimal-minute watch gives an accuracy of 1 part in 100. When short, highly repetitive elements or operations are involved, this difference in accuracy could have a large effect in the final PS.

Exhibit 6–1
Decimal-Minute Watch

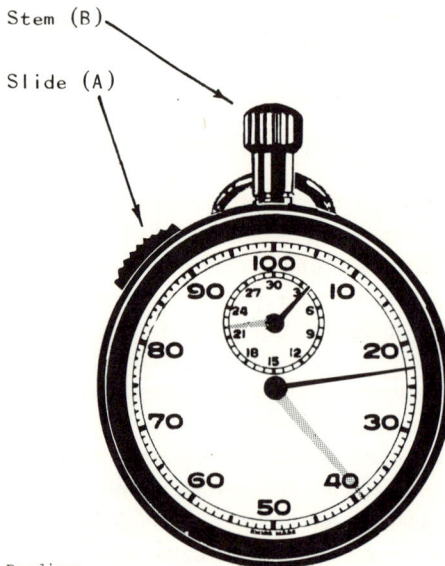

```
Readings

  Black  =  4.23 minutes

  Gray   = 22.39 minutes
```

**Exhibit 6–2
Sixty-Second Watch**

```
Readings

    Black   =   4 minutes,  9 seconds

    Gray    =   9 minutes, 53 seconds
```

Observation Board and Sheet

A lightweight board, slightly larger than the observation sheet, is used to hold the paper and stopwatch. Exhibit 6–3 illustrates a typical board. Most time-study observation forms have two sides: the front for recording the physical data of the product or part being studied, the watch readings and "run" delays. The back of this form is used to show work area layout or part sketch, summary of all delays and the calculation of the final standard time. Exhibits 6–4 and 6–5 show the details of a Timestudy Observation Form as used by Martin & Tucker, Inc.

Reading the Watch and Recording

While taking the timestudy, the observer should hold the board against his body with the lower left arm in such a way that the watch be operated by the thumb and index finger of the left hand thereby leaving his right hand free to record the data. The observer must position the board so that the work, the worker, the dial of the watch, and the recording area all fall in his direct line of vision.

The positioning described above applies to right-handed people. The reverse would apply to left-handed observers.

The two most common methods of reading the stopwatch are

1. Continuous timing.
2. Snap-back timing.

Continuous Timing. With this method of timing, the observer starts the watch at the beginning of the first element and permits it to run continuously during the period of the study. The observer notes the reading of the watch at the end of each element and records this reading on the observation sheet opposite the description of the element. Obviously, the ending of the first

Exhibit 6–3
Timestudy Observation Sheet Mounted on an Observation Board with Stopwatch

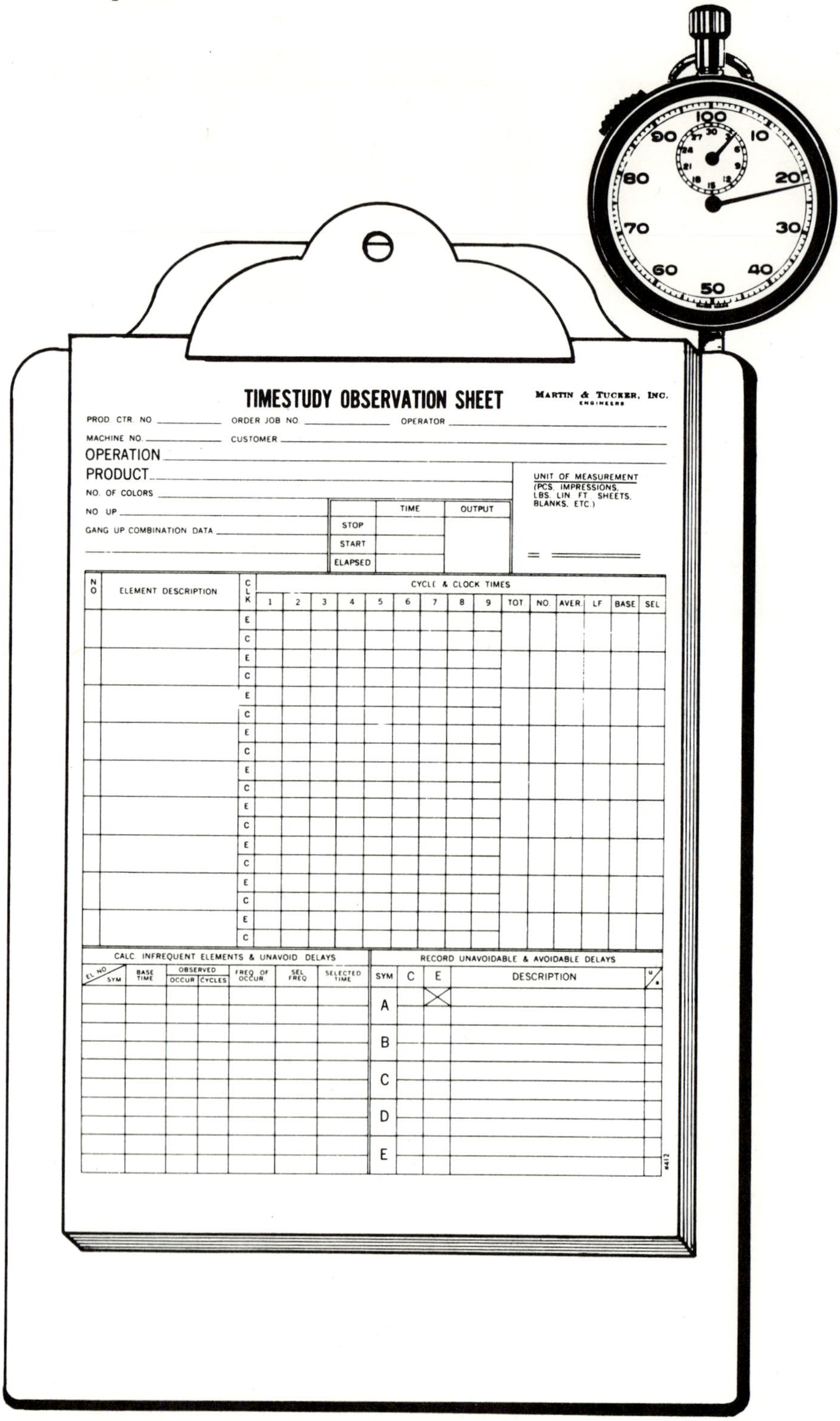

Exhibit 6–4
Timestudy Observation Sheet, Side 1

TIMESTUDY OBSERVATION SHEET

MARTIN & TUCKER, INC.
ENGINEERS

PROD. CTR. NO. ________ ORDER/JOB NO. ________ OPERATOR ________

MACHINE NO. ________ CUSTOMER ________

OPERATION ________

PRODUCT ________

NO. OF COLORS ________

NO. UP ________

GANG UP/COMBINATION DATA ________

	TIME	OUTPUT
STOP		
START		
ELAPSED		

UNIT OF MEASUREMENT
(PCS, IMPRESSIONS, LBS. LIN. FT., SHEETS, BLANKS, ETC.)

= ________

NO.	ELEMENT DESCRIPTION	CLK	CYCLE & CLOCK TIMES 1	2	3	4	5	6	7	8	9	TOT.	NO.	AVER.	LF	BASE	SEL
		E															
		C															
		E															
		C															
		E															
		C															
		E															
		C															
		E															
		C															
		E															
		C															
		E															
		C															
		E															
		C															
		E															
		C															

CALC. INFREQUENT ELEMENTS & UNAVOID. DELAYS

EL NO / SYM	BASE TIME	OBSERVED OCCUR	OBSERVED CYCLES	FREQ. OF OCCUR.	SEL. FREQ.	SELECTED TIME

RECORD UNAVOIDABLE & AVOIDABLE DELAYS

SYM	C	E	DESCRIPTION	u/a
A				
B				
C				
D				
E				

#412

Exhibit 6–5
Timestudy Observation Sheet, Side 2

TIMESTUDY OBSERVATION SHEET

MARTIN & TUCKER, INC.
ENGINEERS

STUDY NO. _____

METHODS SHEET NO. _____

OBSERVER _____

CLIENT CO. _____

DATE _____

DEPT. _____

FOREMAN _____

UNION REP. _____

WORK AREA LAYOUT

SCALE =

MATERIAL PARAMETERS	EQUIPMENT PARAMETERS	OTHER PARAMETERS
_____	_____	ORDER QTY. _____
_____	_____	PROD. SIZE _____
_____	_____	PROD. STYLE _____
_____	_____	_____
_____	_____	_____
_____	_____	_____

NOTES & REMARKS

STD. CREW _____

UNIT _____

UNITS PER CYCLE _____

NO. UP = NO. IN x DIRECTION X NO. IN y DIRECTION

_____ = _____ X _____

_____

_____

_____

_____

FOREMAN'S OK _____   DATE _____

M & T OK _____   APPROVED _____

SUMMARY

ITEM	MINUTES	
	MACH.	MAN.
BASE TIME: REG. ELEMENTS		
BASE TIME: INFREQ. ELEMENTS		
BASE TIME: UNAVOID. DELAYS		
TOTAL BASE TIME		
POLICY DELAYS _____ %		
POLICY DELAYS _____ %		
INCENTIVE ALLOW _____ %		
STANDARD MIN. PER CYCLE		
STANDARD HRS. PER CYCLE		
STANDARD HRS. PER _____ UNITS		
STANDARD _____ UNITS PER HR.		

element is the beginning of the timing of the second, and so on. The time for each element is determined later by subtraction.

Snap-Back Timing. With this method, the hands of the watch are snapped back to zero at the end of each element. At the beginning of the first element, the observer snaps the hand back to zero by pressing on the stem of the watch. The moving hand instantly begins to measure the time of the first element. At the end of the first element, the observer reads the watch, snaps the hand back to zero, and records this reading. In a similar manner, the rest of the elements are timed. This method gives the elemental time directly without later need for subtractions. In addition, the times for each element are more visible to the observer, thereby noting the variations while making the study. This may aid in rating the operator. A practical disadvantage of snap-back timing, where an incentive plan is in use, is the possible objections by workers or union representatives. Sometimes they question whether the snap-back method, where the watch does not run continuously, might inadvertently omit legitimate delay times which should be included in developing the PS. Proper delays are never omitted by trained professional timestudy observers, but it is well to anticipate this type reaction.

Recording the Stopwatch Readings

In order to record the stopwatch reading on the observation sheet, the time-study engineer must do three things almost simultaneously:

1. observe the operator
2. read the watch instantly
3. record the data.

While this might seem to be a difficult task, it is accomplished with practice and experience. Often, the start and stop of an element is accompanied by a click, or a definite noise. Sometimes, it can be triggered by a flash of light or a vibration. These sights and sounds are what aid the observer in taking the readings and he soon learns to make use of them.

7 Preparing for the Timestudy

The exact procedure used in making direct observation time studies may vary somewhat, depending on the type of operation being studied and the intended application of the data obtained. The following minimum steps are usually required:

1. Obtain and record information about the operation, the part or product, the machine, the material and the operator being studied.
2. Divide the operation into major elements and record a complete description of the agreed-upon standard method to be used during the study, viz,
   a. makeready or setup
   b. run cycle
   c. infrequent element
3. Observe and record the time taken by the operator and/or machine.
4. Rate the operator's performance.
5. Determine the allowance.
6. Calculate the time standard for the operation.

Approach for Making the Timestudy

There is a basic required procedure to follow before the timestudy begins:

1. *Request for a Timestudy.* This will generally emanate from the plant if a wage incentive plan is being used. Otherwise, the request will come from the plant manager, chief engineer, cost accountant, profit planner, production planner, or others in the company.
2. *Is the Job Ready for Timestudy?* The timestudy analyst should review the operation to be timed with the supervisor of the department, and make sure that the job methods are standardized, that the materials meet spec-

ifications, that the machine is in satisfactory condition, and that optimum speed has been determined (with a view to limiting waste at uneconomically high speeds; see Chapter 12). The timestudy engineer examines all aspects of the operation for the purpose of suggesting any changes that should be made before the timestudy. If the supervisor approves of these suggestions, then the changes should be placed in effect, and if necessary, the study delayed until these are in place. The questioning by the timestudy engineer was discussed in an earlier chapter.

3. *Recording Information.* All information asked for in the observation form should be completed; timestudies made hastily and incompletely are of little value. It should be kept in mind that the completeness of the data will permit future use in developing standard data, formula constructions—perhaps months later. The observer should record such items as part description, part number, product, product code, material, customer, order number, lot size, machine, machine number, machine capabilities, department, material handling devices, jigs, fixtures, gages, and other instruments. A sketch of the layout or of the piece being processed is also desirable.

4. *Record Description of Method.* The standard time for the operation applies only to that particular operation. Therefore, the observer must record a complete description of the method, preferably on a separate Methods Sheet, similar to Exhibit 7–1. Note the statement on the bottom of that page. Exhibit 7–2 shows a completed methods writeup.

5. *Divide the Operation into Elements.* Timing an entire operation as if it was one element is not the objective of the timestudy. Breaking the operation down into parts (elements) and timing each of them separately is the whole idea behind stopwatch timestudy. Elements which occur regularly are usually listed first, followed by all other elements which are a necessary part of the job. Sometimes it is desirable to attach a separate piece of paper to the observation sheet to describe the starting and end points for each element.

In many cases (particularly with highly repetitive operations), it is possible to list the elements before the timing begins—in other situations, however, the observer must be prepared to record unanticipated elements as they occur.

The *reasons* for elemental breakdown are:

a. An operator may not work at the same tempo throughout the operation. A timestudy permits separate performance (effort) ratings to be applied to each element of the job.

b. A timestudy may show that excessive time is being taken to perform certain elements of the job or that too little time is being spent on other elements.

c. An analysis of an operation by elements may show variations in method that could not otherwise be detected if the entire operation was timed as one element.

d. Standard time values for individual elements can be determined and later applied to other operations synthetically (standard data), if those elements are common to more than one operation. This reduces the time for setting production standards.

Exhibit 7–1
Methods Sheet: Blank

SHEET No._____

METHODS SHEET

MARTIN & TUCKER, INC.
ENGINEERS

PAGE _____ OF _____

MACHINE No._____   STD. No._____   DATE WRITTEN_____

PROD. CTR. No._____   CHART No._____   BY_____

NAME OF OPERATION_____

NAME OF ELEMENT_____

DESCRIPTION OF METHODS

LIMITATIONS, QUALIFICATIONS, CONSTRAINTS

CLIENT COMPANY:_____   MANAGEMENT OK:_____

DIVISION/PLANT:_____   M & T OK:_____

The methods, procedures, layout, etc., described refer specifically to the production standard captioned above, as of the date written. Any alteration in said methods must be reported to enable revision in the production standard, if required.

#410

Exhibit 7–2
Methods Sheet: Completed for 2-Color Press

SHEET No._____

METHODS SHEET

MARTIN & TUCKER, INC.
ENGINEERS

PAGE _____ OF _____

MACHINE No. __179, 188__   STD. No. ___4___   DATE WRITTEN_____

PROD. CTR. No. __20__   CHART No. ___2___   BY_____

NAME OF OPERATION __Print 2-Colors: Harris Offset Press__

NAME OF ELEMENT __Makeready__

DESCRIPTION OF METHODS Standard crew = 2 per Press

1. First Step (First Two Colors)

   A. Read job ticket.
   B. Load and set feeder.
   C. Set front stop and guides.
   D. Adjust cylinder pressure to caliper of sheet.
   E. Set press for register.
   F. Set delivery for sheet (joggers, etc.) and run several blanks.

2. Second Step

   A. Strap plates into press; check that caliper is equal to calibration setting on both units.
   B. Make additional adjustment after initial run.
   C. Open blanket cylinder on both units and cut packing to fit sheet size being run. (A. and C. could be reversed.)

3. Third Step

   A. Adjust fountain to ink coverage required on plates, ink up unit I.
   B. Repeat A. for unit II.
   C. Make water adjustment for each unit. (depending on ink concentration)
   D. Stop press. Wash off plate in unit I with wool sponge prior to obtaining first proof.
   E. Adjust dampener to printing plate unit I. Engage ink rollers, and check water balance.
   F. Start up sheets (by book procedure):
      Book 1 (8 sheets) -- square sheet for register.
      Book 2 (8 sheets) -- adjust to die cutting.
   G. Repeat D, E, F, for second color unit II until position is properly obtained.
   H. Book 3 (50 sheets) -- run and check both colors for proper match. Stop to get foreman's ok.
   I. RUN may begin at this point.

4. Fourth Step (Press Wash and Remove MR)

   A. Wash up both units I and II.
   B. Remove plates, etc., for next job.

CLIENT COMPANY:_____   MANAGEMENT OK:_____

DIVISION/PLANT:_____   M & T OK:_____

The methods, procedures, layout, etc., described refer specifically to the production standard captioned above, as of the date written. Any alteration in said methods must be reported to enable revision in the production standard, if required.

#410

6. *How to Divide an Operation into Elements*. Three general rules apply for dividing an operation into elements:
   a. Make the elements as short in duration as possible and still allow accurate timing.
   b. Manual elements should be separated from machine elements.
   c. Constant elements should be separated from variable elements.

Duration of an Element. If the time span of each element is too short, it is impossible to accurately measure it with a stopwatch. Elements taking 0.03 or 0.04 minute are probably the shortest that can be conveniently measured with a stopwatch. If there are consecutive short elements, different combinations can be timed to determine the time for each individual one. If, for example, the job requires five short elements in a row, the first, second, and third could be timed together, and the same can be done for the fourth and fifth. In other sequences, the first and second could be taken together and then the remaining three, and so on down the line. By a series of subtractions, the time span for each element can be calculated. However with work sampling it may be possible to pick them up if sufficient observations are made.

Separate Manual and Machine Time. When power speeds and feeds are being used on the machine, it is possible to calculate the time required for the machine-controlled elements and then check it against the actual stopwatch data. Also, the beginning and end of the machine's work cycle are excellent start and stop points for an element. Where standard data and formulas are to be developed, it is essential that machine time be separated from manual time.

Constant and Variable Elements. A constant element usually takes the same amount of time on each occurrence since there are no variables. A variable element is influenced by factors such as: the size, weight, length, shape, and so on, of a piece or part. For example, in a timestudy of an office operation, (in the accounts receivable department) typing an invoice is a variable element because it may have a different number of line items, and the time will vary accordingly. However, the typing of the envelope would be a constant element if the time were usually the same.

The time necessary for a machine to automatically strap a unit load might be a constant, but the time necessary to manually tie a load might be a variable because the number and type of items on the load could affect the time required.

In the application of standards for cost estimating, greater accuracy will be obtained if the variable factors are identified wherever necessary.

8

Developing a Production Standard from Timestudy

A discussion of the major steps involved in selecting an operator, determining the necessary number of observations, rating the operator's performance, measuring elemental frequencies, and completing the calculations of the production standard on the timestudy form is now appropriate.

Number of Cycles to be Timed

The number of cycles to be timed, in order for the timestudy to be representative of the work being done, depends on the nature of the work. These factors include: the length of the cycle, the number of elements in the cycle, variations in the length of the cycle, the consistency of the operator, and the relationship between machine-time and manual-time.

A competent and skilled operator working in a consistent and uniform manner will enable the observer to make a better study with fewer observations than will an erratic operator. An observer must be careful, however, not to assume that consistent operators are working at a normal pace. Sometimes, their pace can be consistently above or below normal.

The number of cycles also depends on the skill and experience of the observer. An inexperienced observer invariably requires more observation cycles.

Rating the Operator's Performance

While recording the data, the observer is also evaluating the operator's speed in relation to his own trained concept of what a normal pace or tempo should be. The timestudy engineer needs enough stopwatch readings of each element to provide a representative sample, thereby applying an average speed rating to a representative actual elemental time—or applying speed ratings to each actual elemental time and then determining a representative average of these "normalized" readings.

The purpose of "rating" or "leveling" is to convert the observed time into a normal time for the element or operation. This depends on the judgment and experience of the observer. Rating must be done on the spot while the operator is working and the tempo is fresh in the observer's mind. Generally, the timestudy person first rates the entire operation and then proceeds, during the study, to rate each element separately. Rating is essential to the setting of production standards because of the different tempos used by different operators on the same job.

Note that although the terms "speed," tempo, or pace are used in this text (because they are common in many companies), it is really "effectiveness" that the observer is judging. An operator with poor dexterity for instance, can be applying a great deal of effort, or appear to be making rapid motions but his effectiveness might be poor.

Some workers tend to be nervous during timestudy; others indifferent. Some workers will speed up during study; others will slow down; and still others will work at their usual pace. As a result, the observer must normalize the readings to arrive at what is normal time irrespective of which operator works on the job. For example, an operator performs an operation in an observed time of 0.40 minute and is working, according to the judgment of the observer, at a productivity level of 75%. He rates the operator at 0.75 thus, producing a normal time of 0.40 × 0.75, or 0.30 minute. Conversely, a faster (more effective) operator may get a reading of 0.24 minute. Rating this worker at 125%, normal time is 0.24 × 1.25, or 0.30 minute. The time of both workers has been normalized and is common to the operation, not the operator.

The skill in rating comes from experience. Knowledge of a specific industry's operation and exposure to its operational characteristics is of inestimable value. Experienced timestudy engineers, observing the same operation, will usually develop standards within 5% of each other.

Selecting the Operator to be Timed

Very often there is more than one operator doing the same job and therefore the timestudy engineer may study several of them providing that they are all using the same method. If the observer makes a brief survey of these operators and finds a wide variance in speed or pace among them, the choice might be to select the one working at close to normal speed.

As long as rating factors are used, theoretically it does not make any difference whether the slowest or fastest operator is studied. However, it is more difficult to rate correctly the tempo of a very slow or very fast operator. For example, in some timestudy departments, no standards can be set on an operator rated below 60%. New operators should not be used as well, since their methods are likely to change as they gain more experience and proficiency.

From a practical and psychological viewpoint it is better to timestudy operators who work closer to normal pace, rather than the fastest of the workers. If the fast operator is the basis for the time standard, other workers may be concerned that the standard will not allow sufficient time for them and that it will be impossible to meet.

Elemental Frequencies

Assume that your Industrial Engineers have developed a very accurate standard time for each elemental activity of a particular job. Does this imply that the production standard is also accurate? Not necessarily; there is a critical factor called "frequency" that must be considered. The time value for performing a certain element (such as, adjusting a machine) might be determined to be 0.82 standard minute. But the most important question is, "How many times does this occur during the cycle or each hour of machine operation?" Load machine, replace empty skid, change roll of material, move finished box of parts, and so on, are typical elements whose frequency must be identified.

Elemental times must be multiplied by the frequency (see Exhibit 8–1) in order to come up with the base time for the job. Therefore, the frequency is just as important—and in many cases, it is the more difficult value to obtain. It can be fairly easy to determine that the base time is 0.82 per occurrence, but it can be difficult to determine that the element should occur once, twice, or twenty times per hour of machine operation. If this adjustment occurs every 150 pieces, the time per piece (for this element) would be $0.82/150 = 0.55$ minute per 100 pieces. If the frequency is in error by 20%, the elemental base time can not be any more accurate than 80%.

Those responsible for profit planning, and those involved with estimating and pricing, should recognize that there are techniques available to assure required accuracy. Work sampling studies (described in Chapter 5) can be used effectively to identify frequencies. These are often invaluable in establishing unavoidable delay allowances. Frequency data can also be obtained as a by-product of time studies or production studies.

Too often the elemental time values are finely tuned, but the occurrences are crudely estimated. This can be a problem with any type of standard data obtained from the outside. If MTM data are used to measure elements whose frequencies are not evident, studies must be made in the local environment. In some cases, the standard time values can also be obtained from the same studies, thereby obviating the need to use outside standard data except for reference purposes.

In some situations it is not necessary to develop frequencies because elemental values are not used. For instance with work sampling, an "application" standard can be derived directly from the observations—that is, the standard time per hour or per job can be identified without knowing what the elemental values or frequencies are. This does not provide as much analytical information but the application standards can be set up more quickly.

Taking the Actual Timestudy

Exhibit 8–1 is an example of an observation sheet for a timestudied operation, showing all the steps from the initial readings through to the standard time.

1. The operation is broken down into four elements with one infrequent element "Reload" (reloading materials).

Exhibit 8–1
Timestudy Observation Sheet, Side 1 (Actual Study)

TIMESTUDY OBSERVATION SHEET

MARTIN & TUCKER, INC.
ENGINEERS

PROD. CTR. NO. __26__ ORDER/JOB NO. __17983__ OPERATOR __J. Smith__

MACHINE NO. __H-04__ CUSTOMER __ABC Corporation__

OPERATION __Assembly Parts (2 Pieces per Cycle)__

PRODUCT __Assembly 016-R__

UNIT OF MEASUREMENT
(PCS, IMPRESSIONS, LBS. LIN. FT.. SHEETS, BLANKS, ETC.)

NO. UP __2 Units per Cycle__

GANG UP/COMBINATION DATA _____

__Measured Daywork__

	TIME	OUTPUT	
STOP	8.79.11		
START	8.50.00	18	= __Pieces__
ELAPSED	29.11 min.		

NO.	ELEMENT DESCRIPTION	CLK	1	2	3	4	5	6	7	8	9	TOT.	NO.	AVER.	LF	BASE	SEL
							CYCLE & CLOCK TIMES										
1	A	E	.40	.36	.44	.918	.38	.59	.38	.37	.39	3.66	9	.407	1.0	.407	
		C	.40	3.17	6.89	11.77	14.68	17.86	20.61	23.53	26.53						
2	B	E	1.21	1.44	1.38	1.32	1.26	1.18	1.31	1.36	1.34	11.80	9	1.31	.8	1.048	
		C	1.61	4.61	8.27	13.09	15.94	19.04	21.92	24.89	27.87						
3	C	E	.88	.90	.96	.89	1.00	.88	.94	.95	.93	8.33	9	.9255	.8	.74	
		C	2.49	5.51	9.23	13.98	16.94	19.92	22.86	25.84	28.80						
4	D	E	.32	.94A	.21	.32	.33	.31	.30	.30	.31	2.72	9	.302	1.0	.302	
		C	2.81	6.45	9.44	14.30	17.27	20.23	23.16	26.14	29.11						
5	Reload	E			1.42							1.42	1	—	1.0	.178	
		C			10.86												
		E															
		C															
		E															
		C															
		E															
		C															
		E															
		C															

CALC. INFREQUENT ELEMENTS & UNAVOID. DELAYS

EL. NO. SYM	BASE TIME	OBSERVED OCCUR.	OBSERVED CYCLES	FREQ OF OCCUR.	SEL. FREQ.	SELECTED TIME
1/3	.56	1	9	.111	.05	.028
5	1.42	1	9	.111	.111	.158

RECORD UNAVOIDABLE & AVOIDABLE DELAYS

SYM	C	E	DESCRIPTION	u/a
A	5.51	✕		
	6.13	.62	Dumped pan	a
B	10.86			
	11.42	.56	Jam up	u
C				
D				
E				

#412

2. The study is taken on a continuous basis starting at 8.50.00 (30 minutes past 8 A.M.) and ending at 8.79.11. The duration of the timestudy is 29.11 minutes.
3. Nine cycles were studied, each of which produced 2 units, or a total of 18 pieces.
4. After filling in all data (before the study is started) and checking methods, the timestudy engineer starts the study. The watch is set at zero and at the end of each element, the watch reading is recorded in the lower portion of the split space marked C (C for cumulative reading).
5. Without stopping the watch, a record is kept of clock time from one cycle onto the next. After the third element (C) of the second cycle, the operator accidentally drops the pan of material and has to pick up the pieces. The observer waits until the worker straightens out the mess and the instant that he returns to work on the fourth element, the timestudy engineer records the end of this avoidable delay in the space provided in the lower right portion of the observation sheet as 6.13 minutes. (Later, this will provide the basis for getting the delay time, viz., 6.13 minus 5.51, or 0.62 minute). The engineer also writes in the cause of the delay and how this time will be treated in building the standard. Since it was deemed an avoidable delay, it will not be included in the standard. The first delay is recorded in line A, and later it will be subtracted to construct the standard.
6. At the end of the third cycle, the operator stops to reload materials (having used up the few parts left from the previous shift) and the observer drops down a space to create a fifth element and records the watch reading at the end of the reload element. Of course, this is considered an infrequent element.
7. Immediately after reloading the materials, there is a jamup at the assembly position and the watch reading is taken after the jamup has been cleared. The jamup starting at 10.86 minutes and ending at 11.42, is recorded on line B. It is considered to be an unavoidable delay and is therefore marked u.
8. The study then proceeds to the end of 9 cycles and is completed at 29.11 minutes.
9. The observer then returns to his desk and makes all the subtractions to get E, (the Elapsed time) for each element per cycle. Obtaining an average time for each element, among those considered valid, the observer applies the speed rating or leveling factor (LF) and calculates the base normal cycle time.
10. The unavoidable time of 0.56 minute for the jamup is transferred to the lower left box area and a decision is made on how often such a delay is likely to occur. The observed frequency of occurrence is one time out of 8 cycles, i.e., 12.5% of the time, or 0.125. After checking with the supervisor and some personal investigation, it is decided that the jamup will occur less frequently and therefore, 0.05 is selected as the frequency of occurrence. By multiplying 0.05 times the base time of 0.56 minute, a selected time of 0.028 minute *per cycle* is obtained.
11. The frequency of the reloading element is not a matter of estimate but is based on the number of parts that can be loaded at a time. If reloading

54

Developing a Production Standard from Timestudy

is done every 8 cycles, both the actual and selected frequency is 0.125 and the selected time 0.178 minute.

12. On the reverse side of the observation sheet (Exhibit 8–2), the timestudy engineer inserts the total base time of the regular elements, the infrequent elements, and the unavoidable delay time for each cycle.

13. To this total is added the policy, personal and fatigue allowances expressed in percentages. (Note that some timestudy departments express these allowances as number of minutes per day, but these allowed minutes are easily converted into percentages).

14. The total of base time and allowances is called the standard time. Standard time can be expressed in various ways, as shown. It is important to bear in mind that the standard must ultimately be converted into time per unit or units per minute, hour, and so on and these calculations are also given. In the final figures, the standard is 2.61 standard hours per 100 units, or 38.20 units per standard hour.

Other Comments on the Observation Sheet

Standard Crew. This number is an important factor in the operation because labor hours affect costs. Some operations are unaffected by the size of the crew but for others, it has a marked effect on output per hour.

Units per Cycle. In the operation timestudied in Exhibit 8–1, the operator (or machine) produced two units simultaneously. In other operations, only one or more than two units might be produced simultaneously.

In machine operations, it is sometimes impractical to get readings per piece on high-speed equipment because of the human limitations in reading the watch. An example is a punch press that may be operating at a speed of 1,000 pieces per hour. For that type of operation, the observer may elect to take his reading once every 50, 100, or 300 pieces. This decision must be recorded immediately in order to arrive at the correct standard time later during desk calculations.

Number ''Up.'' This refers to a continuous operation where pieces are produced from a coil, roll, or web. For instance, an unprocessed roll of material is fed into a die, or a printing plate, and at one stroke, punch or impression, 4 pieces are produced. In another case, the operation splits the roll and 6 pieces are produced lengthwise and 4 pieces are produced across the roll thereby giving 24 units per stroke. Again, this must be recorded for purposes of later calculation.

Parameter. As mentioned in a previous chapter, this term refers to physical characteristics of the operation that cause the unit time to vary. For example, the time standard for a milling machine that processes a metal part cannot be expressed as one number but rather as a series of numbers relating to the material's size, weight, and so on. Each part to be machined may require a different feed, speed and depth of cut, thus requiring a different standard time. In this example, the parameters are feed and depth of cut. If different metals are processed through that machine, then additional parameters would

Exhibit 8–2
Timestudy Observation Sheet, Side 2 (Actual Study)

TIMESTUDY OBSERVATION SHEET

MARTIN & TUCKER, INC.
ENGINEERS

STUDY NO. _174_

METHODS SHEET NO. _Ref. 174 rev._

OBSERVER _THL_

CLIENT CO. _ABC Corporation_

DATE _4-17-8X_

DEPT. _Assembly_

FOREMAN _J. Jones_

UNION REP. _D. Stewart_

WORK AREA LAYOUT

SCALE =

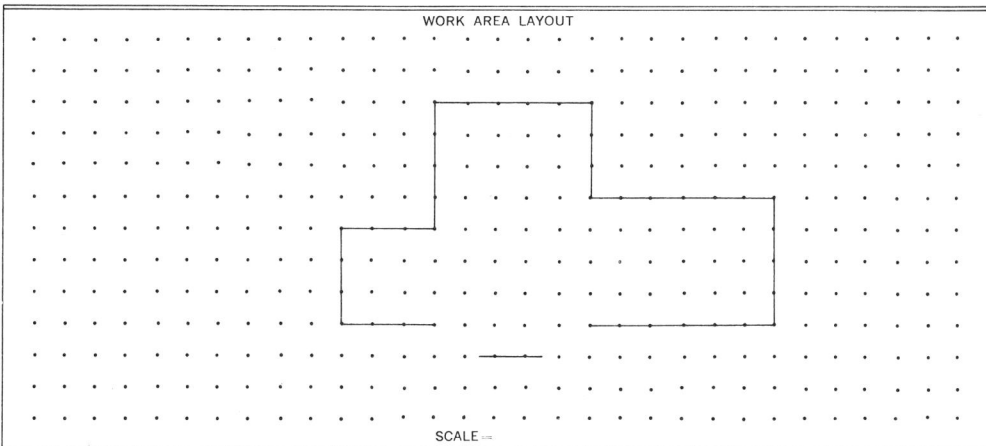

MATERIAL PARAMETERS	EQUIPMENT PARAMETERS	OTHER PARAMETERS
		ORDER QTY. _450_
		PROD. SIZE _6 X 7 X 10_
	Fixture Type B	PROD. STYLE _4Y 37 AK_

NOTES & REMARKS

STD. CREW _1_

UNIT _Pieces_

UNITS PER CYCLE _2_

NO. UP = NO. IN x DIRECTION X NO. IN y DIRECTION

_____ = _____ X _____

_N/A_

FOREMAN'S OK _J.J._   DATE

M & T OK _SAT_   APPROVED _4/23/8X_

SUMMARY

ITEM	MINUTES	
	MACH.	MAN.
BASE TIME: REG. ELEMENTS		2.497
BASE TIME: INFREQ. ELEMENTS		0.158
BASE TIME: UNAVOID. DELAYS		0.028
TOTAL BASE TIME		2.683
POLICY DELAYS _4_ %		0.107
POLICY DELAYS _12_ %		0.322
INCENTIVE ALLOW _____ %		0
STANDARD MIN. PER CYCLE		3.112
STANDARD HRS. PER CYCLE		0.05187
STANDARD HRS. PER _C_ UNITS		2.954
STANDARD _____ UNITS PER HR.		3855

be brass, steel, aluminum, and so on. Hardness of the metal could be another parameter, together with finish specified.

In operations requiring a gradual buildup to cruising speed, a typical parameter would be the quantity of the run as mentioned previously.

It is rare that an equitable PS is one number since, recognized or not, there are parameters that affect the selected speeds and output. For convenience in many instances, management will choose one average figure to use in its cost calculations. This could have a dramatic effect on the direct production cost and contribution measurements, as the actual time departs from the averaged "standard" time. An example of this follows:

| | Optimum Speeds | | |
| | Size of Pieces | | |
Type of Base Material	Up to 10"	11" to 19"	20" and Over
a	1,000	800	600
b	700	550	400
c	600	500	400

Comment

1. Average historical speed = 600.

2. Error between 600 and 1,000 = 67% by not employing or recognizing the parameters of base material and size of piece.

9 Determining the Time Allowances

As discussed in previous chapters, allowances of various types must be added to the normal (base) time for each element or operation. These are classified into personal, fatigue, and unavoidable delay categories.

When normal times are developed through one of the observation techniques, these allowances must be observed or determined separately from the normal base time. (If historical data are the only source of standards, the allowances are in effect, already reflected in the data but the content is unknown.)

Delays affect machine-paced as well as manual-paced operations. In addition, the manual-paced operations are affected by the personal needs of the operating personnel and their need for rest. These do not usually become evident during an observation. Or if they do, they may not be consistent. Is the observed personal or fatigue time appropriate for a standard that will be used to measure costs and contribution? Not likely. Therefore, certain guidelines described below must be used to be sure that the allowances are representative.

People do not work at the same tempo through the day, hence the need for rating. (See Chapter 8.) Neither do they uniformly use personal and fatigue time. Therefore, the normal time must be developed, and then these allowances must be separately applied.

Personal Allowance. This allowance is provided to recognize the fact that every worker needs personal time in the washroom, etc. For light work, this allowance is about 2% to 5%. Although the amount of personal time will vary with the worker more than with the work done, it has been established that workers need more personal time when the work is heavy and done under unfavorable conditions, particularly in a hot humid atmosphere. Under such conditions, more than 5% may have to be allowed.

Fatigue (Rest) Allowance. In spite of advances in modern industry, in terms of improved machinery, materials handling equipment and the like, workers still get tired as the day progresses. An operator could work at a high rate of speed and energy until midmorning, for example, and then slow down towards lunch time. After lunch, the pace may be even slower and then pick up again. While this type of pace change is a function of the day's progression, there are other types that relate to physical exertion, such as having to stack heavy boxes, moving loaded trucks, and so on. Such physical demands cause fatigue more directly than simply the passage of time. Although these demands are rather obvious, there are others that are more subtle, such as demanding mental activity, working under adverse conditions of heat, cold, dust, and noise, and so forth. And, if a worker is exposed to the hazards of accidents, he certainly needs more rest. This is one reason for the management policy of enforced rest periods. Another factor contributing to fatigue is the monotony of the operation. In any case, there is no objective way of measuring fatigue except in terms of daily output. Output achieved by people on incentive plans (performing manually controlled work) has provided useful guidelines for the application of these allowances. Studies of workers taken on a sampling basis throughout the day often provide a close estimate of the fatigue allowance. The allowance is usually a percentage to be added to normalized time. See Appendix for other methods of applying this allowance.

Fatigue allowances will range from about 5% to 20% or more. Some physically or mentally demanding jobs require allowances of up to 50% or more.

Since there is some overlap between personal and fatigue allowances, some industrial engineers apply them as a single combined allowance.

Delay Allowances. Some delays are inherent in every operation. These are classified as *unavoidable* and should be reflected in PS. There are also other delays that should not be included in PS because they could be eliminated if the operating and support people were performing their jobs properly. These are classified as *avoidable*. If avoidable delays are buried in PS, the costs and contribution are distorted, and management's efforts to remove them are subverted. Consequently the company's competitive position in the market-place may suffer.

The classification of delays, therefore, is a serious, practical matter—not an academic issue. Each company has to measure and critically analyze all delay times, and then decide which of them should be reflected in its cost estimating via their PS.

There are no hard and fast rules for treating delays. As a matter-of-fact, the same type delay may be classified differently in different companies. For instance, suppose that one envelope company has a plant that is air-conditioned throughout the year. Since humidity is controlled, paper curling is almost nonexistent. Another envelope company without air-conditioning facilities experiences considerable delays resulting from curled paper jamming its processing machinery.

The question is: Should this latter company classify these delays as "avoidable" or "unavoidable"? The answer is, probably unavoidable because of the fixed environment that induces these delays. On the other hand, referring to the first envelope company, suppose its air-conditioning equipment breaks down because of poor maintenance. How should jamming delays be treated? Avoidable, because the situation can be remedied.

The key to these classifications is an understanding of what should be considered normal for a reasonably well-controlled plant, considering its existing environment.

Suppose that downtime delays are caused by absenteeism. A less-qualified operator was assigned to temporarily replace the regular operator who was absent and was not able to run the machine as well. Should the company consider the *additional* downtime delays as unavoidable? To answer that question, we must know more about the situation. If the company feels that the additional delays constitute a normal situation that it will continue to live with, it might include this increment in the PS. But if the company intends to control the problem (highlighted by the analysis) and does not want the excess time included in the cost estimates, it will treat those delays as avoidable.

Good measurement data are needed before these classifications can be made with any degree of reliability. As described in this book, some of the delays that occur can be classified when a timestudy or sampling study is being made. An obvious example: an operator knocks over a pallet load of material because he moves the fork lift truck carelessly. We would classify this delay as avoidable on the spot.

The pattern of occurrence of some delays is random and erratic. Therefore, it is important to determine their representative frequencies, as we discussed in Chapter 8. When a classification decision cannot be a clear yes or no, a percentage for each may be applied, viz: 60% avoidable; 40% unavoidable.

The classification process can be confusing and frustrating if adequate information about the nature of the delays, their causes and patterns of occurrence, etc., is not available. Once the data are provided, however, the classifications fall into place. Basically, you must first determine what is causing the delay and who is responsible for it. Then, a judgment is made relative to management policy. From a management viewpoint, does the company accept the situation as normal, or does it intend (within practical limits) to reduce or eliminate the problem?

Machine Interference (discussed in Chapter 10) is normally considered unavoidable because it is the result of deliberate assignments to service people. That is, it is not an out-of-control situation the company plans to eliminate.

Infrequent elements such as, reload materials, replace tools, clean machine, get instructions, etc., are not delays because they are an essential part of the operation. These elements are always included in PS after the proper frequency is determined.

With unlimited financial resources and management attention, any delay could be eliminated, theoretically. But in the real business world, a company should not ignore those that are going to persist. In some companies, delays are excluded from PS to be "competitive." This is an exercise in self-deception regardless of the rationales used. To obtain a rational measurement of contribution, unavoidable delays must be included in building PS.

An invaluable by-product of the delay classification process is providing management with target data with which they can take remedial and corrective action.

Policy Allowances. A policy allowance covers activity that is required by management directive. Typical among these is the end-of-the-shift cleanup where a worker is required to stop a few minutes before the end of his shift to clean his machine, tools, workplace, and so forth. Falling into the same category are preventive maintenance checks made during the working day.

Application and Computation of Allowances

The PS states that the press is to run at 5,000 sheets per hour. For an eight-hour shift, that would be equivalent to 40,000 pieces. The actual production turns out to be only 25,000. Is something wrong with the count? Is the standard correct? How could they lose 15,000 sheets?

Does this sound familiar? Are your standards this far from "reality"? This is a serious but not unusual situation. The performance against the standard (in this case 25,000/40,000, or 63%) indicates a substantial loss. Is this acceptable or don't the standards have any *credibility*? If the performance is as low as this case, there should be grave concern. But on the other hand, if everyone knows that there are no allowances in the standards, the performance will receive little credence, making it easy for the production department to rationalize *any* performance.

The basic reason for including allowances in the standards is to provide a realistic, credible target for the production department to shoot for, and to provide a known performance on which to base the cost estimates or any other economic production measurement. See Appendix for additional material.

10 Manual versus Machine Time

Is the time required to produce a product determined by an operator or by a machine? That is, is the operation man- or machine-controlled? Since most plants are operated with both, we must be able to measure and establish standards for both.

Most of the traditional Industrial Engineering techniques were developed from a need to measure and evaluate factory labor because the operators, in most cases, controlled the rate of production. Machine-controlled operations continue to increase however, and require some special measurement techniques.

In an operation where a machine is being used, there are in many cases, both man- and machine-controlled elements. Engineering analysis and measurement are important in order to achieve the best utilization of both, the human and mechanical resources and to establish meaningful standards.

Machine Assignment/ Machine Interference

The number of machines assigned to a service person is a subject of serious consideration. When PS are being established, it can have a significant effect on costs and facility utilization. Basically, when *two or more* machines are assigned to a service person (whether or not the machines have individual operators), there is always the chance (which occurs with measurable probability) that two or more of the machines will require service *at the same time*. In this event, since the service person can do only one thing at a time, only one machine will be serviced and the others will have to wait. This is called *machine interference*.

Some companies try to keep the servicepeople busy by assigning them a greater number of machines. However, a large percentage of machine interference may exist and the company may not realize as much production from

**Exhibit 10–1
Example of Machine
Interference Curves**

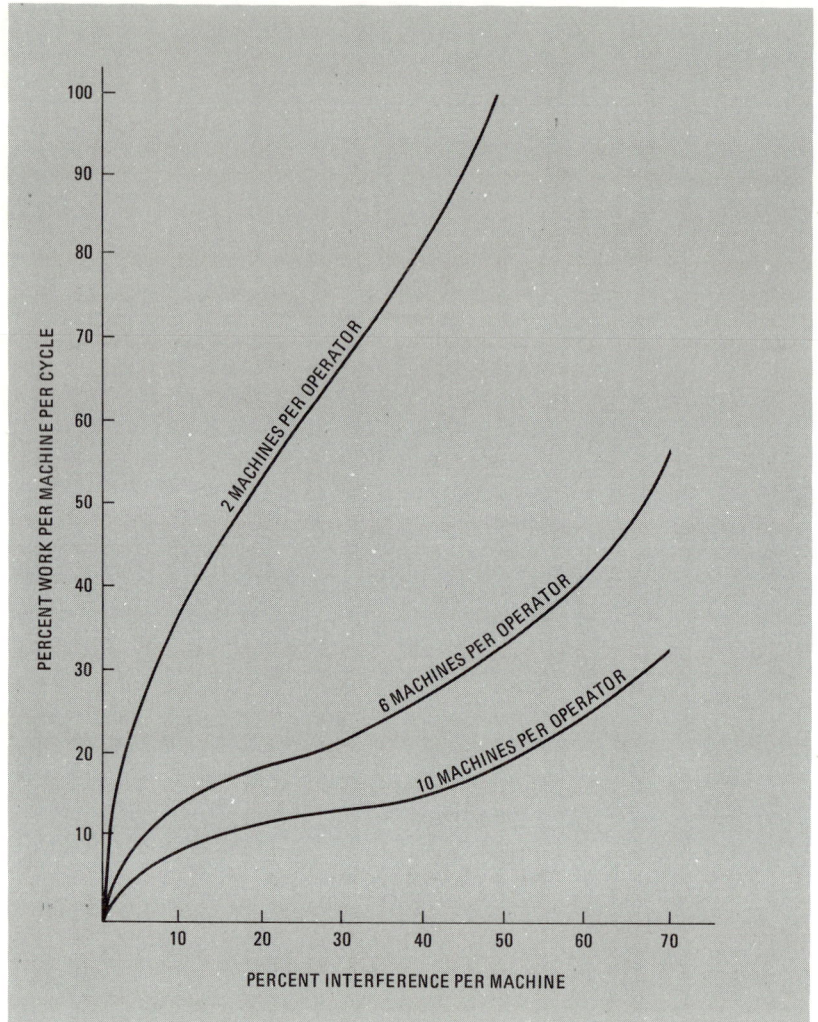

its equipment as it would if fewer machines were assigned. It may also reduce the company's return on its investment.

The amount of machine interference is a function of the machine and the job being run. Selecting the optimum number of machines to be assigned will minimize costs and be consistent with the company's production requirements. To make this decision, some basic data must first be obtained concerning the characteristics of the machines and the work that is being processed. For example, if infrequent elements and downtime can be predicted, it is easier to synchronize the machine cycles and minimize interference. On the other hand, if much of the downtime requires the service person and that time is unpredictable (occurs at random frequencies), it is impossible to synchronize the machines, and interference will increase at a higher rate with a greater machine assignment.

Machine interference is not proportionate to the number of machines assigned. For instance, when a second machine is assigned, the interference downtime for each machine might be 13% (waiting for service). When a third machine is added, the downtime may increase by an additional 13%. But when a fifth machine is added, the increase in this downtime will be less, perhaps only 8%.

Effect on Profit Planning

Why is machine interference so important to profit planning? The standards must include adequate allowances, and therefore must include an amount for machine interference. If the interference is not carefully measured, or if the number of service people varies (resulting in a different number of machines assigned to each person) without using a different standard, the estimated cost could be wrong by 20% to 30% or more.

Are machine assignments treated casually? Has any analysis been made to determine the machine interference patterns? Are the PS based on the optimum assignments? If your company has multiple machine assignments for service people (setup people, adjusters, makeready personnel, and so on) *or* for operators, an analysis should have been made. This is one of the tasks involved in the establishment of *engineered* standards.

The basic data required for a multimachine assignment analysis can be obtained through work sampling (described in Chapter 5). Sometimes testing is necessary. Thus, different assignments are tried and the resulting machine interference measured empirically. In some cases, a simulation can be developed. With some measurement of the machine's cycle and the service person's work, it is possible to calculate how much downtime (due to machine interference) will occur if he is assigned 2, 3, 4, 5, 6, or more machines. This simulation can be done on a computer, in complex cases, but a satisfactory calculation can often be done manually. Your industrial engineering service will be able to supply the best technique.

Exhibit 10–1 illustrates how in one situation the interference related to the workload of the service person and the number of machines assigned. For instance, if the work per machine is 20% and there are six machines being serviced, the interference is about 23% for each machine.

Summary

Management must understand that multiple machine assignments will affect the costs (through utilization of machines and workers). These decisions should be made on the basis of rational measurements.

For practical and economic reasons, a different number of machines may be assigned to a service person at various times because of disparate quantities to be processed. Therefore, a *set* of production standards as well as a *set* of MHRs should be available. The cost estimate for any particular job or for any economic measurement will then require selection of the appropriate combination.

Internal and External Work

This does not refer to work done inside or outside of the building, rather it applies to manual work in relation to machine cycle. It is extremely important to identify elements of jobs that involve man and machine because of the way they affect the job *cycle*, the standard, and the *cost* of producing the product.

Internal Work refers to those manual activities that *can* be performed while the machine is operating (that is, producing salable product). The key word is "can," because you may find that some of this work is not done while the machine is operating. This can be caused by the manning (crew) or the methods. Therefore, it may be beneficial to analyze this kind of situation to determine whether it would be economically attractive to try to perform it "internally."

External Work, on the other hand, refers to activities which *cannot* be performed while the machine is operating. External work will obviously increase the job cycle. The job *cycle* is the sum of machine cycle and the external work, as long as it is possible for the operator or service person to perform all internal work while the machine is operating. This may be affected by the *number of machines assigned* to one person.

When the job is studied and analyzed, the engineer must identify which elements can be performed internally. If there is too much work for one person to perform internally, a second person might be assigned, if there is an overall economic benefit. This might be the case of one operator having to obtain and prepare the material to be fed into the machine and a too short machine cycle to allow enough time to do it.

The rate of accomplishment (speed rating) required to perform the work internally is one factor that is often overlooked in internal work analyses. Good industrial engineering practice normally would require up to 100% productivity internally. In other words, when it is said that the work can be done internally, it is assumed that this work will be done at 100% where necessary. There are situations, however, when the internal work might be a relatively small part of the operator's total work and might require a performance of more than 100%.

When the job cycle is measured (for the job standard), the external work (such as roll changes, clearing jams, etc.) is also expected to be done at 100%. But, if this also represents only a minor portion of the total manual work, the performance might exceed 100%.

Summary

The *job cycle* identifies the standard to be used for costing, as well as decisions on price acceptances, and so forth. Cost and contribution measurements can be dramatically affected by the crewing and the determination of internal and external work. Whatever designation is made, it must be *practical* since the operating personnel must be able to *actually* perform it in the manner prescribed. Many times we have found that with some minor *alteration* in the machine or in the methods being used, work that was formerly done externally could be done internally, with a beneficial reduction in the cycle time.

Economic Crew Size

Economic crew size considers the number of people assigned to work exclusively on one machine. Where fractional people are assigned (more than one machine per worker), the considerations are covered in the previous discussions.

How many people are required to run one machine? If just one person operates it, there is no economic consideration other than trying to run the machine as fast as possible, with due consideration for quality requirements and optimum waste. The work should first be measured to determine whether one or more people are needed to run the machine at various speeds. Speed variations may be directly related to the parameters of operation, or they may be affected by the ability of the crew to keep up (working at a maximum of 100% productivity for any sustained period). In other words, the supervisor may elect to run the machine slower than the rated speed because he cannot assign another person, or chooses not to do so.

How are these decisions made? In some plants, we find that the supervisor is called upon to use personal judgment; in other instances, it is the management that dictates a policy regarding crew size. Often, arbitrary data are used that lead to uneconomical decisions. In other cases, the extra people are not available. Management should consider making extra people available if the economic benefits are attractive. Even if a constant-size plant or departmental work force is desired or necessary, an economic evaluation would indicate where the people should be assigned to optimize the costs.

What is the effect on profit contribution due to a change in crew size? Suppose that with one person, a machine can be run at 1,000 units per hour. If the cost of the labor including fringes is $10 per hour, the unit cost of labor would be $10/1,000 = $10 per M. Assume the remaining part of the MHR is $8.50. The total cost would then be $18.50 per M. Incidentally, the machine may not be running at 1,000 units per hour but the standard (from work measurement) indicates that at 100% productivity (performance), it could be run at 1,000 units per hour. Therefore, this is the reference point from which the analysis should be made.

Now, assume that the machine could be run (with good quality of product) at 1,800 units per hour with an extra person to handle the offcoming product. If the cost of the second person is $8 per hour, the total labor (CCT) cost would be $18. The other portions of the MHR might increase somewhat, viz, DCB up $1.50, making the total MHR $28. The unit cost now becomes $28/1,800 = $15.56 per M. This is a substantial saving of $2.94 per M and results in an equal increase in contribution. Whether the company can provide the additional worker when needed, especially if the need is sporadic, is the question that remains to be answered. A strategy can now be developed since a rational yardstick is available.

This yardstick is possible only if equitable PS are used. Guesses lead to expensive decisions—contribution-draining decisions. As is true in many cases, management does not take action on these matters because they suspect that the guesses are invalid. The key is the ability to measure (after suitable methods analysis) how much manpower is needed at different speeds. In other words, management must know the true contributing effect of higher machine speeds and be aware of the offsetting cost of additional personnel to support these speeds.

For example, a machine can produce a good product at speeds of 10,000, 20,000, 30,000, 40,000, and 50,000 units per hour. As the speed is set higher, more people are required at the end of the line to catch the units and pack them. When the relationship between speeds and crew size is nonlinear (not proportionate), there must be an optimum speed at which the unit cost is lowest. Although this is the economic choice, there are situations where this optimum relationship must be disregarded, such as when facilities are loaded and critical deliveries of product must be made.

A final note—the economic crew size analysis is one of the important factors used when making return-on-capital evaluations for machinery acquisitions, in make-buy decisions, and so on.

The Effect of Speed and Selling Price. Consider a typical operation in which one or two packers might be used at the end of a packing line, depending on the running speed. First, the labor standard must be developed from the data obtained through timestudy, viz:

Work Element	Normal Min. per Occurrence	Frequency per 100	P & F Allowance	Std. Min. per 100
Pick up 50, inspect and put in box	.08	2-1	10%	.176
Aside full box, position empty box	.12	1/5	12%	.027
Aside or straighten defective piece	.03	1/2	10%	.017
Total				.220

This indicates that a packer needs .220 minutes per 100 units, when working at 100% to pack them 50 to a box. The speed of the machine is variable and can produce satisfactory product over a certain range. (We'll assume for purposes of this example, that the quality or waste is about the same at any speed. This will be explored further in Chapter 12.) The following table shows the machine time required over the available range:

Run Speed (Pieces/Minute)	Minutes per 100 Pieces
400	.250
500	.200
600	.167
700	.143
800	.125

From these data it is clear that if the packer works at 100%, a second person will be needed to keep up with the machine as the speed is increased somewhat over 500 per minute. (The exact speed is 100 pieces per .220 minutes.)

What are the o.o.p. conversion costs and contributions with these conditions? The following table shows these calculations, given a MHR of $22 for one packer and a MHR of $33 for two packers.

	1 Packer		2 Packers						
Speed: pcs/min	400	450	500	550	600	650[a]	700	750	800
M/hr.	24	27	30	33	36	39	42	45	48
MHR (given)	$22	22	33	33	33	33	33	33	33
O.o.p. conver. cost/M	$.917	.815	1.10	1.00	.917	.846	.786	.733	.688
Change in contrib. per M (vs. 450 per min.)			$(.285)	(.185)	(.102)	(.031)	.029	.082	.127

[a]675/min. At this speed the o.o.p. conversion cost/M and the conversion contribution/M will be the same as one packer at 450/minute.

This clearly shows that the o.o.p. cost per M and contribution per M is better with two packers at a speed of about 700 per minute or better. (The exact speed can be calculated as 675 per minute.)

If this machine will not run faster than 600 per minute, should a second packer be assigned? More production can be obtained, but the contribution per M will be less than if it were to run at 450 per minute with one packer. The answer lies in the need for the extra production, and the price at which it can be sold.

The following table shows the contribution per 40-hour week, if the product is sold for $1.00 per M. As an example, the previous table shows that at 450 per minute, the o.o.p. cost is $.815 per M. The contribution is $.185 per M, and the contribution per hour is $.185 per M $\times$ 450 $\times$ 60/1000 = $5.00, or $200 per 40-hour week.

	1 Packer		2 Packers						
Speed: pcs/min	400	450	500	550	600	650	700	750	800
@ S.P. = $1.50/M:									
S. P. per hour	$ 24	27	30	33	36	39	42	45	48
Contribution/	$ 80	200	(120)	—	120	240[a]	360	481	559

[a]AT 633 pcs/min., the contribution per hour is $200, same as one packer at 450 pcs/min. Therefore, a 2nd packer is justified above 633 pcs/min.

This illustrates that two packers will provide a higher contribution if the machine is run at 633 per minute or faster. Therefore, as stated earlier, if the machine will not run faster than 600 per minute, it would be better from a contribution viewpoint also, to run it with one packer at 450 per minute. Note, however, that there may be legitimate sales reasons for using the faster speeds irrespective of contribution consequences in order to fulfill customers present needs.

Let's see now what effect a price increase would have. If the selling price is $1.50 per M, the following table results:

Manual versus Machine Time

	1 Packer		2 Packers						
Speed: pcs/min	400	450	500	550	600	650	700	750	800
@ S.P. = $1.50/M:									
S. P. per hour	$ 36	41	45	50	54	59	63	68	72
Contribution/	$560	740	480	660	840	1020	1200	1381	1559

[a]AT 578 pcs/min., the contribution per hour is $740, same as one packer at 450 pcs/min. Therefore, a 2nd packer is justified above 578 pcs/min.

The speed at which the two-packer arrangement begins to provide more contribution is 578 pieces per minute. Therefore, at this selling price there is no question about the advantage or running at the maximum speed of 600 per minute. Of course, if the sales volume is less than this capacity, the contribution per M pieces must be the criterion.

11 Cross Section of Industry Production Standards

This chapter presents a variety of PS, with different formats and parameters, used presently in industry. These are examples of applications previously discussed in the book. However, we will comment briefly on each to show the ways in which PS are developed.

Fifty Actual Industry Production Standards

Exhibits 11–1 and 11–2 show the "run" standards for a flexo-graphic press. Exhibit 11–1 expresses the standards in "standard impressions per hour" and Exhibit 11–2, in "standard hours per thousand impressions." One is the reciprocal of the other; i.e., the standard of 10,925 per hour is the same as 0.092 standard hours per thousand. Either may be used on the cost estimate sheet. The cost estimate sheet is used in scheduling and developing performance variances; this will be discussed in a later chapter. Either form may be used when placing PS on the computer for estimating, performance measurements, scheduling, and so forth.

Thus, it would be inequitable to have only one speed figure for that facility since many different types of work are processed through it, each of which requires a different speed. Therefore, PS is rarely one number, but rather a set of values to account for the physical characteristics that make the time values change.

The parameters in these two standards are

1. *The size of the order (feet on order)*. This parameter is essential to show that running time is neither linear nor proportionate at all times. For a small order, such as 20M feet, getting the press up to "cruising" speed is recognized and will reduce the average running speed during the processing of that order. Perhaps, during such a small run, the press is up

to cruising speed at the last 5M feet of the order; the first 15M feet being the period during which the press speed is being inched up.

2. *Numbers of colors (color combination)*. In this example, the number of colors are not recognized on small orders. But starting with 25M, the effect of the number of colors to be printed comes into play. Here, the parameter accounts for the drying time of the various ink colors; i.e., greater care (and slower speed) must be used when printing 3 or 4 colors, in addition to other technical processing factors.

3. *Allowances*. Technical factors which can be applied regardless of the size of the order or number of colors (in this instance) are treated as overall allowances added to standard time. These generally refer to variations in quality or the nature of the material being processed. These factors affect the running time and, according to definition, should be considered as parameters. However, to introduce these factors as parameters would cause a multivariable presentation of the PS making it difficult to apply. There- fore, since the presence of these technical factors can manifest themselves together with any of the major parameters, it is practical to treat them as "additives" or "subtractives." These allowances are parametric in be- havior and have nothing at all to do with delay allowances that are built into the basic standard.

Exhibit 11–3 is a computation sheet. It informs the estimator how the data are to be used in predetermining the standard direct cost of a job inquiry.

Exhibit 11–4 uses the parameters of number of cuts to be made (in slitting), and the form of material; viz., whether supplied in sheeting or tubing (in rewinding).

Exhibit 11–5 is a standard which explains the physical factors of the operation and suggests, using a nomogram, how to extract standard times within the practical range of operation. Exhibit 11–6 tabulates these data according to two parameters: (1) bag length and (2) gauge of the material. The size of the order in this standard is handled more equitably as an allow- ance, listed under Quantity Variation.

Exhibit 11–7 shows the parameters of bag width and gauge. The allowances provide for the small order, extra-heavy gauge, and special items which differ from the major product mix.

Exhibits 11–8 through 11–10 deal with the standardization of a facility that can handle a variety of materials in different ways. Exhibit 11–8 shows the variations in the materials; viz., type, gauge and adhesives, coatings and the mechanical specifications of the process. Exhibit 11–9 shows the standards for any type of generic product; i.e., "2-ply laminations," the practical combinations of material-to-material-to-adhesive-to-coating. Thus, there are 15 combinations for this product whereas in Exhibit 11–10, for 3-ply lami- nations, the number of combinations is 7. The lamination components and the way in which they are combined reflect the parameters for this operation.

Exhibit 11–11 represents a "makeready" or setup standard. The work in this preparatory operation is identified with a job and is considered chargeable time. This makeready operation is broken down into three steps: basic make- ready, press washup, and remove makeready. Not all makereadies require the same degree of preparation, and these variations are reflected in the parameter "number of colors."

Exhibit 11–12 is a run standard for a given set of styles of folding cartons, namely, seal end, reverse tuck end, and straight tuck end (SE, RTE, STE). For other styles, different standards should be used. The 3 parameters affecting running speed are: (1) inches of feed length, (2) size of the order, and (3) the thickness or caliper of the paperboard being used. In addition, allowances would be used for heavier board: narrow width cartons; shallow depth cartons; and the use of different devices on the gluing machine.

Exhibit 11–13 illustrates a folding operation in a bindery department using both setup and run. Notice that each has its own specific parameters.

Exhibit 11–14 is a run standard for a camera operation in the printing and folding-carton industry. The two major parameters are obvious.

Exhibits 11–15 and 11–16 show PS for *one element* of a makeready on a web-fed printing press in the label industry involving the changing of copy-design plates. The standard hours apply to 8 presses which are grouped into 3 production centers. The time values developed account for the fact that the changes apply to the same number of colors; viz, from 1 color to 1 color, etc. Exhibit 11–16 illustrates standards that require different color combinations because these affect the number of plates.

Exhibit 11–17 shows the standards for another element in the makeready of the same type of press, i.e., changing the ink colors. In this PS, there is an allowance for time differences due to the change in kind of ink. Within the general categories of ''standard mixed inks,'' ''process inks,'' ''mixed inks,'' and ''varnish,'' the variations in going from light and dark oil-based inks to light and dark moisture-set (MS) inks and vice versa are illustrated.

Exhibit 11–18 represents the run standards for one type of product on the same press, namely, pressure-sensitive matrix removed labels. Here, the parameters are the number of colors from 0 to 5 and the specific die to be used in running the order.

Exhibit 11–19 is the standard for the *element* of ''change print cylinder'' as part of the makeready in a 5-color gravure printing press. In order to provide standard-hours for the three sequential steps (first through fifth color), the elemental steps to accomplish these operations are listed.

Exhibit 11–20 is not a production standard; it shows the standardization of waste cost for estimating purposes. *Material Standard* is created to recognize that a waste allowance cannot be handled as a flat percentage added to raw material cost. Basically, there are two kinds of waste in production.

1. *Makeready*. That caused by some or all of the elements of a makeready setup; i.e., waste that unavoidably occurs during the makeready up to the point where the makeready is completed and the operator starts his ''run.'' This excess cost (in this instance) is a function of the color-to-color change, the type of material, the length of the stroke, the standard speed of the press, and the roll width. These latter factors are the parameters of this material standard.
2. *Run*. That caused by the material, the machine, or the job characteristics while it is running. Standard waste allowances can usually be developed for each production center based on those parameters. The machine speed may also affect waste. Chapter 12 describes how this should be considered in the selection of the correct speed when establishing the Run standard.

Exhibit 11–21 is a PS which combines all elements of the makeready of a small printing press in an envelope converting plant. The type of makeready has been broken down into classes and areas. These are parameters. The additives not only provide for variations in quality required, but also give standard times for once-a-day operations, such as, morning startup.

Exhibit 11–22 shows a chart of *washup* production standards on an envelope printer. If a washup can be identified with a specific job, the specific PS can be applied to that job. If the washup is not identifiable with any specific job, it should be included in an average MR standard for all jobs on that facility. In some printing plants, the washup time range can be appreciable. In this PS, the washup cycle time is from a low of 0.177 to 1.5 standard hours—a multiple of almost 8.5.

Exhibit 11–23 is one sheet of a multisheet set of PS for an envelope folding machine involving a product parameter and an envelope size parameter under each product type. The major parameter is the size of the order (lot), followed by the weight of the paper used, and whether the blank is plain or printed —a total of 5 parameters. Referring to the printed line of 40M lot and over, 20 lb, the range in time is from 0.1015 to 0.1608 standard hours per thousand, or an increase in time of 58%. If a "one number" average is used, in this case and in others, the effect on the estimate of direct conversion costs and contribution measurement at the pricing point would be serious.

Exhibit 11–24 illustrates an interesting aspect of standards-setting using the same machine as in the previous exhibit. This sheet deals with the development of standard delay allowances, which relate to the machine changes, waiting times, and policy delays. Such an approach forms the backup data for the delay allowances included in the PS. This documentation is recommended for a high quality standards program.

Exhibit 11–25 is a set of run standards for a taping operation in the corrugated container industry. The two major parameters within the type of corrugated board furnished are: (1) the length times width of the box, and (2) the width of the blank.

Exhibit 11–26 is another PS from the same industry, using three parameters: area, number cutout, and the length of the cutout.

Exhibit 11–27 is a setup standard developed in the automatic screw industry. Here, the parameters are the diameter of the spindle and the steps to be performed in accomplishing the setup operation.

Exhibit 11–28 is a machine-shop PS for a boring mill with a formula to calculate the standard time. The parameters are diameter of the boring mill, type of metal, and tooling.

Exhibit 11–29 is a production standard of a hand operation — hand soldering of electrical terminals. The parameters are, for one type of solder: wire gauge and the area of the terminal cross section. Note the guideline, i.e., the wattage (heat) of the soldering iron. An additive is used where soldering is required all around the terminal, or on both sides of the wire.

Exhibits 11–1 through 11–29 gave a fairly representative cross section of various standards, parameters, allowances, and formats to form a basis for establishing selection and design criteria.

Additional standards, Exhibits 11–30 through 11–50, are given without comment. These show different methods of presenting standards, and the reader is encouraged to identify parameters by himself or herself.

Exhibit 11–1
Actual Production Standard

STD. NO. ___IV (a)___   **PRODUCTION STANDARD**   **MARTIN & TUCKER, INC.** ENGINEERS

CHART NO. ___7___   PAGE _2_ OF _4_

MACHINE NO. _2_   DESCRIPTION: Hudson Sharpe 4-C Printing Press; Production Center #13

OPERATION: Print Flexo-Aniline   ELEMENT: Run

Standard Impressions per Hour

(5) Feet on Order	12M-25M	25,000-60,000		60,000-160,000		160,000-over	
Color Combination	1,2,3, or 4 Colors	3 or 4 Colors	1 or 2 Colors	3 or 4 Colors	1 or 2 Colors	3 or 4 Colors	1 or 2 Colors

#2 Press Output, for 1 out, Impressions/hr or Bags/hr
Foot per Minute Settings

Circumference of Printing Cylinders, in Inches	250	300	350	400	450	500	550
12½	10,925	13,100	15,275	17,475	19,650	21,825	24,025
13½	10,100	12,125	14,150	16,175	18,200	20,225	22,225
14½	9,400	11,300	13,175	15,050	16,950	18,825	20,700
15 3/4	8,650	10,400	12,125	13,850	15,600	17,325	19,050
16	8,525	10,225	11,950	13,650	15,350	17,050	18,750
16¼	8,400	10,075	11,750	13,425	15,125	16,800	18,475
16 3/4	8,150	9,775	11,400	13,025	14,650	16,300	17,925
17½	7,800	9,350	10,925	12,475	14,025	15,600	17,150
18¼	7,475	8,975	10,475	11,950	13,450	14,950	16,450
18½	7,375	8,850	10,325	11,800	13,275	14,750	16,225
19¼	7,075	8,500	9,925	11,350	12,750	14,175	15,600
20 3/4	6,575	7,900	9,200	10,525	11,825	13,150	14,475
21¼	6,425	7,700	9,000	10,275	11,550	12,850	14,125
22¼	6,125	7,350	8,575	9,800	11,025	12,275	13,500
23¼	5,875	7,050	8,225	9,400	10,575	11,725	12,900
24¼	5,625	6,750	7,875	9,000	10,125	11,250	12,375

Allowances

1. For close register printing: decrease Standard IPH 10%.
2. For tone and process printing: decrease Standard IPH 10%.
3. For tubing over 2.5 mil up to 3.5 mil: decrease Standard IPH 20%.
4. For tubing over 3.5 mil up to maximum: decrease Standard IPH 30%.
5. See Page 4 of 4, Standard No. IV for determining lineal feet on order.

To determine pounds per hour use formula (3).

(3) Lbs/hr = Roll Width x Gauge x .800 x fpm x 60

$$\boxed{\text{Lbs/hr} = 48 \times \text{Roll Width} \times \text{Gauge (in inches)} \times \text{fpm}}$$ (Tubing)

CLIENT COMPANY: _____ DATE ISSUED: _____ REVISION DATES: _____
DIVISION/PLANT: _____ M. & T. ENGINEER: _____
SUPERVISORY ACCEPTANCE: _____ M. & T. APPROVAL BY: _____

THE STANDARDS CONTAINED HEREIN ARE APPLICABLE TO THE MACHINE OR OPERATION AND METHODS EMPLOYED AS OF_____
AND ARE SUBJECT TO REVISION PENDING ANY ALTERATION OR CHANGE IN METHODS OR EQUIPMENT.

Exhibit 11–2
Actual Production Standard

STD. NO. __IV (a)__

CHART NO. __7__

MARTIN & TUCKER, INC.
ENGINEERS

PRODUCTION STANDARD

PAGE __3__ OF __4__

MACHINE NO. __2__ DESCRIPTION: __Hudson Sharpe 4-C Press; Production Center #13__

OPERATION: __Print Flexo-Aniline__ ELEMENT: __Run__

Standard Hours per M Impressions

(5) Lineal Feet on Order	12,000-25,000	25,000-60,000		60,000-160,000		160,000-over	
Color Combination	1, 2, 3, or 4 Colors	3 or 4 Colors	1 or 2 Colors	3 or 4 Colors	1 or 2 Colors	3 or 4 Colors	1 or 2 Colors

#2 Press Standard Time, for 1 out, hr/M Impressions or, hr/M Bags

Foot per Minute Setting

Circumference of Printing Cylinder, in Inches	250	300	350	400	450	500	550
12½	.092	.076	.065	.057	.051	.046	.042
13½	.099	.082	.071	.062	.055	.049	.045
14½	.106	.088	.076	.066	.059	.053	.048
15 3/4	.116	.096	.082	.072	.064	.058	.052
16	.117	.098	.084	.073	.065	.059	.053
16¼	.119	.099	.085	.074	.066	.060	.054
16 3/4	.123	.102	.088	.077	.068	.061	.056
17½	.128	.107	.092	.080	.071	.064	.058
18¼	.134	.111	.095	.084	.074	.067	.061
18½	.136	.113	.097	.085	.075	.068	.062
19¼	.141	.118	.101	.088	.078	.071	.064
20 3/4	.152	.127	.109	.095	.085	.076	.069
21¼	.156	.130	.111	.097	.087	.078	.071
22¼	.163	.136	.117	.102	.091	.081	.074
23¼	.170	.142	.122	.106	.095	.085	.078
24¼	.178	.148	.127	.111	.099	.089	.081

Allowances

1. For close register printing: increase Standard hours 10%.
2. For tone and process printing: increase Standard hours 10%.
3. For tubing over 2.5 mil up 3.5 mil: increase Standard hours 20%.
4. For tubing over 3.5 mil up to maximum: increase Standard hours 30%.
5. See Page 4 of 4, Standard No. IV for determining lineal feet on order.

To determine pounds per hour use formula (3).

(3) Lbs/hr = Roll Width x Gauge x .800 x fpm x 60

Lbs/hr = 48 x Roll Width x Gauge (in inches) x fpm   (tubing)

CLIENT COMPANY: _____ DATE ISSUED: _____ REVISION DATES: _____

DIVISION/PLANT: _____ M. & T. ENGINEER: _____

SUPERVISORY ACCEPTANCE: _____ M. & T. APPROVAL BY: _____

THE STANDARDS CONTAINED HEREIN ARE APPLICABLE TO THE MACHINE OR OPERATION AND METHODS EMPLOYED AS OF _____ AND ARE SUBJECT TO REVISION PENDING ANY ALTERATION OR CHANGE IN METHODS OR EQUIPMENT.

Exhibit 11–3
Actual Production Standard

PRODUCTION STANDARD

STD. NO. ___IV (a) & (b)___

CHART NO. ___7___   PAGE __4__ OF __4__

MACHINE NO. ___1, 2___ DESCRIPTION: Hudson Sharpe or Kidder Press; Production Center #13, #14

OPERATION: _____ ELEMENT: _____

Computation Sheet

To compute "Lineal Feet on Order" follow this example:

1.	Quantity of bags	20,000
2.	Percent overage	7%
3.	Bag style, BS or SW	SW
4.	Bag size, width first	9½ x 12 x 3" BG & ½" lip
5.	Number of colors (parameter)	3
6.	Which press?	H/S
7.	Mil thickness (for allowances)	1.25
8.	Sheeting or tubing (for allowances)	Tubing, "J" Film
9.	Circumference of printing cylinder (parameter)	19¼"
10.	Number up (= number around x number across)	2

a. Feet length = 20,000 x 1.07 x 9.5 ÷ 12 = 17,000 ft. This information indicates the length of press run. At 250 fpm, it will take 68 min. plus standard allowances of 24.2% = 84 min.

b. To determine hr/M impressions use Chart No. 7: at 250 fpm and circumference of printing cylinder 19¼"
with 1 up = .141 hr/M
with 2 up = .0705 hr/M
for 20,000 bags = .0705 hr/M x 20,000 = 1.41 hr = 84 min.

c. To get pounds and pounds per hour
lbs = .8 x Roll Width x Gauge x Feet Length (tubing)
lbs = .4 x Roll Width x Gauge x Feet Length (sheeting)

lbs/hr = 48 x Roll Width x Gauge x fpm (tubing)-from chart
lbs/hr = 24 x Roll Width x Gauge x fpm (sheeting)

In the above example
lbs = .8 x 13 3/4" x .00125" x 17,000 (tubing) = 233 lbs
lbs/hr = 48 x 13 3/4" x .00125" x 250 (tubing) = 207 lbs/hr

less 24.2% standard allowance = 158 lbs/hr

Standard hours = 233 ÷ 158 = 1.47 hr -- same as method (b).

CLIENT COMPANY: _____ DATE ISSUED: _____ REVISION DATES:_____

DIVISION/PLANT: _____ M. & T. ENGINEER: _____

SUPERVISORY ACCEPTANCE: _____ M. & T. APPROVAL BY: _____

THE STANDARDS CONTAINED HEREIN ARE APPLICABLE TO THE MACHINE OR OPERATION AND METHODS EMPLOYED AS OF_____

Exhibit 11–4
Actual Production Standard

STD. NO. V		
CHART NO. 1		

PRODUCTION STANDARD

MARTIN & TUCKER, INC.
ENGINEERS

PAGE 1 OF 1

MACHINE NO. 1   DESCRIPTION: Slitter-Dusenberry; Production Center #16

OPERATION: Slitting and Rewinding   ELEMENT: Run Standard Output ft/hr
                                              Standard Time hr/M ft

Poly[a]

Rewind Only	Sheeting 550 fpm = .031 hr M/ft	Plus Additional 3 Minutes or .050 Hours per Roll Change[b]
	Tubing 500 fpm = .033 hr M/ft	

Slitting Plain[d]	ft/min.[c]	450	350	250	175	100
	Number of cuts	1	3	5	7	15
	OR Number out	2	4	6	8	16
	ft/hr / hr/Mft	27,000 / .037	21,000 / .048	15,000 / .067	10,500 / .095	6,000 / .167
Plus Additional Time to Load Original Roll and Remove Slit Rolls	EA. 3 min. .050 hr	8 min. .134 hr	12 min. .200 hr	15 min. .250 hr	20 min. .330 hr
	You Must Determine Number of Rolls to be Slit					

To determine the roll length in feet use formula (a)

Pounds = .4 x Roll Width x Gauge x Feet Length (sheeting)

(a) 1 Foot Length = $2.5 \left(\dfrac{\text{Pounds}}{\text{Roll Width x Gauge}} \right)$ (sheeting)

(a) 2 Feet Length = $1.25 \left(\dfrac{\text{Pounds}}{\text{Roll Width x Gauge}} \right)$ (tubing)

<u>Footnotes</u>

[a] <u>For CELLO, Rewind run:</u> 650 fpm = .025 hr/M ft. <u>Slitting run:</u> 20% faster than poly (roll change--same)

[b] For example to rewind 10 sheeted rolls, each 3,300 ft, standard hours = 3.3 x 10 x .031 + 10 x .050 = 1.05 + .5 = 1.55 hr. That is 93 min. or about 9 min./roll.

[c] When slitting printed poly: reduce run speed by 10%.

[d] Plain poly, gauge range 1-3 mil.

CLIENT COMPANY: _____ DATE ISSUED: _____ REVISION DATES: _____
DIVISION/PLANT: _____ M. & T. ENGINEER: _____
SUPERVISORY ACCEPTANCE: _____ M. & T. APPROVAL BY: _____

THE STANDARDS CONTAINED HEREIN ARE APPLICABLE TO THE MACHINE OR OPERATION AND METHODS EMPLOYED AS OF_____
AVAILABLE _____ TO REVISION PENDING ANY ALTERATION OR CHANGE IN METHODS OR EQUIPMENT

Exhibit 11–5
Actual Production Standard

STD. NO. I. A.
CHART NO. 1

PRODUCTION STANDARD

MARTIN & TUCKER, INC.
ENGINEERS

PAGE 1 OF 2

MACHINE NO. P1, 2, 6, 5   DESCRIPTION: Bag Making -- Poly; Production Center #1, #1A, #6

OPERATION: Bottom Seal Machines   ELEMENT: Standard Output M/hr
                                                            Standard Time hr/M

Practical Range of Bag Dimension	2" – 20" Width [a]	Gauge	Code
	2" – 24" Length [a]	.5 mil – 1.99 mil	L
		2.0 mil – 2.99 mil	M
	On P5 only: to 37½		
	Width to 60" Length	3.0 mil – 5.00 mil	H

Step 1   Determine number of lanes (Number Up) to be used.

Bag Width [a]		Number Up	Note: Since the standards are
2"	– 4½"	4	issued on a per lane basis,
4½"	– 6½"	3	multiply the M/hr by the
6½"	– 9½"	2	Number Up.
Over 10"	–	1	

Step 2   Select Bag Length and Gauge Code and read off the nomogram or, chart the standard in M/hr or hr/M.

Standard per Lane: hr/M   M/hr

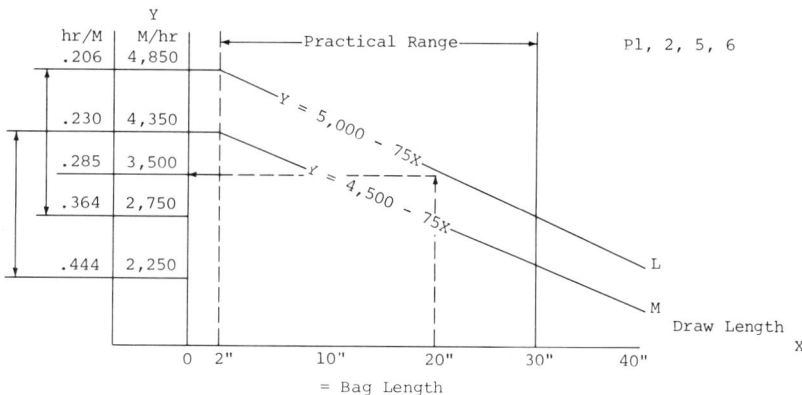

Example

Bag is 8" wide x 20" long x 1.5 mil (code L) Number Up = 2
Draw Length = 20"
Per Lane Standard M/hr = 3,500 bags/hr, use 2 up -- Standard Output = 7,000 bags/hr. or
Standard hr/M = .286 hr/100, use 2 up -- Standard Time = .143 hr/M.

Footnote

[a] Except P5.

CLIENT COMPANY: _____ DATE ISSUED: _____ REVISION DATES: _____
DIVISION/PLANT: _____ M. & T. ENGINEER: _____
SUPERVISORY ACCEPTANCE: _____ M. & T. APPROVAL BY: _____

THE STANDARDS CONTAINED HEREIN ARE APPLICABLE TO THE MACHINE OR OPERATION AND METHODS EMPLOYED AS OF_____
AND ARE SUBJECT TO REVISION PENDING ANY ALTERATION OR CHANGE IN METHODS OR EQUIPMENT.

78

Exhibit 11–6
Actual Production Standard

STD. NO. I.A.
CHART NO. 1

PRODUCTION STANDARD

MARTIN & TUCKER, INC.
ENGINEERS

PAGE 2 OF 2

MACHINE NO. Pl, 2, 6, 5   DESCRIPTION: Bag Making -- Poly; Production Centers #1, #1A, #6

OPERATION: Bottom Seal Machines   ELEMENT: Standard Output M/hr -- Run

The following table represents the standard output and standard time for each size bag (length) in increments of 2 inches.

Select bag length, gauge code, and number of lanes.

x Bag Length in Inches	Code L Gauge = 1-2 mil		Code M Gauge = 2-3 mil	
	M/hr[a]	hr/M	M/hr[b]	hr/M
2	4,850	.206	4,350	.230
4	4,700	.213	4,200	.238
6	4,550	.220	4,050	.247
8	4,400	.227	3,900	.256
10	4,250	.235	3,750	.267
12	4,100	.244	3,600	.278
14	3,950	.253	3,450	.290
16	3,800	.263	3,300	.303
18	3,650	.274	3,150	.317
20	3,500	.286	3,000	.333
22	3,350	.299	2,850	.351
24	3,200	.313	2,700	.370
26	3,050	.328	2,550	.392
28	2,900	.345	2,400	.417
30	2,750	.364	2,250	.444
32	2,600	.385	2,100	.476
34	2,450	.408	1,950	.513
36	2,300	.435	1,800	.556
38	2,150	.465	1,650	.606
40	2,000	.500	1,500	.667

Notes

Quantity variation

Subtract 15% for orders under 10M
10% for orders from 10M - 25M
5% for orders from 25M - 50M

[a] Formula is 5,000 - 75x.
[b] Formula is 4,500 - 75x.

CLIENT COMPANY: _____ DATE ISSUED: _____ REVISION DATES: _____
DIVISION/PLANT: _____ M. & T. ENGINEER: _____
SUPERVISORY ACCEPTANCE: _____ M. & T. APPROVAL BY: _____

THE STANDARDS CONTAINED HEREIN ARE APPLICABLE TO THE MACHINE OR OPERATION AND METHODS EMPLOYED AS OF_____ AND ARE SUBJECT TO REVISION PENDING ANY ALTERATION OR CHANGE IN METHODS OR EQUIPMENT.

Exhibit 11–7
Actual Production Standard

STD. NO. 1
CHART NO. 2

PRODUCTION STANDARD

MARTIN & TUCKER, INC.
ENGINEERS

PAGE_____ OF__

MACHINE NO. 9 Machines   DESCRIPTION: Schjeldahl, G. T. 208 or 201; Production Center #9

OPERATION: Bag Making -- Side Weld   ELEMENT: Run

Standard Crew = 1 Operator   Unit of Output = Bags

Order Quantity Equal or Over 25 M
Sheet Stock: Flat Bottoms or Gussetted

Bag Width (= Draw Length)	Gauge Code L 1.25 - 1.75 mil		Gauge Code M 2.00 - 3.00 mil		Gauge Code H 3.25 - 5.0 mil	
	M/hr	hr/M	M/hr	hr/M	M/hr	hr/M
3" to 6"	11,500	.087	8,640	.116	6,000	.167
6+" to 9"	10,560	.095	8,000	.125	5,600	.178
9+" to 12"	9,600	.104	7,420	.135	5,280	.189
12+" to 16"	8,640	.116	7,000	.143	5,000	.200
16+" to 20"	7,680	.130	6,200	.161	4,800	.208
20+" to 24"	6,720	.149	5,500	.182	4,320	.231

Schedule of Allowances

Number	Type of Allowance	Change in Standard Hours per M
1.	Order quantity under 25 M	Add 50% to Std. hr/M
2.	Solid roll run (1 up)	Add 45% to Std. hr/M
3.	Gauge .75 to 1.0 mil	Add 15% to Std. hr/M
4.	Gauge over 5.0 mil	Add 20% to Std. hr/M
5.	Gussetted bags, gauge code H only	Add 40% to Std. hr/M
6.	"Square" bags	Add 20% to Std. hr/M
7.	Specialty bags	Add to Std. hr/M:
	7.1 Header	20%
	7.2 Reinforced header	30%
	7.3 Serration (across the web)	40%
	7.4 Wicket, or other small quantity pack	20% to 40% depending on quantity of bags/wicket
8.	Duplex bags (2 ply)	Add 35% to Std. hr/M

Definitions

(1)   "Ideal" bag is a bag in which the ratio of width to length is under .85.

(2)   "Square" bag is a bag in which the ratio of width to length is over .85.

CLIENT COMPANY:_____ DATE ISSUED:_____ REVISION DATES:_____
DIVISION/PLANT:_____ M. & T. ENGINEER:_____
SUPERVISORY ACCEPTANCE:_____ M. & T. APPROVAL BY:_____

THE STANDARDS CONTAINED HEREIN ARE APPLICABLE TO THE MACHINE OR OPERATION AND METHODS EMPLOYED AS OF_____
AND ARE SUBJECT TO REVISION PENDING ANY ALTERATION OR CHANGE IN METHODS OR EQUIPMENT.

Exhibit 11–8
Actual Production Standard

STD. NO. _3_		
CHART NO. _1_		

PRODUCTION STANDARD

MARTIN & TUCKER, INC.
ENGINEERS

PAGE _1_ OF _3_

MACHINE NO. __60__   DESCRIPTION: Inta Roto, 3 Ply, 44", 2 Station Applicator

OPERATION: Laminate/Coat Production Center #2   ELEMENT: Derivative Data

---

Standard Crew = 3 = 1 Operator + 2 Helpers   Unit of Output = M ft
                                                                               MM sq. in.
                                                                               lbs.
                                                                               M imp.

Machine Specifications

Maximum web width	44"	
Minimum web width	22"	
Maximum number of plies	3	(2 unwind stations w/flying splicers)
Maximum O.D. unwind roll	28"	+ (1 portable foil unwind station, 12" O.D.
Maximum O.D. rewind roll	28"(or 1,000 lbs)	limit, 18" O.D. other materials)
Core I.D. (rewind)	6"	

Cylinders: impression;   coating;   combining.
            (rubber, edge-   (Gravure   (chrome-plated
            trimmed)   engraved)   steel)

Laminating or coating standards are issued for running 1 up (= 1 web across).

   Material: Polyethylene (laminating grade) with either one, or two of the following:
        Mylar, Cello, Foil, Polypropylene, Polyethylene, Nylon, and Paper.

	Film	Foil	Paper
Gauge: Maximum	.005	.00200	.0200 (soft)
Minimum	.001	.00035	.0025

   Adhesive Material: Solvent diluted adhesives, and some water-based adhesives.

   Coating Material: Solvent based coatings.

For the purpose of lamination production standards the following are categorized.

   Film includes: Polyethylene, Mylar, Cello, Polypropylene, Polystyrene, and Nylon.

   Paper includes: Glassine, Pouch paper, and other papers.

   Foil includes: Aluminum only.

Exhibit 11–9
Actual Production Standard

STD. NO. ___3___
CHART NO. ___2___

PRODUCTION STANDARD

MARTIN & TUCKER, INC.
ENGINEERS

PAGE ___2___ OF ___3___

MACHINE NO. ___60___ DESCRIPTION: Inta Roto, 3 Ply, 44", 2 Station Applicator

OPERATION: Laminate/Coat; Production Center #2 ELEMENT: ___Run___

Standard Crew = 3 = 1 Operator + 2 Helpers   Unit of Output = M ft
                                                                           MM sq. in.
                                                                           lbs
                                                                           M imp.

Order Quantity Equal or Over 30 M ft[c]
2-Ply Lamination

Lamination Components	Standard ft/min	Standard ft/hr	Standard hr/M ft
1. Film to Film[a]			
1.1 Cello/Cello	440	26,400	.0379
1.2 Cello/OPP	420	25,200	.0397
1.3 Cello/PE	400	24,000	.0417
1.4 Mylar/PE	360	21,600	.0463
1.5 OPP/OPP	320	19,200	.0521
1.6 Nylon/PE[d]	260	15,600	.0641
1.7 PE/PE[d]	240	14,400	.0694
2. Film to Foil			
2.1 Cello/AL	400	24,000	.0417
2.2 OPP/AL	400	24,000	.0417
2.3 Mylar/AL	340	20,400	.0490
2.4 PE/AL	280	16,800	.0595
3. Film to Paper	360	21,600	.0463
4. Foil to Paper	360	21,600	.0463
5. Foil to Foil[b]			
6. Paper to Paper[b]			

Abbreviations   PE = Polyethylene
                AL = Aluminum
                OPP = Oriented polypropylene

Footnotes

[a] This group represents 80% of existing lamination possibilities/orders.

[b] These combinations are rarely applied.

[c] 30M ft = app. 550 lbs/ply in 1.25 mil, PE, 36" web.

[d] These standards represent the average condition of roll formation, the extra care required in laminating printed to plain film, etc.

CLIENT COMPANY: _____ DATE ISSUED: _____ REVISION DATES: _____
DIVISION/PLANT: _____ M. & T. ENGINEER: _____
SUPERVISORY ACCEPTANCE: _____ M. & T. APPROVAL BY: _____

THE STANDARDS CONTAINED HEREIN ARE APPLICABLE TO THE MACHINE OR OPERATION AND METHODS EMPLOYED AS OF _____
AND ARE SUBJECT TO REVISION PENDING ANY ALTERATION OR CHANGE IN METHODS OR EQUIPMENT.

Exhibit 11–10
Actual Production Standard

STD. NO. 3		
CHART NO. 3		

PRODUCTION STANDARD

MARTIN & TUCKER, INC.
ENGINEERS

PAGE 3 OF 3

MACHINE NO. 60   DESCRIPTION: Inta Roto, 3 Ply, 44", 2 Station Applicator

OPERATION: Laminate/Coat; Production Center #2   ELEMENT: Run

Standard Crew = 3 = 1 Operator + 2 Helpers   Unit of Output = M ft
MM sq. in.
lbs
M imp.

Order Quantity Equal or Over 22M ft[c]
3-Ply Lamination

	Required Number of Passes	Standard Feet per Minute	Standard Feet per Hour	Standard Hours per M ft
1. Film/Foil/Double H.S. Category[a]	3	240	14,400	.0694
2. Paper/Foil/Film	1	320	19,200	.0521
3. Film/Foil/Film	2	260	15,600	.0641
4. Film/Film/Film	2	240	14,400	.0694
5. Foil/Film/Film or H.S. Category	2	240	14,400	.0694
6. Film or H.S. Category/Paper/ Film or H.S. Category	1 or 2	280	16,800	.0595
7. Film/Foil/Paper[b]				

Footnotes

[a] This type of lamination "considered" as 3 ply even though it consists of 2 plies only.

[b] This and other 3 ply combinations are rarely applied, at present.

[c] 22M ft = app. 400 lbs/ply in 1.25 mil, PE, 36" web.

CLIENT COMPANY: _____ DATE ISSUED: _____ REVISION DATES: _____
DIVISION/PLANT: _____ M. & T. ENGINEER: _____
SUPERVISORY ACCEPTANCE: _____ M. & T. APPROVAL BY: _____

THE STANDARDS CONTAINED HEREIN ARE APPLICABLE TO THE MACHINE OR OPERATION AND METHODS EMPLOYED AS OF_____
AND ARE SUBJECT TO REVISION PENDING ANY ALTERATION OR CHANGE IN METHODS OR EQUIPMENT.

Exhibit 11–11
Actual Production Standard

STD. NO. 4		
CHART NO. 3		

PRODUCTION STANDARD

MARTIN & TUCKER, INC.
ENGINEERS

PAGE 1 OF 1

MACHINE NO. 179   DESCRIPTION: 2-C Harris Offset: Production Center #20

OPERATION: Print 2-Colors, or Coat Varnish   ELEMENT: Makeready

Standard Hours[a]

Number of Colors	Basic MR	PWU[b]	RMR[c]	Total MR
1st 2-colors	3.50	.70	.30	4.50
3rd color, same set up	1.75	.50	.15	2.40
1-color complete set up	2.75	.50	.30	3.55
Varnish coat	.30	.25	.15	.70
3rd and 4th color same set up	2.55	.70	.30	3.55

Notes

1. For a separate varnish plate: Add .70 Std. Hr.

2. For running against grain: Add .50 Std. Hr.

3. For heavy solids: Add 1.00 Std. Hr.

Footnote

[a] Standard allowance for P, F, and D included: 10%.

[b] Press washup.

[c] Remove makeready.

CLIENT COMPANY: _____ DATE ISSUED: _____ REVISION DATES: _____

DIVISION/PLANT: _____ M. & T. ENGINEER: _____

SUPERVISORY ACCEPTANCE: _____ M. & T. APPROVAL BY: _____

THE STANDARDS CONTAINED HEREIN ARE APPLICABLE TO THE MACHINE OR OPERATION AND METHODS EMPLOYED AS OF_____
AND ARE SUBJECT TO REVISION PENDING ANY ALTERATION OR CHANGE IN METHODS OR EQUIPMENT.

Exhibit 11–12
Actual Production Standard

PRODUCTION STANDARD

MARTIN & TUCKER, INC.
ENGINEERS

PAGE 1 OF 2

MACHINE NO. 122   DESCRIPTION: Speedking Gluer; Production Center #16

OPERATION: Fold, Glue, and Pack   ELEMENT: Run

Styles: SE, RTE, STE, Sleeves

Standard Blanks per Hour and Standard Hours per M Blanks

Inches of Feed Length	Quantity			
	10M–50M		50M–Over	
	Board Caliper			
	.014"–.025"	.026"–.040"	.014"–.025"	.026"–.040"
4	27,000 / .037	23,000 / .044	30,000 / .034	25,000 / .040
5	27,000 / .037	23,000 / .044	30,000 / .034	25,000 / .040
6	27,000 / .037	23,000 / .044	30,000 / .034	25,000 / .040
7	27,000 / .037	23,000 / .044	30,000 / .034	25,000 / .040
8	26,000 / .038	22,500 / .045	28,500 / .035	24,500 / .041
9	25,000 / .040	21,000 / .048	28,000 / .036	23,500 / .043
10	24,000 / .042	20,000 / .050	26,500 / .038	22,000 / .046
11	22,000 / .046	18,000 / .055	25,500 / .041	20,500 / .049
12	20,000 / .050	16,700 / .060	22,000 / .045	18,500 / .054
13	18,500 / .054	15,500 / .065	20,500 / .049	17,000 / .059
14	17,300 / .058	14,300 / .070	19,500 / .052	16,000 / .062
15	16,000 / .062	13,500 / .074	18,000 / .056	15,000 / .067
16	15,000 / .066	12,500 / .079	17,000 / .059	14,000 / .071
17	14,300 / .070	12,000 / .084	16,000 / .063	13,000 / .076
18	13,500 / .074	11,500 / .089	15,000 / .067	12,500 / .080
19	12,500 / .079	10,500 / .095	14,000 / .071	12,000 / .085
20	12,000 / .084	10,000 / .100	13,300 / .075	11,000 / .090
21	11,000 / .090	9,500 / .108	12,500 / .081	10,500 / .097

Practical Range (left margin)

Range of Straight Linear Relation of Output to Feed Length (right margin)

CLIENT COMPANY: _____ DATE ISSUED: _____ REVISION DATES: _____

DIVISION/PLANT: _____ M. & T. ENGINEER: _____

SUPERVISORY ACCEPTANCE: _____ M. & T. APPROVAL BY: _____

THE STANDARDS CONTAINED HEREIN ARE APPLICABLE TO THE MACHINE OR OPERATION AND METHODS EMPLOYED AS OF _____ AND ARE SUBJECT TO REVISION PENDING ANY ALTERATION OR CHANGE IN METHODS OR EQUIPMENT.

Exhibit 11–13
Actual Production Standard

STD. NO. 117	**PRODUCTION STANDARD**	MARTIN & TUCKER, INC.
CHART NO. 1		ENGINEERS

STD. NO. 117
CHART NO. 1

PRODUCTION STANDARD

MARTIN & TUCKER, INC.
ENGINEERS

PAGE 1 OF 1

MACHINE NO. 1042   DESCRIPTION: Baum Folder 31 x 46 (Continuous Air Wheel)

OPERATION: Fold   ELEMENT: Setup and Run

Setup Operation	Standard Hours per Folding Section			
	Parallel	8 Page (1st Ra)	16 Page (2nd Ra)	32 Page (3rd Ra)
One fold	.33	.16	.16	.16
Two folds	.45	.29	.29	.29
Three folds	.57	.41	.41	
Four folds	.69	.53	.53	
Five folds				
First score, slit, or perf.	.09	.09	.09	
Each Add'l. score, slit, or perf.	.06	.06	.06	

Running

Folding Factor
 Parallel only -- Use sheet travel length.
 Right angle -- Use 3/4 width plus parallel folded length, Or sheet travel length
            whichever is greater

Folding Factor	Production per Hour	Hours per M	Folding Factor	Production per Hour	Hours per M	Folding Factor	Production per Hour	Hours per M
3			16	10,225	.098	36	4,690	.213
3½			17	9,650	.104	37	4,570	.219
4			18	9,150	.109	38	4,460	.224
4½			19	8,690	.115	39	4,345	.231
5			20	8,280	.121	40	4,275	.234
5½			21	7,900	.127	42	4,040	.248
6			22	7,550	.133	44	3,860	.259
6½			23	7,250	.138	46	3,700	.271
7	21,700	.046	24	6,950	.144	48	3,545	.282
7½	20,420	.049	25	6,690	.149	50	3,410	.293
8	19,300	.052	26	6,445	.155	52	3,275	.305
8½	18,300	.055	27	6,210	.161	54	3,160	.316
9	17,380	.058	28	5,990	.167	56	3,045	.329
9½	16,525	.061	29	5,795	.173	58	2,945	.340
10	15,790	.064	30	5,600	.179	60	2,850	.351
11	14,480	.069	31	5,430	.184	63		
12	13,375	.075	32	5,260	.190	66		
13	12,410	.081	33	5,110	.196	69		
14	11,575	.086	34	4,965	.202	72		
15	10,850	.092	35	4,820	.208	75		

CLIENT COMPANY: _____ DATE ISSUED: _____ REVISION DATES: _____

DIVISION/PLANT: _____ M. & T. ENGINEER: _____

SUPERVISORY ACCEPTANCE: _____ M. & T. APPROVAL BY: _____

THE STANDARDS CONTAINED HEREIN ARE APPLICABLE TO THE MACHINE OR OPERATION AND METHODS EMPLOYED AS OF_____
AND ARE SUBJECT TO REVISION PENDING ANY ALTERATION OR CHANGE IN METHODS OR EQUIPMENT.

Exhibit 11–14
Actual Production Standard

STD. NO. __201__
CHART NO. __1__

PRODUCTION STANDARD

MARTIN & TUCKER, INC.
ENGINEERS

PAGE __1__ OF __1__

MACHINE NO. __14A__   DESCRIPTION: __Rutherford RMT 12499 Step and Repeat__

OPERATION: __Platemaking -- Photocomposing__   ELEMENT: __Run__

Standard Hours per Plate

Steps	Films									
	1	2	3	4	5	6	7	8	9	10
1	.37									
2	.42	.57								
3	.47	.62	.78							
4	.52	.67	.83	.98						
5	.57	.72	.88	1.03	1.20					
6	.62	.77	.93	1.08	1.25	1.40				
7	.67	.82	.98	1.13	1.30	1.45	1.62			
8	.72	.87	1.03	1.18	1.35	1.50	1.67	1.83		
9	.77	.92	1.08	1.23	1.40	1.55	1.72	1.88	2.04	
10	.82	1.07	1.13	1.28	1.45	1.60	1.77	1.93	2.09	2.25
11	.88	1.12	1.18	1.33	1.50	1.65	1.82	1.98	2.14	2.30
12	.94	1.18	1.23	1.38	1.55	1.70	1.87	2.03	2.19	2.35
13	1.00	1.24	1.29	1.43	1.60	1.75	1.92	2.08	2.24	2.40
14	1.06	1.30	1.35	1.50	1.65	1.80	1.97	2.13	2.29	2.45
15	1.12	1.36	1.41	1.56	1.71	1.85	2.02	2.18	2.34	2.50
16	1.18	1.42	1.47	1.62	1.77	1.91	2.07	2.23	2.39	2.55
17	1.24	1.48	1.53	1.68	1.83	1.97	2.13	2.28	2.44	2.60
18	1.30	1.54	1.59	1.74	1.90	2.03	2.19	2.34	2.49	2.65
19	1.36	1.60	1.65	1.80	1.96	2.09	2.25	2.40	2.55	2.70
20	1.42	1.66	1.71	1.86	2.02	2.15	2.31	2.46	2.61	2.75
21	1.48	1.72	1.77	1.92	2.08	2.20	2.36	2.51	2.66	2.80

CLIENT COMPANY:_____ DATE ISSUED:_____ REVISION DATES:_____

DIVISION/PLANT:_____ M. & T. ENGINEER:_____

SUPERVISORY ACCEPTANCE:_____ M. & T. APPROVAL BY:_____

THE STANDARDS CONTAINED HEREIN ARE APPLICABLE TO THE MACHINE OR OPERATION AND METHODS EMPLOYED AS OF_____
AND ARE SUBJECT TO REVISION PENDING ANY ALTERATION OR CHANGE IN METHODS OR EQUIPMENT.

Exhibit 11–15
Actual Production Standard

STD. NO. 1-01/14							

CHART NO. 38E

PRODUCTION STANDARD

MARTIN & TUCKER, INC.
ENGINEERS

PAGE 1 OF 2

MACHINE NO. All L.P.   DESCRIPTION: New Era 9 x 12 Presses

OPERATION: Makeready   ELEMENT: Change -- Copy-Design Plates

Full copy = Complete design change for each color in design.

Partial copy = Design change for one color in multicolor design after original full copy design or single line or one word change (in same position all copies) on one color copy design.

Standard Hours per Plate

Machine Numbers	Production Centers	Full Copy Standard Hours					Partial Copy[a]
		1 Color to 1 Color	2 Color to 2 Color	3 Color to 3 Color	4 Color to 4 Color	5 Color to 5 Color	
1,2,3,4	A	.155	.325	.548	X	X	.107
5	B	.155	.325	.548	.706	X	.107
6,7,8	C	.155	.325	.548	.706	.986	.107

Note

[a] Use when estimating an order with multiple copy changes on one copy design color. (Multiply: Number of partial copy changes x Partial copy/Plate Standard hour) for total Standard hours. For partial partial copy change, add partial copy Standard hour total to original copy change Standard hours for total "All Plate Changes"/ Order.

CLIENT COMPANY: _____ DATE ISSUED: _____ REVISION DATES: _____

DIVISION/PLANT: _____ M. & T. ENGINEER: _____

SUPERVISORY ACCEPTANCE: _____ M. & T. APPROVAL BY: _____

THE STANDARDS CONTAINED HEREIN ARE APPLICABLE TO THE MACHINE OR OPERATION AND METHODS EMPLOYED AS OF_____
AND ARE SUBJECT TO REVISION PENDING ANY ALTERATION OR CHANGE IN METHODS OR EQUIPMENT.

88

Exhibit 11–16
Actual Production Standard

STD. NO. 1-01/14
CHART NO. 38E

PRODUCTION STANDARD

MARTIN & TUCKER, INC.
ENGINEERS

PAGE 2 OF 2

MACHINE NO. All L. P.   DESCRIPTION: New Era 9 x 12 Presses
OPERATION: Change -- Copy-Design Plates   ELEMENT: Makeready

Machine Numbers	Production Centers	Full Copy Standard Hours					X
		1 Color to 2 Color or 2 Color to 1 Color	2 Color to 3 Color or 3 Color to 2 Color	3 Color to 4 Color or 4 Color to 3 Color	4 Color to 5 Color or 5 Color to 4 Color	1 Color to[a] No Color	X
1,2,3,4	A	.299	.522	X	X	.027	X
5	B	.299	.522	.679	X	.027	X
6,7,8	C	.299	.522	.679	.9597	.027	X

Note

[a] For in-between changes more drastic than those shown above use this Standard hour example: 5 color copy-design to 1 color copy-design. Full change use 5 color to 5 color Standard hour (1 color to none Standard hour x 4).

CLIENT COMPANY: _____   DATE ISSUED: _____ REVISION DATES: _____
DIVISION/PLANT: _____   M. & T. ENGINEER: _____
SUPERVISORY ACCEPTANCE: _____   M. & T. APPROVAL BY: _____

THE STANDARDS CONTAINED HEREIN ARE APPLICABLE TO THE MACHINE OR OPERATION AND METHODS EMPLOYED AS OF_____
AND ARE SUBJECT TO REVISION PENDING ANY ALTERATION OR CHANGE IN METHODS OR EQUIPMENT.

Exhibit 11–17
Actual Production Standard

STD. NO. 1-01/14
CHART NO. 39E

PRODUCTION STANDARD

MARTIN & TUCKER, INC.
ENGINEERS

PAGE 1 OF 1

MACHINE NO. All L.P.   DESCRIPTION: New Era 9 x 12 Presses

OPERATION: Change: Ink Color (Standard Mixed Process Inks and Varnish)   ELEMENT: Makeready

---

No allowance in these standards for ink roller changes on print heads.

"Standard Inks" Standard Hours per Change

From	To	PC 1,5	PC 2,3,4, 6,7,8
None	Dk Oil or Dk MS	.0354	.0354
Lt oil	None	.1085	.1085
Lt MS	None		
Lt oil Dk oil	Lt oil Dk oil, Dk, MS, and none	.1592	.1592
Dk MS None	None Lt MS		
Lt oil Lt MS	Dk oil or Dk MS Lt oil or Lt MS Dk oil or Dk MS	.2411	.2250
Dk oil Dk MS	Lt oil or Lt MS Lt oil Dk oil or Dk MS		
Lt oil Dk MS	Lt MS Lt MS	.2880	.2660

"Process Ink" Standard Hours per Change[a]

From	To	PC 1,5	PC 2,3,4, 6,7,8
Dk MS Dk oil	None Dk MS	.3013	.2867
Lt oil Dk oil Lt MS	Dk MS Lt MS Lt MS	.3611	.3370
	Dk MS		
Dk MS	Dk MS		
Lt oil Dk MS	Lt MS Lt MS	.4269	.3941
[a] For Each full day of run time add for wash up required.		.1090	.1090

"Mixed Inks" Standard Hours per Change

From	To	PC 1,5	PC 2,3,4, 6,7,8
Lt oil Lt MS None Dk oil Dk MS	None None Dk MS None None	.1387	.1387
None Lt oil Dk oil	Lt oil Lt oil Lt oil Dk MS	.2544	.2793
Lt oil Dk oil Lt MS Dk MS	Dk oil or Dk MS Lt oil or Lt MS Lt oil or Lt MS Dk oil or Dk MS Lt oil Dk oil or Dk MS	.3510	.2958
Lt oil Dk oil Dk MS	Lt MS Lt MS Lt MS	.4049	.3572

"Overprint Varnish" Standard Hours per Change[b]

From	To	PC 1,5	PC 2,3,4, 6,7,8
Lt oil	Varnish #1159	.6627	.6307
Lt MS	Varnish #1159	.7652	.7168

NOTE

[b] Never go from Dk ink to overprint varnish.

CLIENT COMPANY: _____ DATE ISSUED: _____ REVISION DATES: _____

DIVISION/PLANT: _____ M. & T. ENGINEER: _____

SUPERVISORY ACCEPTANCE: _____ M. & T. APPROVAL BY: _____

THE STANDARDS CONTAINED HEREIN ARE APPLICABLE TO THE MACHINE OR OPERATION AND METHODS EMPLOYED AS OF _____
AND ARE SUBJECT TO REVISION PENDING ANY ALTERATION OR CHANGE IN METHODS OR EQUIPMENT.

Exhibit 11–18
Actual Production Standard

STD. NO. 1-01/14
CHART NO. 55E

PRODUCTION STANDARD

MARTIN & TUCKER, INC.
ENGINEERS

PAGE 1 OF 1

MACHINE NO. PC 7   DESCRIPTION: New Era 9 x 12 L.P.

OPERATION: PS Matrix (Waste) Removed Labels   ELEMENT: Run

Ink: oil, moisture set and all combinations.

Die Design Group	Die Design Number Up	Standard Imprints per Hour / Standard Hours per M Imprints				
		Blank or 1 Color	2 Color	3 Color	4 Color	5 Color
Standard dies	3-15	4,745	4,396	3,962	3,557	3,192
Special dies		.2107	.2275	.2524	.2811	.3133
1/16" Stroke	3-15	4,458	4,112	3,718	3,352	2,957
Premium (X)		.2243	.2432	.2690	.2983	.3382
Standard dies	16-28	4,026	3,687	3,336	3,010	2,688
Special dies		.2484	.2712	.2998	.3322	.3720
1/16" Stroke	16-28	3,811	3,403	3,058	2,736	2,352
Premium (X)		.2624	.2939	.3270	.3655	.4252

CLIENT COMPANY: _____ DATE ISSUED: _____ REVISION DATES: _____

DIVISION/PLANT: _____ M. & T. ENGINEER: _____

SUPERVISORY ACCEPTANCE: _____ M. & T. APPROVAL BY: _____

THE STANDARDS CONTAINED HEREIN ARE APPLICABLE TO THE MACHINE OR OPERATION AND METHODS EMPLOYED AS OF_____
AND ARE SUBJECT TO REVISION PENDING ANY ALTERATION OR CHANGE IN METHODS OR EQUIPMENT.

Exhibit 11–19
Actual Production Standard

MARTIN & TUCKER, INC.
ENGINEERS

PRODUCTION STANDARD

STD. NO. _____
CHART NO. _____   PAGE 1 OF 1

MACHINE NO. 75   DESCRIPTION: Champlain 5 Color Gravure Press
OPERATION: Makeready   ELEMENT: Change Print Cylinder

Standard Hours per Occurrence

Step Number	Element Change	First Color		Color 2 and 3 each		Color 4 and 5 each	
		Min. Occ.	Accum.	Min. Occ.	Accum.	Min. Occ.	Accum.
1.0	Remove doctor blade	2.80	2.80	2.30	2.30	1.60	1.60
1.1	Raise applicator	.20	3.00	.20		.30	1.90
2.0	Unlock chase	.45	3.45	.45	2.95	.45	2.35
3.0	Disconnect ink pump, put up cradle and remove chase from head	2.25	5.70	1.10	4.05	1.10	3.45
3.1	Wash cylinder = (get solvent, rags, wash, pumis cylinder and load cylinder onto truck)	5.60	11.30	-0-	-0-	-0-	-0-
3.2	Wash cylinder = (wash, pumis cylinder and load cylinder onto truck)	-0-	-0-	3.20	7.25	3.20	6.65
4.0	Remove cylinder from chase						
4.1	Remove collars, wash shafts, remove sling rings, scrape chase, wrap cylinder and put into storage rack	16.10	27.40	12.35	19.60	13.70	20.35
5.0	Get cylinder for next order	2.03	29.43	2.03	21.63	2.03	22.38
6.0	Reassemble chase and print cylinder						
6.1	Attach bearings, sling rings, collars, etc.	11.11	40.54	10.96	32.59	10.96	33.34
7.0	Put chase into print head, (Raise applicator as necessary)	5.05	45.59	2.35	34.94	1.60	34.94
8.0	Copy register for 1st off OK	5.00	50.59	5.90	40.84	7.78	42.72
9.0	Observed time		50.59		40.84		42.72
10.0	Levelled time (observed x 1.10)		55.65		44.92		46.92
11.0	Allowed (Standard time) time = (Levelled time x 1.238)		68.89		55.61		58.18
12.0	Standard Hours (Std. min./60 min.)		1.15		.93		.97

NOTE

Element 4.1 can vary with inks that have run several days and have hardened on sling rings. This variance has been included in ink allowance. Poorly stepped copy can cause variance in element 8. This variance is in MHR.

CLIENT COMPANY: _____ DATE ISSUED: _____ REVISION DATES: _____
DIVISION/PLANT: _____ M. & T. ENGINEER: _____
SUPERVISORY ACCEPTANCE: _____ M. & T. APPROVAL BY: _____

THE STANDARDS CONTAINED HEREIN ARE APPLICABLE TO THE MACHINE OR OPERATION AND METHODS EMPLOYED AS OF _____ AND ARE SUBJECT TO REVISION PENDING ANY ALTERATION OR CHANGE IN METHODS OR EQUIPMENT

92

Exhibit 11–20
Actual Production Standard: Material Standard

STD. NO. 1-01/14
CHART NO. 38WM

MATERIAL STANDARD

MARTIN & TUCKER, INC.
ENGINEERS

PAGE 1 OF 1

MACHINE NO: PC 1 thru 8   DESCRIPTION: Letterpress/New Era 9 x 12 Presses

OPERATION: Change -- Copy-Design Plates   ELEMENT: Waste (Makeready)

MATERIAL: Heat Seal WKK and Gemkote

Run Standard Imprints per Hour	Roll Width, in Inches	1C to 2C PC 1-8	2C to 3C PC 1-8	3C to 4C PC 5,6,7,8	4C to 5C PC 6,7,8
Stroke: 4½" thru 7½"					
6,000 to 6,499	10 and 10 3/4	3.43	5.99	7.81	11.03
	11½	3.67	6.41	8.35	11.79
	12½	3.99	6.97	9.08	12.83
5,500 to 5,999	10 and 10 3/4	3.16	5.52	7.19	10.15
	11½	3.37	5.89	7.68	10.85
	12½	3.67	6.41	8.36	11.80
5,000 to 5,499	10 and 10 3/4	2.88	5.04	6.56	9.27
	11½	3.08	5.39	7.01	9.91
	12½	3.35	5.85	7.63	10.77
4,500 to 4,999	10 and 10 3/4	2.61	4.56	5.93	8.39
	11½	2.79	4.87	6.35	8.96
	12½	3.03	5.29	6.91	9.75
4,000 to 4,499	10 and 10 3/4	2.33	4.08	5.31	27.49
	11½	2.49	4.36	5.68	8.03
	12½	2.71	4.73	6.17	8.72
3,500 to 3,999	10 and 10 3/4	2.05	3.60	4.68	6.61
	11½	2.20	3.84	5.01	7.08
	12½	2.40	4.19	5.45	7.69
Stroke: 7-9/16" thru 9"					
6,000 to 6,499	10 and 10 3/4	4.08	7.13	9.29	13.13
	11½	4.37	7.63	9.93	14.04
	12½	4.75	8.29	11.56	15.27
5,500 to 5,999	10 and 10 3/4	3.76	6.56	8.55	12.08
	11½	4.01	7.01	9.15	12.92
	12½	4.37	7.64	9.95	14.05
5,000 to 5,499	10 and 10 3/4	3.43	5.99	7.81	11.03
	11½	3.67	6.41	8.35	11.80
	12½	3.99	6.97	9.08	12.83
4,500 to 4,999	10 and 10 3/4	3.11	5.43	7.07	9.97
	11½	3.32	6.41	7.56	10.67
	12½	3.61	6.97	8.21	11.60
4,000 to 4,499	10 and 10 3/4	2.77	4.85	6.32	8.93
	11½	2.97	5.19	6.76	9.55
	12½	3.23	5.64	7.35	10.37
3,500 to 3,999	10 and 10 3/4	2.45	4.28	5.57	7.88
	11½	2.63	4.57	5.96	8.43
	12½	2.85	4.97	6.48	9.16

Cost of Waste Material per Change

CLIENT COMPANY:_____ DATE ISSUED:_____ REVISION DATES:_____
DIVISION/PLANT:_____ M. & T. ENGINEER:_____
SUPERVISORY ACCEPTANCE:_____ M. & T. APPROVAL BY:_____

THE STANDARDS CONTAINED HEREIN ARE APPLICABLE TO THE MACHINE OR OPERATION AND METHODS EMPLOYED AS OF_____ AND ARE SUBJECT TO REVISION PENDING ANY ALTERATION OR CHANGE IN METHODS OR EQUIPMENT.

Exhibit 11–21
Actual Production Standard

STD. NO. _____		MARTIN & TUCKER, INC.
CHART NO. _____	**PRODUCTION STANDARD**	ENGINEERS
		PAGE _____ OF __

MACHINE NO. 77, 78, 79   DESCRIPTION: Winkler Rotary Printer

OPERATION: Makeready Press _____ ELEMENT: All _____

Work Class and Area	Makeready Element	Standard Hours
Class 1		
3 sq. in.	Address change only	.1152
5 sq. in.	+ Form	.1403
Class 2		
3-14 sq. in.	One side, one color, one plate	.2572
15-35 sq. in.	One side, one color, one plate	.2772
76-95 sq. in.	One side, one color, one plate	.5172
Class 5		
5-14 sq. in.	One side, two colors, two plates	.2792
36-55 sq. in.	One side, two colors, two plates	.4242

Additives

a.	Close or hairline register, per side	.0443
b.	Setup pot and fountain, aniline ink	.0535
c.	Makeready perforating complete	.2100
d.	Washup for ink change, per color -- Machine No. 77	.0967
	Washup for ink change, per color -- Machine No. 77, 78	.1500
e.	Replace Cylinder Jacket: remove jacket, cut new one, repack and install on cylinder, complete	.1630
f.	Morning startup: remove ink covering, install and adjust rubber rolls, ink for running	.1048
g.	Remove worn, cut new and replace tail	.0196
h.	Clean cylinders and rolls to remove ink build up after running bleeding solids	.2140

CLIENT COMPANY: _____ DATE ISSUED: _____ REVISION DATES: _____

DIVISION/PLANT: _____ M. & T. ENGINEER: _____

SUPERVISORY ACCEPTANCE: _____ M. & T. APPROVAL BY: _____

Exhibit 11–22
Actual Production Standard

STD. NO. _____
CHART NO. _____

PRODUCTION STANDARD

MARTIN & TUCKER, INC.
ENGINEERS

PAGE _____ OF __

MACHINE NO. All described   DESCRIPTION: W & D 18Q and 20F Printers

OPERATION: Washup   ELEMENT: All -- Top and Bottom Oil Units; Flexo Unit

Element Number	Description of Washup	Standard Minutes per Washup	Standard Hours per Washup
1	Complete 2-colors to 2 light colors	49.31	.821
2	Complete 2-colors to 2 dark colors	30.14	.502
3	Complete 2-colors to 1 light and 1 dark color	35.69	.595
4	Complete 1-color to 1 light color and 1 general washup	28.89	.481
5	Complete 1-color to 1 dark color and 1 general washup	18.99	.317
6	Complete 1-color to dark color	17.08	.285
7	Complete 1-color to light color	27.22	.453
8	General 2-color washup	17.00	.283
9	General 1-color washup	10.59	.177
10	Complete washup of Flexo unit	90.00	1.500
A	Morning preparation	18.20	.303
B	Clean up top and bottom drip pan	9.45	.159
C	Clean up top or bottom drip pan	4.67	.078

EN

CLIENT COMPANY: _____ DATE ISSUED: _____ REVISION DATES: _____
DIVISION/PLANT: _____ M. & T. ENGINEER: _____ _____
SUPERVISORY ACCEPTANCE: _____ M. & T. APPROVAL BY: _____
THE STANDARDS CONTAINED HEREIN ARE APPLICABLE TO THE MACHINE OR OPERATION AND METHODS EMPLOYED AS OF_____
AND ARE SUBJECT TO REVISION PENDING ANY ALTERATION OR CHANGE IN METHODS OR EQUIPMENT.

Exhibit 11–23
Actual Production Standard

STD. NO. _____

CHART NO. _____

PRODUCTION STANDARD

MARTIN & TUCKER, INC.
ENGINEERS

PAGE _____ OF __

MACHINE NO. 21,22,23,24,25   DESCRIPTION: Wide Range Window (WRW)

OPERATION: Open Side Folding _____ ELEMENT: Run _____

Standard Pieces per Hour and Standard Hours per M[a]

Run Size	Commercials, Pennysavers, and Bankers Flap			Glassine Windows	
Paper Weight	3½ x 6 thru 4½ x 9	4 3/4 x 11	6 x 12	4½ x 10 3/8	5 x 11½
Printing	#6¼ thru 10½	#12	#16	#11	#14
40M Lot and over					
20#-24#-28#					
Plain	9,950 / .1005	8,300 / .1205	7,300 / .1370	6,780 / .1475	6,330 / .1580
Printed	9,850 / .1015	8,200 / .1220	6,570 / .1522	6,670 / .1499	6,220 / .1608
13#					
Plain	7,950 / .1258	7,160 / .1397	5,975 / .1674		
Printed	7,890 / .1267	7,040 / .1420	5,930 / .1696		
Under 40M Lot					
32#					
Plain	8,300 / .1205	7,300 / .1370	6,180 / .1618		
Printed	8,200 / .1220	7,225 / .1384	6,120 / .1634		
16#					
Plain	7,625 / .1311	6,950 / .1439	5,975 / .1674		
Printed	7,550 / .1325	6,900 / .1449	5,930 / .1686		

[a] Includes a 30% incentive factor in addition to standard delay allowances.

EN

CLIENT COMPANY: _____ DATE ISSUED: _____ REVISION DATES: _____

DIVISION/PLANT: _____ M. & T. ENGINEER: _____

SUPERVISORY ACCEPTANCE: _____ M. & T. APPROVAL BY: _____

THE STANDARDS CONTAINED HEREIN ARE APPLICABLE TO THE MACHINE OR OPERATION AND METHODS EMPLOYED AS OF_____
AND ARE SUBJECT TO REVISION PENDING ANY ALTERATION OR CHANGE IN METHODS OR EQUIPMENT.

Exhibit 11–24
Actual Production Standard

MARTIN & TUCKER, INC.
ENGINEERS

PRODUCTION STANDARD

STD. NO. _____

CHART NO. _____

PAGE_____ OF__

MACHINE NO. 21 thru 25 _____ DESCRIPTION: Wide Range Window (WRW) _____

OPERATION: Standard Delay Allowances _____ ELEMENT: All _____

Delay Elements	Nonwindow Commercials, Baronials; Booklets				Cellophane Window			
	Minute Each	Occurrence Hour	Day	Chargeable Minute per Day	Minute Each	Occurence Hour	Day	Chargeable Minute per Day
Paper jams	.61	2.6	20.8	12.69	.77	7.00	56	43.10
Minor machine adjusting	2.88	1.2	9.6	27.65	2.88	1.20	9.6	27.65
Waiting for adjuster	1.51	.167	1.25	1.89	1.51	.167	1.25	1.89
Wash and/or scrape rollers or machine parts	1.67	.50	4	6.68	1.67	1.00	4	6.68
Reload machine	2.25	.25	2	4.50	2.25	.25	2	4.50
Change glassine or cello roll	-	-	-	-	.90	.25	2	1.80
Washup before lunch	10.00	.125	1	10.00	10.00	.125	1	10.00
Washup at end of shift	10.00	.125	1	10.00	15.00	.125	1	15.00
Total Delay Time				73.41 minutes				100.72 minutes

Allowances[a]

Unavoidable delay	16.8%		20.9%
Personal (relief girls; machine not idle)	-		-
Fatigue	4 %		4 %
Total	20.8%		24.9%

[a] not including incentive factor

EN

CLIENT COMPANY:_____ DATE ISSUED:_____ REVISION DATES:_____

DIVISION/PLANT:_____ M. & T. ENGINEER:__

SUPERVISORY ACCEPTANCE:_____ M. & T. APPROVAL BY:_____

THE STANDARDS CONTAINED HEREIN ARE APPLICABLE TO THE MACHINE OR OPERATION AND METHODS EMPLOYED AS OF_____ AND ARE SUBJECT TO REVISION PENDING ANY ALTERATION OR CHANGE IN METHODS OR EQUIPMENT.

Exhibit 11–25
Actual Production Standard

STD. NO. 14
CHART NO. 2

PRODUCTION STANDARD

MARTIN & TUCKER, INC.
ENGINEERS

PAGE 1 OF 1

MACHINE NO. 417   DESCRIPTION: Semi-automatic Taper
OPERATION: Tape Containers   ELEMENT: Run

350 Test double wall -- 600# test double wall.
Crew size -- 1 feeder, 1 bundler.   Standard machine hours per 1000 boxes run.

Box				Blank Width (Inches)						
Length (Inches)		Width (Inches)		0	10	20	30	40	50	60
Over	Including	Over	Including	10	20	30	40	50	60	
0	4	0	4	0.57	0.62	1.55	1.69	1.80	1.93	
4	8	0	4	0.75	0.83	0.92	1.79	1.89	2.08	2.62
4	8	4	8	0.70	0.73	0.79	0.91	1.90	2.11	2.41
8	12	0	4	0.95	1.06	1.19	1.23	2.03	2.18	2.78
8	12	4	12	0.87	0.90	0.98	1.07	1.26	2.27	2.56
12	16	0	4	1.03	1.14	1.28	1.38	2.13	2.34	2.91
12	16	4	16	0.93	0.97	1.10	1.20	1.32	1.90	2.00
16	20	0	4	1.09	1.22	1.41	1.47	1.54	2.45	3.08
16	20	4	20	1.01	1.05	1.20	1.30	1.45	1.70	1.97
20	24	0	4	1.15	1.28	1.49	1.58	1.61	2.57	3.25
20	24	4	20	1.05	1.13	1.28	1.37	1.50	1.81	2.04
20	24	20	24	1.11	1.15	1.31	1.52	1.67	1.88	2.11
28	32	0	4	1.23	1.41	1.62	2.44	2.48	2.64	3.20
28	32	4	24	1.37	1.47	1.63	1.81	1.93	2.10	2.25
28	32	24	32	1.99	2.11	2.38	2.62	2.81	3.17	3.42
36	40	0	4	1.55	1.79	2.06	2.70	2.82	3.01	3.59
36	40	4	8	1.68	1.76	1.96	2.61	2.84	3.04	3.10
36	40	12	24	1.89	2.01	2.22	2.47	2.62	3.48	3.23
36	40	24	36	2.14	2.27	2.58	2.85	3.04	3.44	3.59
36	40	36	40	2.39	2.47	2.80	3.04	3.42	3.59	3.71
44	48	0	4	1.81	2.01	2.32	3.14	3.21	3.38	4.14
44	48	4	8	1.85	1.99	2.19	2.99	3.18	3.37	3.85
44	48	8	20	2.03	2.17	2.39	2.69	2.80	3.20	3.48
44	48	20	28	2.18	2.32	2.64	2.97	3.23	3.54	3.69
44	48	28	36	2.41	2.52	2.90	3.07	3.55	3.69	3.84

CLIENT COMPANY: _____ DATE ISSUED: _____ REVISION DATES: _____
DIVISION/PLANT: _____ M. & T. ENGINEER: _____
SUPERVISORY ACCEPTANCE: _____ M. & T. APPROVAL BY: _____

THE STANDARDS CONTAINED HEREIN ARE APPLICABLE TO THE MACHINE OR OPERATION AND METHODS EMPLOYED AS OF_____
AND ARE SUBJECT TO REVISION PENDING ANY ALTERATION OR CHANGE IN METHODS OR EQUIPMENT.

Exhibit 11–26
Actual Production Standard

STD. NO. 33A		MARTIN & TUCKER, INC.
CHART NO. 4	**PRODUCTION STANDARD**	ENGINEERS
		PAGE____ OF__

MACHINE NO. 17 ___ DESCRIPTION: Band and Gang Saws

OPERATION: Cut Pads ___ ELEMENT: Run (Lift = 20 pieces)

Standard Man-Minutes per 1000 Sheets

Square foot area per M	Length of Cut in Inches								
	0 to 5	5.01 to 10	10.01 to 15	15.01 to 20	20.01 to 25	25.01 to 30	30.01 to 35	35.01 to 40	40.01 to 45
One Out									
0- 400	12.53	13.06	13.38	13.75	14.13	14.50	15.00	15.50	16.00
400.01- 800	13.03	13.56	13.88	14.25	14.63	15.00	15.50	16.00	16.50
800.01-1,200	13.28	13.81	14.00	14.50	14.88	15.25	15.75	16.25	16.75
1,200.01-1,600	13.75	14.31	14.63	15.00	15.38	15.75	16.25	16.75	17.25
1,600.01-2,000	14.28	14.81	15.13	15.50	15.88	16.25	16.75	17.25	17.75
Four Out									
0- 400	5.90	6.44	6.75	7.13	7.50	7.89	8.38	8.88	9.38
400.01- 800	6.19	6.73	7.04	7.41	7.79	8.16	8.66	9.16	9.66
800.01-1,200	6.46	7.00	7.31	7.69	8.06	8.44	8.94	9.44	9.94
1,200.01-1,600	6.84	7.38	7.69	8.06	8.44	8.81	9.31	9.81	10.31
1,600.01-2,000	7.13	7.66	7.98	8.35	8.73	9.10	9.60	10.10	10.60
Seven Out									
0- 400	4.95	5.49	5.80	6.18	6.55	6.93	7.43	7.93	8.43
400.01- 800	5.28	5.81	6.13	6.50	6.88	7.25	7.75	8.25	8.75
800.01-1,200	5.60	6.14	6.45	6.83	7.20	7.58	8.08	8.58	9.08
1,200.01-1,600	6.03	6.56	6.88	7.25	7.63	8.00	8.50	9.00	9.50
1,600.01-2,000	6.35	6.89	7.20	7.58	7.95	8.33	8.83	9.33	9.83

CLIENT COMPANY:_____ DATE ISSUED:_____ REVISION DATES:_____

DIVISION/PLANT:_____ M. & T. ENGINEER:_____

SUPERVISORY ACCEPTANCE:_____ M. & T. APPROVAL BY:_____

THE STANDARDS CONTAINED HEREIN ARE APPLICABLE TO THE MACHINE OR OPERATION AND METHODS EMPLOYED AS OF_____ AND ARE SUBJECT TO REVISION PENDING ANY ALTERATION OR CHANGE IN METHODS OR EQUIPMENT.

Exhibit 11–27
Actual Production Standard

STD. NO. 118				
CHART NO. 4	**PRODUCTION STANDARD**		MARTIN & TUCKER, INC. ENGINEERS	
			PAGE_____ OF__	

MACHINE NO. 51 ML _____ DESCRIPTION: Single Spindle, B & S Automatic

OPERATION: Setup Screw Machine _____ ELEMENT: All

Tool or Operation	Minutes per Setup		
	Machine Capacity		
	1/2"	3/4"	1 1/4"
Remove, replace and time cams, change holders, gears, collet and finger	65	65	65
Box tools (single blade)	22	22	33
Box tools (double blade)	32	42	54
Cut off tools	17	17	21
Centering and facing tools	32	32	36
Drills	22	22	32
Form tools	16	16	22
Knurls, top or bottom	32	32	42
Reamers	33.	33	36
Stock stop	5	5	5
Swing tools, turning	32	32	44
Spinning operations	42	42	53
Taps	21	21	26
Thread rolling	42	42	53

CLIENT COMPANY:_____ DATE ISSUED: _____ REVISION DATES:_____

DIVISION/PLANT:_____ M. & T. ENGINEER:_____

SUPERVISORY ACCEPTANCE: _____ M. & T. APPROVAL BY:_____

THE STANDARDS CONTAINED HEREIN ARE APPLICABLE TO THE MACHINE OR OPERATION AND METHODS EMPLOYED AS OF_____
AND ARE SUBJECT TO REVISION PENDING ANY ALTERATION OR CHANGE IN METHODS OR EQUIPMENT.

Exhibit 11–28
Actual Production Standard

STD. NO. 7C									
CHART NO. 2									

PRODUCTION STANDARD

MARTIN & TUCKER, INC.
ENGINEERS

PAGE _____ OF __

MACHINE NO. 334   DESCRIPTION: 36" to 120" Boring Mill

OPERATION: Bore Cast Iron   ELEMENT: Run

TOOLING: High-Speed Steel

Depth of cut, in inches	Size of Boring Mill								
	36- to 42-Inch Mill			54- to 60-Inch Mill			72- to 120-Inch Mill		
	S	F	C	S	F	C	S	F	C
1/8	47.5	.080	.00135	47.5	.109	.00099	42.5	.25	.00049
1/4	45.0	.080	.00143	47.5	.083	.00122	45.0	.125	.00091
3/8	45.0	.062	.00182	47.5	.068	.00159	47.5	.094	.00115
1/2	42.5	.062	.00192	45.0	.068	.00167	45.0	.094	.00121
5/8	40.0	.062	.00204	42.5	.068	.00177	42.5	.094	.00128

Notes

1. S = Surface speed in feet per minute

2. F = Feed per revolution in inches

3. C = Time factor

To get hours required to complete one cut:

    multiply C (the time factor) by outside diameter of chip circle and length of cut.

Time factor C includes delay allowances.

CLIENT COMPANY: _____   DATE ISSUED: _____ REVISION DATES: _____

DIVISION/PLANT: _____   M. & T. ENGINEER: _____

SUPERVISORY ACCEPTANCE: _____   M. & T. APPROVAL BY: _____

THE STANDARDS CONTAINED HEREIN ARE APPLICABLE TO THE MACHINE OR OPERATION AND METHODS EMPLOYED AS OF_____
AND ARE SUBJECT TO REVISION PENDING ANY ALTERATION OR CHANGE IN METHODS OR EQUIPMENT.

Exhibit 11–29
Actual Production Standard

STD. NO. 44
CHART NO. 1

PRODUCTION STANDARD

MARTIN & TUCKER, INC.
ENGINEERS

PAGE_____ OF__

MACHINE NO._____ DESCRIPTION: ___Handwork_____

OPERATION: __Solder Terminals (30/70)_____ ELEMENT: 12 to 26 Gauge Wire_____

| Soldering Iron Wattage | Terminal Cross Section in Square Inches | Standard Minutes One Side Only | | | | | | | Add for Solder All Around Terminal |
| | | Gauge of Wire Soldered to Terminal | | | | | | | |
		12	14	16	18	19	20	22 to 26	
95 to 200	.0000 to .0070	.041	.038	.036	.034	.033	.032	.030	.004
150 to 200	.0070 to .0115	.047	.043	.038	.034	.033	.032	.030	.004
120	.0070 to .0115	.047	.043	.038	.034	.033	.032	.030	.009
95	.0070 to .0115	.062	.056	.049	.043	.041	.038	.034	.012
62 to 75	.0000 to .0030	.047	.043	.038	.034	.033	.032	.030	.004
62 to 75	.0030 to .0050	.051	.047	.043	.038	.036	.034	.030	.007
62 to 75	.0050 to .0070	.087	.071	.056	.041	.039	.037	.033	.010
62	.0070 to .0115	.089	.080	.070	.060	.057	.055	.049	.041
75	.0070 to .0115	.060	.056	.051	.047	.045	.043	.038	.022

CLIENT COMPANY: _____ DATE ISSUED: _____ REVISION DATES:_____

DIVISION/PLANT:_____ M. & T. ENGINEER:_____

SUPERVISORY ACCEPTANCE: _____ M. & T. APPROVAL BY:_____

THE STANDARDS CONTAINED HEREIN ARE APPLICABLE TO THE MACHINE OR OPERATION AND METHODS EMPLOYED AS OF_____

AND ARE SUBJECT TO REVISION PENDING ANY ALTERATION OR CHANGE IN METHODS OR EQUIPMENT.

Exhibit 11–30
Actual Production Standard

STD. NO. __172__

CHART NO. __1__

MARTIN & TUCKER, INC.
ENGINEERS

PRODUCTION STANDARD

PAGE_____ OF__

MACHINE NO. __1122__ DESCRIPTION: __Sheridan Gathering, Saddle Stitch and Trim__

OPERATION: __Gather, Saddle Stitch, and Trim__ ELEMENT: __Makeready and Run__

Book Size _____ Book Size Previous Run _____ Quantity_____

Number of Signatures_____ Spec. Allowance Signatures_____

1. Makeready Time (in Hours and Operation Number.)

No. of Pockets	1	2	3	4	5	6	7
No Change	.42	.52	.58	.70	.80	.90	1.00
Oper. No.	100	101	102	103	104	105	106
[a] Change	.85	1.00	1.10	1.40	1.53	1.66	1.73
Oper. No.	107	108	109	110	111	112	113

[a] Book size is considered the same until, (1) The length, head to foot changes.
By more than ½" (2) there is any variation in Width.

Job Time

1.1 Makeready time (selected from table) ...._____ hr

1.2 Trimmer makeready time (when book size changes) .30 hr ...._____ hr

Special Allowances (Makeready)   hr/M

1.3 Changeover from grip to sucker .... .33/pocket......_____ hr

1.4 Insert of unequal size to book .... .010/pocket......_____ hr

2. Running time (books per hour - hr per M and operation number).

Number of Signatures	Book Width in Inches											
	4½" to 7"			Over 7" to 9"			Over 9" to 11"			Over 11" to 11¾"		
	M Books per Hour			M Books per Hour			M Books per Hour			M Books per Hour		
	Run	Hr/M	Op. No.	Run	Hr/M	Op. No.	Run	Hr/M	Op. No.	Run	Hr/M	Op. No.
1	6530	.191	132	7820	.160	133	6240	.200	134	3070	.408	135
2	5880	.213	137	7040	.178	138	5610	.223	139	2910	.429	140
3	5290	.236	142	6330	.197	143	5050	.247	144	2770	.452	145
4	4760	.262	147	5700	.219	148	4550	.275	149	2630	.476	150
5	4280	.291	152	5130	.244	153	4090	.306	154	2500	.500	155
6	3860	.325	157	4620	.271	158	3680	.340	159	2370	.526	160

Gathering two books at a time—Use 67% of time for actual number of pockets used.
Allowance for length of run.

Jobs up to 6,000	Plus 10% of hr/M
" over 6,000 to 15,000	Plus 5% of hr/M
" over 15,000 to 60,000	As shown in table.
" over 60,000 to 100,000	Minus 5% of hr/M
" over 100,000	Minus 10% of hr/M

2.1 Running time = ..._____ hr/M

3. Special Allowances

3.1 Varnished cover—100% coverage—Plus 10% of hr/M ...._____

3.2 Running on vacuum grip. 4 pg. signature—Plus 25% of hr/M ...._____

3.3 Unusually troublesome—Plus .050 hr/M............................_____

4. Total running time per M (Total 2.1, 3.1, 3.2, and 3.3)............... _____

Time per M x Length of run in M's =

_____ x _____ = _____ hr

5. After job clean-up (.30 hr) .... .30 hr

6. Total time to makeready, run the job and clean-up

Total Items (1,1. 1,2. 1,3. 1,4. 4 and 5) ...._____ hr

CLIENT COMPANY: _____ DATE ISSUED: _____ REVISION DATES:_____

DIVISION/PLANT: _____ M. & T. ENGINEER: _____

SUPERVISORY ACCEPTANCE: _____ M. & T. APPROVAL BY: _____

THE STANDARDS CONTAINED HEREIN ARE APPLICABLE TO THE MACHINE OR OPERATION AND METHODS EMPLOYED AS OF_____
AND ARE SUBJECT TO REVISION PENDING ANY ALTERATION OR CHANGE IN METHODS OR EQUIPMENT.

Exhibit 11–31
Actual Production Standard

STD. NO. 111
CHART NO. 1

PRODUCTION STANDARD

MARTIN & TUCKER, INC.
ENGINEERS

PAGE 1 OF 1

MACHINE NO. 1073   DESCRIPTION: Smyth Number 3 Sewing Machine

OPERATION: Sew   ELEMENT: Makeready and Run

Number of Signatures_____ Size of Signature_____ Weight of Paper_____ Oblong Books_____

Reinforced End Papers_____ Sew with Tapes_____ Number of Books to be Sewn_____ Standard Time_____ Allowed

1. Makeready   Operation Number
    1.1 No size change .... .10 hr/job .... 100 .... _____ hr.
    1.2 Machine adjustment to new size .... .30 hr/job .... 101 .... _____ hr.
    1.3 Setup for tapes, including detachment .... .03 hr/job .... 102 .... _____ hr.

2. Running Time		Allowance by Stock Weight and Book Size				
		Under 35		35 or Over		
(Sewing time = Number of signatures × Signature allowance). (Reinforced end papers are classified as open head signatures)	Number of Signatures	6" x 9" and Under Operation Number	Over 6" x 9" Operation Number	6" x 9" and Under Operation Number	Over 6" x 9" Operation Number	Sewing time hr/M
2.1 Closed head signatures (except 8 pgs.) including quad 16 and duplex 32 (not inserted)		103 2,533/hr .39/M	104 2,222/hr .45 hr/M	105 3,454/hr .29 hr/M	106 3,030/hr .33 hr/M	
2.2 Duplex 64 (32 pgs. inserted into 32 pgs.) and quad 32 (16 pgs. inserted into 16 pgs.)		107 2,000/hr .50 hr/M	108 1,754/hr .57 hr/M	109 2,741/hr .37 hr/M	110 2,381/hr .42 hr/M	
2.3 a) 8 pg. closed head signature b) Open head signature (not including 2.2.) w/8 pgs. bound on either side of center c) 2.1 signatures with tips or other loose pages with 8 pgs. bound on either side of center		111 1,461/hr .68 hr/M	112 1,282/hr .78 hr/M	113 1,900/hr .53 hr/M	114 1,667/hr .60 hr/m	
2.4 All open head signatures other than 2.3 (does not have 8 pgs. bound on either side of center)		115 845/hr 1.18 hr/M	116 741/hr 1.35 hr/M	117 1,036/hr 1.04 hr/M	118 909/hr 1.10 hr/M	
2.5 8 pg. signatures w/6 or more tipped pgs. or signatures with furnished heavy inserts		119 407/hr 2.46 hr/M	120 357/hr 2.80 hr/M	121 542/hr 1.85 hr/M	122 476/hr 2.10 hr/M	

2.6 Sewing with tapes
   Up to 6 signatures per book .... .08 hr/M.
   7 to 12 signatures per book .... .06 hr/M.
   13 to 22 signatures per book .... .03 hr/M.

2.7 Add items 2.1 to 2.6 including .... _____

2.8 Allowance for oblong books, 12% x (item 2.7)
   books sewn on short side) .12 x _____ = _____

2.9 Add items 2.7 and 2.8 ....

3. Total Sewing Time
   Number of books in thousands x sewing time/M book (item 2.9)
   _____ x _____ = ... _____ hr

4. Total Job Time (Add Items 1 and 3) .... _____ hr

CLIENT COMPANY:_____ DATE ISSUED:_____ REVISION DATES:_____
DIVISION/PLANT:_____ M. & T. ENGINEER:_____
SUPERVISORY ACCEPTANCE:_____ M. & T. APPROVAL BY:_____

THE STANDARDS CONTAINED HEREIN ARE APPLICABLE TO THE MACHINE OR OPERATION AND METHODS EMPLOYED AS OF_____ AND ARE SUBJECT TO REVISION PENDING ANY ALTERATION OR CHANGE IN METHODS OR EQUIPMENT.

Exhibit 11–32
Actual Production Standard

STD. NO. ___2___
CHART NO. _1_

PRODUCTION STANDARD

MARTIN & TUCKER, INC.
ENGINEERS

PAGE __1__ OF__1__

MACHINE NO. __185__   DESCRIPTION: <u>1-C Harris Offset; Production Center #8</u>

OPERATION: <u>Print or Coat</u>   ELEMENT: <u>Run</u>

Standard Sheets per Hour			
		Standard Hours per M Sheets	
Up to 10,000 Sheets		10,000 Sheets or More	
Board Caliper		Board Caliper	
.014"-.024"	.025"-.032"	.014"-.024"	.025"-.032"
3,250	2,900	3,600	3,250
.308	.345	.278	.308

Conversion Schedule from Sheets
to Blanks per Hour
and Hours per M Blanks

Number Up				
2	6,500	5,800	7,200	6,500
	.154	.172	.139	.154
4	13,000	11,600	14,400	13,000
	.077	.086	.070	.077
6	19,500	17,400	21,600	19,500
	.051	.057	.046	.051

<u>Limitations</u>

1. <u>Maximum sheet size:</u> 22" x 30¼".
2. <u>Materials:</u> chip, bleached manila, clay coated, solid bleached sulphate.

<u>Notes to Standards</u>

1. <u>For varnishing:</u> subtract 10% from Standard hr/M.

CLIENT COMPANY: _____ DATE ISSUED: _____ REVISION DATES: _____

DIVISION/PLANT: _____ M. & T. ENGINEER: _____

SUPERVISORY ACCEPTANCE: _____ M. & T. APPROVAL BY: _____

THE STANDARDS CONTAINED HEREIN ARE APPLICABLE TO THE MACHINE OR OPERATION AND METHODS EMPLOYED AS OF_____
AND ARE SUBJECT TO REVISION PENDING ANY ALTERATION OR CHANGE IN METHODS OR EQUIPMENT.

Exhibit 11–33
Actual Production Standard

PRODUCTION STANDARD

MARTIN & TUCKER, INC.
ENGINEERS

PAGE 2 OF 2

MACHINE NO. 31 _____ DESCRIPTION: Kidder Flexo Press, 4-C, 36" Production Center #3

OPERATION: Print _____ ELEMENT: Run -- Machine Variables
-- Product Variables

Standard Crew = 2 = 1 Operator + 1 Helper   Unit of Output = M ft

Order Quantity	50M to 150M ft		Over 150M But Under 250M ft		Over 250M ft	
	Number of Colors		Number of Colors		Number of Colors	
	3 or 4	1 or 2	3 or 4	1 or 2	3 or 4	1 or 2
Std. ft/min.	400	450	450	500	500	550
Std. ft/hr	24,000	27,000	27,000	30,000	30,000	33,000
Std. hr/M ft	.0417	.0370	.0370	.0333	.0333	.0303

Allowances

1. For order qty. under 50M ft. use the following:
   a. 10M to 25M ft: 250 ft/min. - .0667 std. hr/M ft
   b. 26M to 49M ft: 300 ft/min. - .0555 std. hr/M ft

2. "J" Film (Tubing):   Up to 2 mil add 10% to Std. hr/M ft
                        Over 2 mil add 20% to Std. hr/M ft

Notes

    These standards represent the average running condition, in a variety
    of materials, structure, and gauge.

CLIENT COMPANY: _____ DATE ISSUED: _____ REVISION DATES: _____
DIVISION/PLANT: _____ M. & T. ENGINEER: _____
SUPERVISORY ACCEPTANCE: _____ M. & T. APPROVAL BY: _____

THE STANDARDS CONTAINED HEREIN ARE APPLICABLE TO THE MACHINE OR OPERATION AND METHODS EMPLOYED AS OF _____
AND ARE SUBJECT TO REVISION PENDING ANY ALTERATION OR CHANGE IN METHODS OR EQUIPMENT.

Exhibit 11–34
Actual Production Standard

STD. NO.		PRODUCTION STANDARD		MARTIN & TUCKER, INC. ENGINEERS
CHART NO. 6-2				PAGE 3 of 5

MACHINE NO. 1   DESCRIPTION: Free-Blown Extruder

OPERATION: Blow Film   ELEMENT: Run

Tubing Lay Flat Size, in inches	Gauge	Feet per Minute	Feet per Hour	Pounds per Hour	Gauge	Feet per Minute	Feet per Hour	Pounds per Hour	Gauge	Feet per Minute	Feet per Hour	Pounds per Hour
36	.00150	69	4,150	180	.00175	59	3,550	180	.00200	52	3,125	180
34	.00150	70	4,200	172	.00175	59	3,550	170	.00200	52	3,125	170
32	.00150	75	4,500	172	.00175	63	3,800	170	.00200	55	3,300	170
30	.00150	78	4,700	170	.00175	66	3,950	165	.00200	57½	3,450	165
28	.00150	79	4,750	160	.00175	68	4,100	160	.00200	59½	3,550	160
26	.00150	86	5,150	160	.00175	73	4,400	160	.00200	64	3,850	160
24	.00150	90	5,400	155	.00175	77	4,600	155	.00200	67½	4,050	155
22	.00150	95	5,700	150	.00175	81	4,850	150	.00200	71	4,250	150
20	.00150	104	6,250	150	.00175	87	5,200	145	.00200	73	4.375	140
20	.00150	104	6,250	150	.00175	87	5,200	145	.00200	73	4,375	140
18	.00150	108	6,500	140	.00175	89	5,350	135	.00200	75	4,500	130
16	.00150	117½	7,050	135	.00175	97	5,800	130	.00200	82	4,900	125
14	.00150	124	7,450	125	.00175	102	6,100	120	.00200	86	5,150	115
20	.00150	59	3,550	85	.00175	51	3,050	85	.00200	44	2,650	85
18	.00150	63	3,800	82	.00175	54	3,250	82	.00200	47	2,800	80
16	.00150	66	3,950	76	.00175	57	3,400	76	.00200	49	2,950	75
14	.00150	72	4,300	72	.00175	61	3,640	72	.00200	52	3,125	70
12	.00150	81	4,850	70	.00175	69	4,150	70	.00200	61	3,650	70
12	.00150	81	4,850	70	.00175	69	4,150	70	.00200	61	3,650	70
10	.00150	90	5,400	65	.00175	77½	4,650	65	.00200	67½	4,050	65
8	.00150	104	6,250	60	.00175	89	5,350	60	.00200	78	4,700	60
6	.00150	127½	7,650	55	.00175	109	6,550	55	.00200	96	5,750	55

Footnotes

1. Set the feet per minute as recommended for gauge and layflat size combination for standard performance.

2. Potential pounds per hour = tubing (layflat size) x gauge x .800 x feet per hour. This is the output generating function. To measure net actual pounds per hour use the formula: Net actual pounds per hour = Net footage x Yield ÷ By running hours.

   This represents net output after allowances for: Scrap, planned losses, and variation in running speed (actual vs. standard).

CLIENT COMPANY: _____ DATE ISSUED: _____ REVISION DATES: _____

DIVISION/PLANT: _____ M. & T. ENGINEER: _____

SUPERVISORY ACCEPTANCE: _____ M. & T. APPROVAL BY: _____

THE STANDARDS CONTAINED HEREIN ARE APPLICABLE TO THE MACHINE OR OPERATION AND METHODS EMPLOYED AS OF _____
AND ARE SUBJECT TO REVISION PENDING ANY ALTERATION OR CHANGE IN METHODS OR EQUIPMENT.

106

Exhibit 11–35
Actual Production Standard

STD. NO. _____
CHART NO. _____

PRODUCTION STANDARD

MARTIN & TUCKER, INC.
ENGINEERS

PAGE_____ OF__

MACHINE NO._31 thru 34____ DESCRIPTION:_Manual Cutter -- Solid Dies_____

OPERATION:_Die Cut Baronial, Booklet, and Open_____ ELEMENT:___Run_____
Side Blanks

20# Stock[a]

Number Out	Envelope Style or Size[b]	500/Lift Std./hr	hr/M	550/Lift Std./hr	hr/M	600/Lift Std./hr	hr/M
10	No. 6¼ wallet	54,400	.0184	59,840	.0167	65,280	.0153
12		56,050	.0178	61,655	.0162	67,260	.0149
3	5 x 11	37,950	.0264	41,745	.0240	45,540	.0220
3	Double fold	36,750	.0272	40,425	.0247	44,100	.0227
20	3 5/8 x 4 3/4	59,700	.0168	65,700	.0152	71,600	.0139
24	Baronial	60,250	.0166	66,275	.0151	72,300	.0138
9	4 3/4 x 6½	51,500	.0194	56,650	.0177	61,800	.0162
10	Booklet	50,750	.0197	55,825	.0179	60,900	.0164

[a] Similar for other weights.

[b] Similar for other styles and sizes.

EN

CLIENT COMPANY:_____ DATE ISSUED:_____ REVISION DATES:_____
DIVISION/PLANT:_____ M. & T. ENGINEER:_____
SUPERVISORY ACCEPTANCE:_____ M. & T. APPROVAL BY:_____

THE STANDARDS CONTAINED HEREIN ARE APPLICABLE TO THE MACHINE OR OPERATION AND METHODS EMPLOYED AS OF_____
AND ARE SUBJECT TO REVISION PENDING ANY ALTERATION OR CHANGE IN METHODS OR EQUIPMENT.

Exhibit 11–36
Actual Production Standard

STD. NO. 1109

CHART NO. _____

PRODUCTION STANDARD

MARTIN & TUCKER, INC.
ENGINEERS

PAGE_____ OF__

MACHINE NO. 5 (Post 50) DESCRIPTION: _____

OPERATION: Gluing _____ ELEMENT: Run _____

Inches Feed Length	Standard Hours per M Cartons			
	Caliper			
	.014"-.020"	.021"-.026"	.027"-.032"	.033"-.040"
4	.024	.025	.027	.029
5	.025	.027	.030	.032
6	.027	.030	.032	.035
7	.029	.032	.035	.038
8	.031	.035	.038	.042
9	.033	.037	.041	.045
10	.035	.040	.044	.048
11	.037	.043	.048	.053
12	.040	.046	.052	.057
13	.044	.050	.056	.063
14	.047	.053	.060	.069
15	.050	.058	.065	.076
16	.055	.063	.072	.083
17	.060	.068	.078	.091
18	.065	.074	.086	.098
19	.070	.080	.092	.106
20	.076	.087	.100	.115
21	.082	.094	.108	.124
22	.088	.102	.117	.133
23	.096	.110	.126	.143
24	.105	.119	.135	.154
25	.113	.128	.144	.164
26	.122	.137	.153	.174
27	.132	.146	.164	.185
28	.143	.156	.175	.196
29	.153	.166	.187	.207
30	.163	.177	.199	.218
31	.174	.188	.210	.229
32	.185	.199	.221	.240
33	.197	.211	.233	.252
34	.209	.223	.245	.264
35	.222	.236	.257	.277

Notes
1. For automatic trays   Add 30% to total hours.
2. For cartons with glued-in cell   Add 40% to total hours.
3. For 5-panel cartons   Add 15% to total hours.

These standards apply to the following carton styles: reverse tuck, straight tuck, seal end, sleeves, double wall, glued-in cell, displays, trays.

Standard Crew: 1 Feeder and 2 Catchers
                1/2 Operator

CLIENT COMPANY: _____ DATE ISSUED: _____ REVISION DATES: _____

DIVISION/PLANT: _____ M. & T. ENGINEER: _____

SUPERVISORY ACCEPTANCE: _____ M. & T. APPROVAL BY: _____

THE STANDARDS CONTAINED HEREIN ARE APPLICABLE TO THE MACHINE OR OPERATION AND METHODS EMPLOYED AS OF_____
AND ARE SUBJECT TO REVISION PENDING ANY ALTERATION OR CHANGE IN METHODS OR EQUIPMENT.

Exhibit 11–37
Actual Production Standard

STD. NO. 100 CHART NO. 1	**PRODUCTION STANDARD**	**MARTIN & TUCKER, INC.** ENGINEERS PAGE 1 OF 3

MACHINE NO._____ DESCRIPTION: Steel Rule Dies for Cutting and Creasing

OPERATION: Diemaking _____ ELEMENT: All _____

		Standard Hours		
		New Die	Die on Hand	
Style of Carton	Number Up	Single Size	Same Layout	Different Layout
Reverse Tuck End Straight Tuck End (A) Regular	1	3.000	2.000	–
	2	4.200	2.900	3.000
	3	5.500	3.900	4.100
	4	6.700	4.800	5.000
	5	7.900	5.700	5.900
	6	9.200	6.700	6.900
	7	10.400	7.600	7.850
	8	11.600	8.500	8.750
	9	12.800	9.400	9.650
	10	14.000	10.300	10.550
	11	15.050	11.050	11.300
	12	16.100	11.800	12.050
	13	17.150	12.500	12.750
	14	18.200	13.300	13.550
	15	19.250	14.050	14.300
	16	20.150	14.700	14.950
	17	21.050	15.350	15.600
	18	21.950	16.000	16.250
	19	22.850	16.650	16.900
	20	23.750	17.300	17.550
	21	24.650	17.950	18.200
	22	25.550	18.600	18.850
	23	26.450	19.250	19.500
	24	27.350	19.900	20.150
	25	28.250	20.550	20.800
	26	29.050	21.050	21.300
	27	29.850	21.550	21.800
	28	30.650	22.050	22.300
	29	31.450	22.550	22.800
	30	32.250	23.050	23.350
	31	33.050	23.550	23.850
	32	33.850	24.050	24.350
	33	34.650	24.550	24.850
	34	35.450	25.050	25.350
	35	36.250	25.550	25.850

CLIENT COMPANY: _____ DATE ISSUED: _____ REVISION DATES:_____

DIVISION/PLANT:_____ M. & T. ENGINEER:_____

SUPERVISORY ACCEPTANCE: _____ M. & T. APPROVAL BY:_____

THE STANDARDS CONTAINED HEREIN ARE APPLICABLE TO THE MACHINE OR OPERATION AND METHODS EMPLOYED AS OF_____
AND ARE SUBJECT TO REVISION PENDING ANY ALTERATION OR CHANGE IN METHODS OR EQUIPMENT.

Exhibit 11–38
Actual Production Standard

STD. NO. __101R__

CHART NO. _____

MARTIN & TUCKER, INC.
ENGINEERS

PAGE _____ OF __

PRODUCTION STANDARD

Setup ☐   Run ☒

PRODUCTION CENTER: __#101__   __78" CORRUGATOR__   DATE: __10/16/79__

EQUIPMENT: BY: THL

NAME: __Combiner (Corrugator)__   MANUFACTURER: __S & S Paper Mach. Co.__   MODEL: _____

SIZE: __78"__   SPEED: __to 450 fpm__   CREW: __7 or 8__

FUNCTION: __Combine single wall or double wall; slit, score, trim, and cut off.__

	Single Wall				Double Wall			
	Brown Box[a]		Preprint		Brown Box[a]		Preprint	
Flute ⟶	E, B, C		B, E, C		CE, BE, BC		BE, BC, CE	
Test ⟶	200	275	200	275	275	350	275	350
Liner weight[b] ⟶	32-47#	64-70#	32-47#	64-70#	32-47#	64-70#	32-47#	64-70#
Run speed (lin. ft/min.)[c]	375	310	375	310	280	270	260	250
Standard lin. ft/hr[d]	16,900	14,000	16,900	14,000	12,600	12,150	11,700	11,300
Standard sq. ft/hr[e]	95,600	79,100			71,400	73,400		

Special Condition Factors

Kraftex (Kt) (as inner liner) _____ Multiply above standards by .90

Tear Tape _____ Multiply above standards by .95

[a] Includes mottled white.

[b] At double backer.

[c] This is the speed while running -- does not reflect nonrun time.

[d] This reflects 25% allowance.

[e] This reflects 25% allowance and is based on an average 68" roll width.

CLIENT COMPANY: _____ DATE ISSUED: _____ REVISION DATES: _____

DIVISION/PLANT: _____ M. & T. ENGINEER: _____

SUPERVISORY ACCEPTANCE: _____ M. & T. APPROVAL BY: _____

THE STANDARDS CONTAINED HEREIN ARE APPLICABLE TO THE MACHINE OR OPERATION AND METHODS EMPLOYED AS OF _____
AND ARE SUBJECT TO REVISION PENDING ANY ALTERATION OR CHANGE IN METHODS OR EQUIPMENT.

Exhibit 11–39
Actual Production Standard

STD. NO. 102R

CHART NO. _____

MARTIN & TUCKER, INC.
ENGINEERS

PAGE_____ OF__

PRODUCTION STANDARD

Setup ☐   Run ☒

PRODUCTION CENTER: #102   86" Corrugator   DATE: 10/16/79

EQUIPMENT: BY: THL

NAME: Combiner (Corrugator) MANUFACTURER: S & S Paper Mach. Co. MODEL:

SIZE: 86"   SPEED: to 650'/min.   CREW: 7

FUNCTION: Combine single wall or double wall; slit, score, trim, and cut off

	Single Wall[a]				Double Wall[a]			
	Brown Box[a]	Preprint			Brown Box[a]	Preprint		
Flute ⟶	B, C, E				BC, EB, EC			
Test ⟶	200	275			275	350		
Liner weight[b] ⟶	32-47#	64-70#			32-47#	64-70#		
Run speed (lin. ft/min.)[c]	450	330			300	275		
Standard lin. ft/hr[d]	21,600	15,800			14,400	13,200		
Standard sq. ft/hr[e]	147,600	108,200			98,400	90,200		

Special Condition Factors

Kraftex (Kt) (as inner liner) _____   Multiply above standards by .90

Short pieces (less than 30" cut length) _____   Multiply above standards by .90

Long pieces (130"-170") _____   Multiply above standards by .85

[a] Includes mottled white.

[b] At double backer.

[c] This is the speed while running -- does not reflect nonrun time.

[d] This reflects 20% allowance.

[e] This reflects 20% allowance and is based on an average 82" roll width.

CLIENT COMPANY: _____ DATE ISSUED: _____ REVISION DATES: _____
DIVISION/PLANT: _____ M. & T. ENGINEER: _____
SUPERVISORY ACCEPTANCE: _____ M. & T. APPROVAL BY: _____

THE STANDARDS CONTAINED HEREIN ARE APPLICABLE TO THE MACHINE OR OPERATION AND METHODS EMPLOYED AS OF_____
AND ARE SUBJECT TO REVISION PENDING ANY ALTERATION OR CHANGE IN METHODS OR EQUIPMENT.

Exhibit 11–40
Actual Production Standard

STD. NO. __100S__

CHART NO. _____

MARTIN & TUCKER, INC.
ENGINEERS

PAGE_____ OF__

PRODUCTION STANDARD

Setup ☒   Run ☐

PRODUCTION CENTER: __#101 and #102__   __Corrugators__   DATE: __10/16/78__

EQUIPMENT: BY: THL

NAME: __Combiner (Corrugator)__ MANUFACTURER: __S & S Paper Mach. Co.__ MODEL: _____

SIZE: __78" x 86"__   SPEED: __to 450 fpm and 650 fpm__   CREW: __7 or 8__

FUNCTION: __Combine single wall or double wall; slit, score, trim, and cut off__

PC Number⟶	#101	#102
	Standard Hours per Order	
Machine size⟶	78"	86"
Basic allowance	.067	.050
Tear tape	.080	
Skid rid		

Exhibit 11–41
Actual Production Standard

STD. NO. 104RS

CHART NO. _____

MARTIN & TUCKER, INC.
ENGINEERS

PAGE_____ OF__

PRODUCTION STANDARD

Setup ☒   Run ☒

PRODUCTION CENTER: __#104___ __Coater___   DATE: __10/19/79__

  EQUIPMENT: BY: THL

  NAME: _Coater_____ MANUFACTURER: _Black Clawson____ MODEL:_____

  SIZE: _87"_____ SPEED: _to 375 fpm_____ CREW: _5_____

  FUNCTION: _Clay coating and calendering of preprint liners_____

Setup   Standard Hours per Order
                              .40^a

Run

Weight of outer liner	38# K	33# White Tag	38# BW
Run speed -- lin. ft/min.^{b}	375	350	
Standard lin. ft/hr^c	17,800	16,600	

^{a} Based on following probabilities for every 5 orders;

          4 orders @ .25 hr
          1 order @ 1.00 hr

^{b} This is the speed while running -- does not reflect nonrun time.

^{c} This reflects 21% allowance.

CLIENT COMPANY:_____ DATE ISSUED:_____REVISION DATES:_____

DIVISION/PLANT:_____ M. & T. ENGINEER:_____

SUPERVISORY ACCEPTANCE:_____ M. & T. APPROVAL BY:_____

THE STANDARDS CONTAINED HEREIN ARE APPLICABLE TO THE MACHINE OR OPERATION AND METHODS EMPLOYED AS OF_____
AND ARE SUBJECT TO REVISION PENDING ANY ALTERATION OR CHANGE IN METHODS OR EQUIPMENT.

Exhibit 11–42
Actual Production Standard

STD. NO. __105RS__

CHART NO. _____

MARTIN & TUCKER, INC.
ENGINEERS

PAGE_____ OF__

PRODUCTION STANDARD

Setup ☒   Run ☒

PRODUCTION CENTER: __#105__   __Gravure Press__   DATE: __10/19/79__

EQUIPMENT: BY: THL

NAME: __Roto Gravure Press__   MANUFACTURER: __Motter Print Press__ MODEL:_____

SIZE: __88"__   SPEED: __to 400 fpm__   CREW: __4__

FUNCTION: __Printing of preprint liners -- 4 colors__

Setup

Job Printing Class	Standard Hours per Order
R = repeat	2.0
N = new	3.0
C = critical	4.0

Run

	38# K/33# WT	38# BW	
Weight of outer liner →			
Run speed -- lin. ft/min.^{a}	385		
Standard lin. ft/hr^b	18,000		

^{a}This is the speed while running — does not reflect nonrun time.

^{b}This reflects 22% allowance.

CLIENT COMPANY:_____ DATE ISSUED:_____ REVISION DATES:_____

DIVISION/PLANT:_____ M. & T. ENGINEER:_____

SUPERVISORY ACCEPTANCE:_____ M. & T. APPROVAL BY:_____

THE STANDARDS CONTAINED HEREIN ARE APPLICABLE TO THE MACHINE OR OPERATION AND METHODS EMPLOYED AS OF_____
AND ARE SUBJECT TO REVISION PENDING ANY ALTERATION OR CHANGE IN METHODS OR EQUIPMENT.

Exhibit 11–43
Actual Production Standard

STD. NO. <u>111R</u>

CHART NO. _____

MARTIN & TUCKER, INC.
ENGINEERS

PAGE _____ OF __

PRODUCTION STANDARD

Setup ☐   Run ☒

PRODUCTION CENTER: <u>#111   Rotary Chain Slotter</u>   DATE: <u>10/30/79</u>

EQUIPMENT: BY: THL

NAME: <u>Press-Printer Slotter</u>   MANUFACTURER: <u>S & S Paper Mach. Co.</u> MODEL: <u>Rotary-Chain</u>

SIZE: <u>78" x 180"</u>   SPEED: _____ CREW: <u>2+</u>

FUNCTION: <u>LP Print (1 color), slot, score, trim, slit</u>

Run Speed (Fed Blanks per Minute)[a]

Fed Blank Size, in Square Feet	Single Wall					Double Wall			
	200#		275#			275#		350#	
	Regular	Special[c]	Regular	Special[c]		Regular	Special[c]	Regular	Special[c]
20	28	25	25	23		23	21		
30	21	19	19	17		17	15		
40	18	16	16	14		14	12		
50	15	14	14	13		13	11		
60	14	13	13	12		12	10		
70+	13	12	12	11		11	9		

Standard Blanks per Hour[b]

20	1,260	1,125	1,125	1,035		1,035	945	932	850
30	945	855	855	765		765	675	689	610
40	810	720	720	630		630	540	565	485
50	675	630	630	585		585	495	525	446
60	630	585	585	540		540	450	485	405
70+	585	540	540	495		495	405	445	365

[a] This is the speed while running -- does not reflect nonrun time.

[b] This reflects 25% allowance.

[c] Special values as apply to heavy print (over 50% coverage), slippery material, chocked loads, skip feed, etc.

CLIENT COMPANY: _____ DATE ISSUED: _____ REVISION DATES: _____

DIVISION/PLANT: _____ M. & T. ENGINEER: _____

SUPERVISORY ACCEPTANCE: _____ M. & T. APPROVAL BY: _____

THE STANDARDS CONTAINED HEREIN ARE APPLICABLE TO THE MACHINE OR OPERATION AND METHODS EMPLOYED AS OF _____

AND ARE SUBJECT TO REVISION PENDING ANY ALTERATION OR CHANGE IN METHODS OR EQUIPMENT.

Exhibit 11–44
Actual Production Standard

STD. NO. 112R

CHART NO. _____

MARTIN & TUCKER, INC.
ENGINEERS

PAGE_____ OF__

PRODUCTION STANDARD

Setup ☐   Run ☒

PRODUCTION CENTER: __#112__   __60 x 140 Press__   DATE: __10/30/79__

EQUIPMENT: BY: THL

NAME: __Press-Printer Slotter__ MANUFACTURER: __Hooper Swift-Koppers__ MODEL: _____

SIZE: __60" x 140"__   SPEED: _____ CREW: __3+__

FUNCTION: __LP Print (2 colors), slot, score, trim, slit__

Run Speed (Fed Blanks per Minute)[a]

Fed Blank	Single Wall				Double Wall			
Size in Square Feet	200#		275#		275#		350#	
	Regular	Special[c]	Regular	Special[c]	Regular	Special[c]	Regular	Special[c]
20	75	56	60	45	56	42		
30	55	41	44	33	41	31		
40	44	33	35	26	33	25		
50	36	27	29	22	27	20		
60	31	23	25	19	23	17		
70+	28	21	22	17	21	16		

Standard Blanks per Hour[b]

20	3,375	2,520	2,700	2,025	2,520	1,890	2,268	1,701
30	2,475	1,845	1,980	1,485	1,845	1,395	1,661	1,256
40	1,980	1,485	1,575	1,170	1,485	1,125	1,337	1,013
50	1,620	1,215	1,305	990	1,215	900	1,094	810
60	1,395	1,035	1,125	855	1,035	765	932	689
70+	1,260	945	990	765	945	720	851	648

[a] This is the speed while running -- does not reflect nonrun time.
[b] This reflects 25% allowance.
[c] Special values as apply to heavy print (over 50% coverage), slippery material, chocked loads, skip feed, etc.

CLIENT COMPANY:_____ DATE ISSUED:_____ REVISION DATES:_____
DIVISION/PLANT:_____ M. & T. ENGINEER:_____
SUPERVISORY ACCEPTANCE:_____ M. & T. APPROVAL BY:_____

THE STANDARDS CONTAINED HEREIN ARE APPLICABLE TO THE MACHINE OR OPERATION AND METHODS EMPLOYED AS OF_____ AND ARE SUBJECT TO REVISION PENDING ANY ALTERATION OR CHANGE IN METHODS OR EQUIPMENT.

Exhibit 11–45
Actual Production Standard

STD. NO. 113R

CHART NO. _____

MARTIN & TUCKER, INC.
ENGINEERS

PAGE_____ OF_

PRODUCTION STANDARD

Setup ☐   Run ☒

PRODUCTION CENTER: __#113__[a]   __50 x 103 Press__

DATE: __11/1/79__

BY: THL

EQUIPMENT:

NAME: __Press-Printer Slotter__   MANUFACTURER: __Hooper Swift-Koppers__ MODEL: _____

SIZE: __50" x 103"__   SPEED: _____   CREW: __3__

FUNCTION: __LP Print (2 colors), slot, score, trim, slit.__

	Run Speed (Fed Blanks per Minute)[b]							
	Single Wall				Double Wall			
Fed Blank Size in Square Feet	200#		275#		275#		350#	
	Regular	Special[d]	Regular	Special[d]	Regular	Special[d]	Regular	Special[d]
10	140	105	112	84	98	78		
20	95	71	76	57	67	54		
30	71	53	57	43	50	40		
40	56	42	45	34	39	31		
50	45	34	36	27	32	26		
Standard Blanks per Hour[c]								
10	6,300	4,725	5,040	3,780	4,410	3,510	3,969	3,159
20	4,275	3,195	3,420	2,565	3,015	2,430	2,714	2,187
30	3,195	2,385	2,565	1,935	2,250	1,800	2,025	1,620
40	2,520	1,890	2,025	1,530	1,755	1,395	1,580	1,256
50	2,025	1,530	1,620	1,215	1,440	1,170	1,296	1,053

[a] Use these standards for 50 x 113 (#114) and 35 x 78 (#115) presses also (on temporary basis).

[b] This is the speed while running -- does not reflect nonrun time.

[c] This reflects 25% allowance.

[d] Special values as apply to heavy print (over 50% coverage), slippery material, chocked loads, skip feed, etc.

CLIENT COMPANY:_____ DATE ISSUED:_____ REVISION DATES:_____

DIVISION/PLANT:_____ M. & T. ENGINEER:_____

SUPERVISORY ACCEPTANCE:_____ M. & T. APPROVAL BY:_____

THE STANDARDS CONTAINED HEREIN ARE APPLICABLE TO THE MACHINE OR OPERATION AND METHODS EMPLOYED AS OF_____
AND ARE SUBJECT TO REVISION PENDING ANY ALTERATION OR CHANGE IN METHODS OR EQUIPMENT.

Page 118

Exhibit 11–46
Actual Production Standard

STD. NO. 131R
CHART NO. _____

PRODUCTION STANDARD

MARTIN & TUCKER, INC.
ENGINEERS

PAGE ____ OF __

Setup ☐   Run ☒

PRODUCTION CENTER: #131   Large Comet -- Finishing   DATE: 10/25/79

EQUIPMENT: BY: THL

NAME: Folder-Gluer   MANUFACTURER: Universal   MODEL: _____

SIZE: 64" x 126"   SPEED: _____   CREW: 4

FUNCTION: Fold, glue, strap bundles

Run Speed (Blanks per Minute)[a]

Blank Size in Square Feet[c]	Number of Boxes per Bundle[c]	Single Wall				Double Wall			
		200#		275#		275#		350#	
		Regular	Special[d]	Regular	Special[d]	Regular	Special[d]	Regular	Special[d]
To 11	25 and up	130	100	120	85	105	75		
12-15	20	120	90	110	80	90	70		
16-21	15	95	80	85	70	75	60		
22-37	10	60	50	55	45	50	45		
38-55	5	30	25	30	30	32	30		

Standard Blanks per Hour[b]

To 11	25 and up	5,850	4,500	5,400	3,830	4,730	3,380	4,260	3,040
12-15	20	5,400	4,050	4,950	3,600	4,050	3,150	3,650	2,840
16-21	15	4,280	3,600	3,830	3,150	3,380	2,700	3,040	2,430
22-37	10	2,700	2,250	2,480	2,030	2,250	2,030	2,030	1,830
38-55	5	1,350	1,130	1,350	1,350	1,440	1,350	1,300	1,220

[a] This is the speed while running -- does not reflect any nonrun time.

[b] This includes 25% allowance.

[c] Either the "Blank Size" or the "Number of Boxes per Bundle" may be the limiting factor. Therefore, use the parameter that specifies the lower speed and hourly production rate.

[d] Use "Special" Standards for Skip feed, heavy printing (more than 50% coverage). Slippery material (e.g., preprint), special shape (panel width < 5", depth < 6" or panel length 2½ times the width panel).

CLIENT COMPANY: _____   DATE ISSUED: _____   REVISION DATES: _____
DIVISION/PLANT: _____   M. & T. ENGINEER: _____
SUPERVISORY ACCEPTANCE: _____   M. & T. APPROVAL BY: _____

THE STANDARDS CONTAINED HEREIN ARE APPLICABLE TO THE MACHINE OR OPERATION AND METHODS EMPLOYED AS OF _____ AND ARE SUBJECT TO REVISION PENDING ANY ALTERATION OR CHANGE IN METHODS OR EQUIPMENT.

Exhibit 11–47
Actual Production Standard

STD. NO. 132R
CHART NO. _____

MARTIN & TUCKER, INC.
ENGINEERS

PAGE_____ OF__

PRODUCTION STANDARD

Setup ☐   Run ☒
PRODUCTION CENTER: #132   Small Comet -- Finishing   DATE: 10/27/79

EQUIPMENT: BY: THL

NAME: Folder-Gluer   MANUFACTURER: Universal   MODEL: _____

SIZE: 38" x 88"   SPEED: _____   CREW: 4-5

FUNCTION: Fold, glue, strap bundles

Run Speed (Blanks per Minute)[a]

Blank Size in Square Feet[c]	Number of Boxes per Bundle[c]	Single Wall				Double Wall			
		200#		275#		275#		350#	
		Regular	Special[d]	Regular	Special[d]	Regular	Special[d]	Regular	Special[d]
To 11	25 and up	145	110	130	100	105	75		
12-15	20	135	105	120	95	95	70		
16-21	15	105	85	95	80	75	60		
	10	70	60	60	50	50	45		

Standard Blanks per Hour[b]

To 11	25 and up	6,530	4,950	5,850	4,280	4,730	3,380	4,260	3,040
12-15	20	6,080	4,730	5,400	4,050	4,280	3,150	3,850	2,800
16-21	15	4,730	3,830	4,280	3,600	3,380	2,700	3,040	2,400
	10	3,150	2,700	2,700	2,250	2,250	2,030	2,030	1,830

[a] This is the speed while running -- does not reflect any nonrun time.

[b] This includes 25% allowance.

[c] Either the "Blank Size" or the "Number of Boxes per Bundle" may be the limiting factor. Therefore, use the parameter that specifies the lower speed and hourly production rate.

[d] Use "Special" Standards for Skip feed, heavy printing (more than 50% coverage). Slippery material (e.g., preprint), special shape (panel width < 5", depth < 6" or panel length 2½ times the width panel).

CLIENT COMPANY: _____ DATE ISSUED: _____ REVISION DATES: _____
DIVISION/PLANT: _____ M. & T. ENGINEER: _____
SUPERVISORY ACCEPTANCE: _____ M. & T. APPROVAL BY: _____

THE STANDARDS CONTAINED HEREIN ARE APPLICABLE TO THE MACHINE OR OPERATION AND METHODS EMPLOYED AS OF_____
AND ARE SUBJECT TO REVISION PENDING ANY ALTERATION OR CHANGE IN METHODS OR EQUIPMENT.

Exhibit 11–48
Actual Production Standard

STD. NO. __133R__

CHART NO. _____

MARTIN & TUCKER, INC.
ENGINEERS

PAGE_____OF__

PRODUCTION STANDARD

Setup ☐   Run ☒

PRODUCTION CENTER: __#133__   ZLR -- Finishing   DATE: __10/23/79__

EQUIPMENT: BY: THL

NAME: __Folder-Gluer-Printer__ MANUFACTURER: __S & S Paper Mach. Co.__ MODEL: __ZLR__

SIZE: __60" x 113"__   SPEED: __to 180/min. (10,800/hr)__   CREW: __4 (or 3)__

FUNCTION: __Flexo print (2 colors), slot, score, trim, fold, glue, strap bundles__

Run Speed (Blanks per Minute)[a]

Blank Size in Square Feet[c]	Number of Boxes per Bundle[c]	Single Wall				Double Wall			
		200#		275#		275#		350#	
		Regular	Special[d]	Regular	Special[d]	Regular	Special[d]	Regular	Special[d]
To 11	25 and up	180	135	150	110	110	80		
12-15	20	170	130	140	105	105	75		
16-21	15	130	107	110	90	80	65		
22-37	10	85	75	70	60	55	50		
38+	5	45	40	40	35	35	32		

Standard Blanks per Hour[b]

To 11	25 and up	8,100	6,080	6,750	4,950	4,950	3,600	4,460	3,240
12-15	20	7,650	5,850	6,300	4,730	4,725	3,380	4,250	3,040
16-21	15	5,850	4,820	4,950	4,050	3,600	2,930	3,240	2,640
22-37	10	3,830	3,380	3,150	2,700	2,480	2,250	2,230	2,030
38+	5	2,030	1,800	1,800	1,575	1,580	1,440	1,420	1,300

[a] This is the speed while running -- does not reflect any nonrun time.

[b] This includes 25% allowance.

[c] Either the "Blank Size" or the "Number of Boxes per Bundle" may be the limiting factor. Therefore, use the parameter that specifies the lower speed and hourly production rate.

[d] Use "Special" Standards for Skip feed, heavy printing (more than 50% coverage). Slippery material (e.g., preprint), special shape (panel width < 5", depth < 6" or panel length 2½ times the width panel).

CLIENT COMPANY:_____ DATE ISSUED:_____ REVISION DATES:_____

DIVISION/PLANT:_____ M. & T. ENGINEER:_____

SUPERVISORY ACCEPTANCE:_____ M. & T. APPROVAL BY:_____

THE STANDARDS CONTAINED HEREIN ARE APPLICABLE TO THE MACHINE OR OPERATION AND METHODS EMPLOYED AS OF_____

AND ARE SUBJECT TO REVISION PENDING ANY ALTERATION OR CHANGE IN METHODS OR EQUIPMENT.

Exhibit 11–49
Actual Production Standard

MARTIN & TUCKER, INC.
ENGINEERS

STD. NO. __134R__

CHART NO. _____

PAGE_____ OF__

PRODUCTION STANDARD

Setup ☐   Run ☒

PRODUCTION CENTER: __#134__   __ZLM - Finishing__   DATE: __10/23/79__

EQUIPMENT: BY: THL

NAME: __Folder-Gluer-Printer__ MANUFACTURER: __S & S Paper Mach. Co.__ MODEL: __ZLM__

SIZE: __38" x 81"__   SPEED: _____ CREW: __3+__

FUNCTION: Flexo print (1 color), slot, score, trim, fold, glue, strap bundles.

Blank Size in Square Inches	Number of Boxes per Bundle [c]	Run Speed (Blanks per Minute) [a]							
		Single Wall				Double Wall			
		200#		275#		275#		350#	
		Regular	Special [d]	Regular	Special [d]	Regular	Special [d]	Regular	Special [d]
To 11	25 and up	180	135	150	110	110	80		
12-15	20	170	130	140	105	105	75		
16-21	15	130	107	110	90	80	65		
22-37	10	85	75	70	60	55	32		
38+	5	45	40	40	35	35	32		

Standard Blanks per Hour [b]									
To 11	25 and up	8,100	6,080	6,750	4,950	4,950	3,600	4,460	3,240
12-15	20	7,650	5,850	6,300	4,730	4,725	3,380	4,250	3,040
16-21	15	5,850	4,820	4,950	4,050	3,600	2,930	3,240	2,640
22-37	10	3,830	3,380	3,150	2,700	2,480	2,250	2,230	2,030
38+	5	2,030	1,800	1,800	1,575	1,580	1,440	1,420	1,300

[a] This is the speed while running -- does not reflect any nonrun time.

[b] This includes 25% allowance.

[c] Either the "Blank Size" or the "Number of Boxes per Bundle" may be the limiting factor. Therefore, use the parameter that specifies the lower speed and hourly production rate.

[d] Use "Special" Standards for Skip feed, heavy printing (more than 50% coverage). Slippery material (e.g., preprint), special shape (panel width < 5", depth < 6" or panel length 2½ times the width panel).

CLIENT COMPANY: _____ DATE ISSUED: _____ REVISION DATES: _____

DIVISION/PLANT: _____ M. & T. ENGINEER: _____

SUPERVISORY ACCEPTANCE: _____ M. & T. APPROVAL BY: _____

THE STANDARDS CONTAINED HEREIN ARE APPLICABLE TO THE MACHINE OR OPERATION AND METHODS EMPLOYED AS OF_____
AND ARE SUBJECT TO REVISION PENDING ANY ALTERATION OR CHANGE IN METHODS OR EQUIPMENT.

Exhibit 11–50
Actual Production Standard

STD. NO. __135R__
CHART NO. _____

MARTIN & TUCKER, INC.
ENGINEERS

PAGE_____ OF__

PRODUCTION STANDARD

Setup ☐   Run ☒

PRODUCTION CENTER: __#135__   __Piemonte -- Finishing__   DATE: __10/25/79__

EQUIPMENT: BY: THL

NAME: __Folder-Gluer-Printer__   MANUFACTURER: __Piemonte__   MODEL:_____

SIZE: __47" x 105"__   SPEED:_____   CREW: __4__

FUNCTION: __Flexo print (2 colors), slot, score, trim, fold, glue, strap bundles.__

Run Speed (Blanks per Minute)[a]

Blank Size in Square Inches[c]	Number of of Boxes per Bundle[c]	Single Wall 200# Regular	Single Wall 200# Special[d]	Single Wall 275# Regular	Single Wall 275# Special[d]	Double Wall 275# Regular	Double Wall 275# Special[d]	Double Wall #350 Regular	Double Wall #350 Special[d]
To 11	25 and up	155	115	135	100	105	75		
12-15	20	145	110	125	95	100	75		
16-21	15	110	90	95	75	75	60		
22-37	10	70	60	60	50	50	45		
	5	40	35	35	30	32	30		

Standards Blanks per Hour[b]

To 11	25 and up	6,980	5,175	6,080	4,500	4,730	3,380	4,260	3,040
12-15	20	6,530	4,950	5,630	4,280	4,500	3,150	4,050	2,840
16-21	15	4,950	4,050	4,280	3,380	3,380	2,700	3,040	2,430
22-37	10	3,150	2,700	2,700	2,250	2,250	2,030	2,030	1,830
	5	1,800	1,580	1,580	1,350	1,440	1,350	1,300	1,220

[a] This is the speed while running -- does not reflect any nonrun time.

[b] This includes 25% allowance.

[c] Either the "Blank Size" or the "Number of Boxes per Bundle" may be the limiting factor. Therefore, use the parameter that specifies the lower speed and hourly production rate.

[d] Use "Special" Standards for skip feed, heavy printing (more than 50% coverage), slippery material (e.g., preprint), special shape (panel width < 5", depth < 6" or panel length 2½ times the width panel).

CLIENT COMPANY:_____   DATE ISSUED: _____   REVISION DATES:_____
DIVISION/PLANT:_____   M. & T. ENGINEER:_____
SUPERVISORY ACCEPTANCE: _____   M. & T. APPROVAL BY:_____

THE STANDARDS CONTAINED HEREIN ARE APPLICABLE TO THE MACHINE OR OPERATION AND METHODS EMPLOYED AS OF_____
AND ARE SUBJECT TO REVISION PENDING ANY ALTERATION OR CHANGE IN METHODS OR EQUIPMENT.

12 Application of PS in Waste Control

Waste must and can be controlled! But it cannot be eliminated. Some amount of waste will be generated at almost every production center and both the value of the material and the *time* spent producing this waste material must be included in the cost estimate. If the waste is related to a specific order or product, the quantity should be increased to provide the time for making waste. Thus, the planned quantity should be increased by the amount of the expected waste. On the other hand, if the waste is characteristic of the product or group of products, which is reflected in the parameters of operation, it can be included in the PS. However, the waste may be characteristic of the processing machine, regardless of the standard, and in that case, it usually should be included in the MHR. The choice of where to include this expected waste production (conversion) cost is sometimes one of convenience. The important thing is to recognize it, measure it correctly, and include it in the estimated production cost.

Measuring Expected Waste Production Cost

Waste can be measured as a percentage of either input or output, but the treatment is different in each case. Suppose for instance, that a production center starts with 100 pieces and runs 100 pieces through the machine to produce 90 good pieces with 10 wasted. The waste percentage will be expressed differently depending on whether the input or output amount is used as the base. The 10 pieces, in this case, are 10% of the input (10/100) or 11.11% of the output (10/90). Either measurement is valid, as long as it is developed and applied consistently. This output-input relationship also can be expressed as a yield. In the above example, the yield is 9/10 = 90%. The yield is always expressed the same way regardless of whether waste is measured as a percent of input or output.

To illustrate how PS relates to the waste, consider an order for 200 pieces and assume a PS of 100 pieces per hour (or 0.01 hours per piece). If this PS is based on input, then the machine will run at a speed of 100 pieces per hour but to get 200 good pieces, it will take longer than 2.0 hours if there is any waste generated. If 10% waste (as a percent of input) is characteristic of this machine, it will produce 10% bad pieces or 90 good pieces per hour. Therefore, to get 200 good pieces, the machine would have to run 200/90 = 2.22 hours.

The same answer would be obtained if the waste was measured as a percent of output; in this case it would be 10/90 = 11.11%; thereby, the required input is 111.11% of 200 pieces, or 222 pieces. And, since the input standard is 100 pieces per hour, it would take 222/100 = 2.22 hours to run.

If the PS was based on output, it would be stated as 90 pieces per hour and the required running time would be calculated directly without considering the waste; viz., 200/90 = 2.22 hours.

To convert from input waste percent to output waste percent or vice versa, the following formulas can be used:

$$(1)\ \left(\frac{\text{Input Waste Percent}}{100 - \text{Input Waste Percent}}\right) \times 100 = \text{Output Waste Percent}$$

$$(2)\ 100 - \left(\frac{100}{1 + \dfrac{\text{Waste \%}}{100}}\right) = \text{Input Waste Percent}$$

When standards are developed from historical data or used to measure performance, they are usually expressed in terms of "good" production per hour (or hours per unit of "good" production).

Yield, rather than waste percentages, can be used in these calculations if the conversion from one to the other is made as follows:

1. If waste is expressed as percent of Input, use: 100 − Waste Percent = Yield Percent
2. If waste is expressed as percent of Output, use

$$\frac{100}{\left(1 + \dfrac{\text{Waste \%}}{100}\right)} = \text{Yield Percent}$$

Yield factors can be used to adjust the standard as follows:

If the quantity and the standard are not both expressed in terms of input or output, the standards can be factored as shown below:

	If Standard Is Expressed As	
If Quantity is Expressed As	*Standard Hours/Input Quantity*	*Standard Hours/Output Quantity*
Output required	Divide PS by yield[a]	Use as is
Input required	Use as is	Multiply PS by yield[a]

[a]Yield expressed as a decimal.

Knowing how the waste percentage is measured and whether the standard is based on throughput rates or effective output rates (in good pieces) is the important point.

The time to process material that cannot be sold (for the full price) must be included in the estimate as a part of direct cost. Otherwise, the contribution will be overstated resulting in the possibility of accepting work that might have otherwise been rejected.

The following table illustrates measurement of waste in a production process that involves four production centers plus shipping. The entire process from Production Center A to Shipping results in an overall yield of 90%:

Production Center	Quantity		Conversion Waste			Conversion Yield (Output/Input)
	In	Out	Pieces	Percent of Input	Percent of Output	
A	100	98	2	2.000	2.041	0.980
B	98	97	1	1.000	1.031	0.990
C	97	94	3	3.000	3.192	0.969
D	94	94	4	4.000	4.444	0.957
Ship	90	90				
Totals	100	90	10	10.000	11.111	0.900

In the process of estimating the direct cost of an order, the waste may be facility- or order-related. If it is facility-related, apply the appropriate waste factor (for any product) for *each* step in the manufacturing process as shown on the above table.

If it is order- (customer-) related, factors must be used that are appropriate to that particular product.

As indicated above, the waste can be reflected either in the quantity or in the production standard. In any process with two or more steps, either technique may be used.

On the other hand, waste may also be included in the MHR. In this case, care must be taken to assure that the complementary MHR and PS are used. These points are illustrated in the following example:

Production Center	Quantity		Yield	MHR (Dollars per hour)		Production Standard Standard Hours per M Pieces	
	In	Out		Without Waste	With Waste	Without Waste	With Waste
A	100	98	.980	$74.80	$76.33	.420	.429
B	98	97	.990	29.66	29.96	1.300	1.313
C	97	94	.969	13.54	13.97	.900	.929
D	94	90	.957	45.11	47.11	2.810	2.935
Total			.900				

Problem. In Production Center B, find the cost (including waste) using three alternate methods, for an order for 50,000 pieces (shipped quantity).
1) Yield = 90/97 = 0.9278
2) We must first determine the quantity required at Production Center B. The yield 90/97 will identify the ratio of the overall production output to the good pieces out of B. This ratio is 0.9278 and therefore, the good output required from B is 50,000/0.9278 = 53,981 pieces. The input to B is 53,981/0.99 = 54,435 pieces.

METHOD 1. FACTOR THE OUTPUT QUANTITY. If we use the input quantity, the waste is excluded and therefore, we should use the MHR and PS that do *not* include waste:

$$(54,435/1,000) \times 1.300 \times \$29.66 = \$2,099$$

METHOD 2. FACTOR THE MHR. If we use the good output, the waste could be included in the MHR but not in the PS:

$$(53,891/1,000) \times 1.300 \times \$29.96 = \$2,099$$

METHOD 3. FACTOR THE PRODUCTION STANDARD. As an alternative to Method 2 (again using the good output), we can use the PS which includes the waste and the MHR which does not include any waste allowance:

$$(53,891/1,000) \times 1.313 \times \$29.66 = \$2,099$$

In all three methods, the same conversion cost ($2,099) is identified for Production Center B.

Waste-Determined Optimum Machine Speed

Minimum o.o.p. *conversion* cost may seem to occur at the highest running speed, but as speeds are increased, waste percentages usually increase. In some plants, the gains from higher speeds are all wiped out by the increased cost of wasted materials. Thus, the cost of material waste exceeds the gain in conversion contribution. The tabular examples show the procedure for determining this *optimum running speed* to achieve an economic balance between speed and waste.

Failure to use quality control statistics in building production standards can substantially reduce a company's annual contribution.

The optimum speed is at the point where for the change in total o.o.p. costs/M at a machine (between 2 speed levels) is zero. At this point, a reduction in total o.o.p. costs/M (o.o.p. conversion costs/M + wasted conversion costs/M + material costs/M + wasted material cost/M), through a further increase in speed, is no longer possible. Above this optimum speed the effect of wasted material cost becomes the dominant cost factor. Below this optimum speed, the effect of o.o.p. conversion cost dominates. At this optimum speed, the contribution/M (for the machine) is maximized.

Example 1 is an analysis of a small 1-color press. Example 2 is for a larger 2-color press.

Calculations for Two Examples

Example 1. Small 1-Color Printing Press

O.o.p. MHR: Run = $20; Material Cost = $10/M; Max. Speed = 8,000 iph

Speeds	5,000	5,500	6,000	6,500	7,000	7,500
Waste generated	6%	7%	9%	13%	19%	27%
O.o.p. costs/hour						
Material	$50.00	$55.00	$60.00	$65.00	$70.00	$75.00
Conversion	20.00	20.00	20.00	20.00	20.00	20.00
Total	70.00	75.00	80.00	85.00	90.00	9˜.00
Waste cost/hour	4.20	5.25	7.20	11.05	17.10	2˜.65
Total o.o.p./hour	74.20	80.25	87.20	96.05	107.10	120.65
Total o.o.p./M	14.84	14.59	*14.53*	14.78	15.30	16.09
Change in o.o.p./M	—	.25	.06	(.25)	(.52)	(.79)

Obviously, the minimum total o.o.p. cost/M is between 6,000 and 6,500 impressions (sheets) per hour. At that speed point, the *change* in total o.o.p. cost/M is zero.

Example 2. Larger 2-Color Printing Press

O.o.p. MHR: Run = $40; Material Cost = $10/M; Speed = 8,000 iph

Speeds	4,500	5,000	5,500	6,000	6,500	7,000
Waste generated	3%	4%	7%	10%	14%	19%
O.o.p. costs/hour						
Material	$45.00	$50.00	$55.00	$60.00	$65.00	$70.00
Conversion	40.00	40.00	40.00	40.00	40.00	40.00
Total	85.00	90.00	95.00	100.00	105.00	110.00
Waste cost/hour	2.55	3.60	6.65	10.00	14.70	20.90
Total o.o.p./hour	87.55	93.60	101.65	110.00	119.70	130.90
Total o.o.p./M	19.46	18.72	18.48	*18.33*	18.42	18.70
Change in o.o.p./M	—	.74	.24	.15	(.09)	(.28)

The minimum total o.o.p. is obviously between 6,000 and 6,500 impressions per hour. In order to pinpoint the exact optimum speed, we can do the calculations for values between 6,000 and 6,500. In this case, we will find that 6,300 impressions per hour is best, assuming that waste is 12%.

$$O.o.p./M = [(\text{MHR} \div \text{Speed}) + (\text{Material Cost}/M)] \times [1 + \text{Waste}]$$
$$= [(\$40 \div 6.3) + \$10] \times [1 + 0.12]$$
$$= (\$6.35 + \$10) \times 1.12$$
$$= \$18.31$$

At this waste percent and speed, the change in total o.o.p. costs/M is zero and contribution/M is maximum.

13 Application of PS in Cost Estimating and Price Evaluation

Direct costs are required when estimating the contribution from an offered price and/or to assist in establishing prices for products. These direct costs have three major components:

1. Direct production or conversion costs
2. Direct material costs
3. Direct order or product costs

Direct Production or Conversion Costs. These are the costs of processing the product or order through all of the operational steps. Each operation has its own MHR, i.e., the direct costs per hour incurred in the running of the machine or work station, and each has its own set of PS, depending on the parameters of the operation. The product of the MHR and the specific PS applied, totaled for all operations results in total direct conversion cost of the product or order.

To illustrate these points, consider *two different orders* or products processed on the *same set of facilities* in the *same sequence*:

Product 1

Operation	PS/M	MHR	Direct Production Cost Per M
B	0.25	$32	$8.00
G	0.008	69	0.55
L	1.225	28	34.30
Total Direct Production Cost/M			$42.85

Product 2

Operation	PS/M	MHR	Direct Production Cost per M
B	0.375	$32	$12.00
G	0.045	69	3.11
L	0.825	28	23.10
	Total Direct Production Cost/M		$38.21

Note that while the PS changes, the facility MHRs remain the same. The changes in the time standards are caused by parameters (variables) of the specific operation. Changes in PS do not change the MHR unless the standard crew is changed.

With the direct production costs available, the next step is to add the other direct cost components.

Direct Material Costs. These consist of material costs that are directly used in the processing of the product or order. The running cost of materials, the setup or makeready material costs, and the packing materials costs should be included; viz,

1. Material running costs: This includes all materials that are part of the product cost, i.e., paper, paperboard, film, foil, steel rods, brass sheets, plastic pellets, and so on.
2. Setup or makeready costs: This includes dies, plates, and cutting tools, required to process the order.
3. Packing costs: This includes corrugated containers, nonreturnable pallets, and partitions, required to pack and ship the order or product.

Direct Order or Product Costs. These are generally nonmaterial costs that are related directly to the processing and selling of the product. These consist of costs such as: selling, freight out, transaction, and storage and warehousing.

The Role of PS Obviously, the effect of PS is reflected in the conversion cost segment of the total direct costs. As stated earlier, to the extent that the PS are incorrect, so will be the conversion costs. Where the conversion costs are a large portion of total direct costs in an order or product, the resulting measurement of contribution will be critically affected. Thus, where the direct costs are understated because of "tight" PS, the measurement of contribution can be seriously overstated and vice versa.

The inequity of such time values can lead the company into accepting poorly contributing business in the mistaken belief that it is good business. And, on the other hand, it can prompt the company into rejecting orders that are in fact high contributors.

Where the company provides only production services on customer supplied materials, the direct costs are mostly conversion costs, and in this instance, the use of improper time values can have a disastrous effect on company profits.

Exhibit 13–1
Cost Estimate and Price Evaluation: Die Casting Industry

Customer: <u>White & Co.</u>   Ordered Quantity: <u>5,000</u>   Metal: <u>Aluminium</u>
Piece weight: <u>2.136 lbs</u>[a]   Expected Waste: <u>4% of output</u>   Overrun: <u>10%</u>
     Planned Quantity: <u>5,500</u>   Estimated Quantity: <u>5,720</u>

	Conversion			
Production Center	Standard Hours Per C	Standard Hours Per C	O.o.p. MHR	Direct Conversion Cost
Preparation				
Setup diecast—800T[b]	—	4.00	$24.79	$ 99.16
Setup trim press[b]	—	.50	16.27	8.14
Setup straighter[b]	—	.50	13.29	6.65
				$113.95
Run				
Diecast—800T	1.25 in	71.50[e]	24.79	1,772.49
First inspection	.625 in	35.75[e]	10.36	370.37
File	2.50 in	143.00[e]	13.29	1,900.47
Trim press	.625 in	35.75[e]	16.27	581.65
Straighten	2.50 in	143.00[e]	13.29	1,900.47
Final inspection	.333 out	18.33[c]	9.82	180.00
Pack	1.000 out	55.00[c]	9.82	540.10
				$7,245.55
		Total Direct Conversion Cost =		$7,359.50

Doc's
Metal: 2.136# per piece @ $.62/# × 5,720 pieces   = $7,575.11
Packaging: 275 @ $.50 ea.   =   137.50
Die Maintenance: 1 hr @ $26.59   =   26.59
Freight out: 117.4 cwt. @ $3.10/cwt.   =   363.94

                                   Total Direct Order Cost[d] = $15,462.64
                                                          Per C = $281.14

[a]Piece weight shown includes net casting weight plus individually allocated metal loss.
[b]Includes dismount time.
[c]For planned quantity.
[d]Before commissions.
[e]For estimated quantity.

Examples of Cost-Estimating and Price Evaluations

Exhibit 13–1 shows an estimate for a die casting product. Note the separation of the preparatory and run operations, thereby allowing estimates for more than one quantity. In this case, the preparatory hours are held constant and the run times vary with the specific quantity. For example, if the quantity required were twice that shown, the direct conversion cost would be $113.95 + (2 × $7,245.55) = $14,605.05.

If the market price of $310 per hundred is to be considered, how much would the contribution be? Contribution is $310 − $281.14 = $28.86 per C and the PV would be $28.86/$310 = 0.093.

This estimate and the following ones illustrate the crucial nature of both the PS and the MHR in arriving at a rational basis for the pricing accept/reject decision. Obviously, if the standards used are "loose," more time than required is used to extend the MHRs, and it can mistakenly show a high enough direct cost to make the contribution measurement low or negative. In turn, the company would turn down the order and lose potential contribution—— maybe at a time they needed it the most. The reverse is also true, causing the company to book a lot of profitless work.

Only *engineered* production standards will give a secure basis for accept/ reject decisions.

Exhibit 13–2 shows an estimate for a product in the flexible packaging industry. Again, makeready and run operations are separated and production standards are used for all operations. If the selling price is $.152 per M square inches, the PV would be $.045/$.152 = 0.296. However, if the standards shown are "tight," it implies that engineered PS would allow greater hours. If 20% more time would be required by *engineered* standards, and the company entered a falling market at $.112 per M square inches, (or $6,720 for this order of 60 MM square inches) what would be the PV?

Exhibit 13–2
Cost Estimate and Price
Evaluation: Flexible
Packaging Industry

Product: PE-Coated, adhesive-laminated foil and paper, 8 colors
Quantity: 60 mil. sq. in. = 4 mil. pkgs. 2½″ × 3″ (pouch stock) = 210 M lineal feet.

		Conversion		
Production Center	Production Standard hrs/M	Estimated hrs	Direct Machine- Hour Rate	Direct Cost
Makeready				
Extruder-laminator	3	3	$16.62	$ 49.86
8c Gravure press	6	6	26.15	156.90
Run				
Extruder-laminator	250 fpm	14	16.62	232.68
8c Gravure press	500 fpm	7	26.15	183.05
Slitter-rewinder	150 fpm	23.3	7.15	166.60
Wrap and palletize		16	2.30	36.80
		Total Conversion Cost		825.89
		Direct Materials Cost		5,610.10
		Total Order Cost		$6,435.99
		Cost per M sq. in.		.107

	(For 60MM—Square Inch Order)	
	Tight (as Shown in Exhibit 13-2)	Engineered (as Revised)
Makeready	$206.76	$248.11
Run	$619.13	$742.96
Materials	$5,610.00	$5,610.00
Total order cost	$6,435.99	$6,601.07
Selling price	$6,720.00	$6,720.00
PV	0.042	0.0177

Obviously, this order is dominated by materials cost; i.e., direct conversion cost is 12.8% of total direct order cost with tight standards (or 15% with engineered standards). However, in situations where the direct production cost is the larger segment, the effect on the standard contribution and PV will be much more dramatic than what is shown above.

The following are typical problems encountered in this industry affecting accept/reject decisions (see Exhibit 13–2):

Problem 1. The customer decides to switch his business away from a competitor (where he has already paid for etching the gravure cylinders) to you, providing you are willing to absorb the cost of reetching your cylinders. Your cost for this operation is $375 per cylinder, or $3,000 for the eight cylinders. Find the minimum order quantity required to insure that you will not wind up selling below your o.o.p. cost at the selling price of $0.152 per thousand spuare inches.

SOLUTION

$$\text{Break-Even Quantity in Units} = \frac{\text{One-Time Constant Cost}}{\text{Unit Contribution per M}}$$

$$= \frac{\$3,000}{\$.045 \text{ per M}}$$

$$= 66.67 \text{ million square inches}$$

This means that if you took the 60 million square inch order at the offered selling price, you would generate a cash loss on 6.67 million square inches. Obviously, for any contribution to be generated, the ordered quantity would have to exceed 66.67 million.

Problem 2. Find the selling price per thousand square inches to give a PV of 0.30 at the estimated quantity of 60 million square inches, with you paying the $3,000 reetching cost.

SOLUTION

$$\text{O.o.p. Cost at 60 million square inches} = \text{Order Cost} + \$3,000$$
$$= \$6,436 + \$3,000$$
$$= \$9,436$$

$$\text{O.o.p. Cost per M} = \$9,436/60 \text{ million}$$
$$= \$.1572$$

Selling Price to give a PV of 0.30:

$$\text{Selling price} = \frac{\text{O.o.p. Cost}}{(1 - \text{PV})}$$

$$= \frac{\$.1572}{.70}$$

$$= \$.2246 \text{ per M square inches}$$

Thus, at the ordered or estimated quantity of 60 million square inches, an increase in selling price from $0.152 to $0.2246 (an increase of 47.8%) offsets the $3,000 reetching cost.

Problem 3. Find the gross order contribution and PV of a 100 million square inch quantity at the selling price of $0.152 per thousand square inches, with the $3,000 reetching cost billed to your company.

SOLUTION

O.o.p. cost at 100 million square inches
= Run + Materials + Makeready + Reetch
= $1,031.90 + $9,350 + $206.76 + $3,000
= $13,588.66
Selling Price at 100 million square inches
= $0.152 per M × 100 million
= $15,200
Contribution
= Selling Price − O.o.p. cost
= $15,200 − $13,588.66
= $1,611.34
PV
= Contribution/Selling Price
= $1,611.34/$15,200
= .106

Standard MHR   The MHR is expressed as a direct cost per *standard hour*. Part of the procedure for developing the MHRs involves identifying performance levels so that a subsidy can be incorporated in the MHR to assure that it is consistent with the standard being used. For example: assume that the 100% standard for a production center is 100 units per hour or 10 standard hours per thousand. The performance against this PS is 80%. Therefore, to produce 1,000 units, the standard time would be 10 hours, but the actual time is 10/.80, or 12.5 hours. If the MHR per chargeable hour is $20, the MHR for a *standard* chargeable hour is therefore $20/.80 or $25, and the hourly subsidy cost is $5 per hour.

The cost for performing this job, using the "standard" approach, is

10 standard hours × $25 = $250

The cost for performing this job on an "actual" basis is

12.5 chargeable hours × $20 = $250

The cost is the same in either case, as long as the MHR is in harmony with the performance, as measured against the standard used in the estimating process. If, in the above example, the PS was refined and the performance changed as a result, and found to be 9 hours instead of 10 hours, the performance would be 9/12.5, or 72% (if the actual chargeable time was still 12.5 hours). The MHR would then be $20/.72 = $27.77. Therefore, the cost based on the standard concept would be

9 standard hours × $27.77 = $250

The estimated cost has not changed of course, because the expected actual time has not changed. When a PS is adjusted or refined, the MHR must also be adjusted using the subsidy mechanism. This is necessary to preserve the accuracy of the cost estimate. On the other hand, if a PS is refined to apply more specifically to individual products as a result of changed parameters, the costs will change. Suppose, for instance, that 80% is an average performance and, through refinements, we find that the PS for this particular product should be 9 hours (performance = 80%). The expected chargeable actual hours would then be 9/.8, or 11.25 hours. The MHR will not change for this production center since the performance is the same. The estimated cost would be:

9 standard hours × $25 = $225

and the cost based on the actual hours:

11.25 actual chargeable hours × $20 = $225

Standard versus Actual

A typical reaction to the use of standard costs is, if both methods produce the same cost, why bother with standards, expected performance and subsidies?

The answer is *management control*. Estimating any cost in actual terms means that management accepts the actual as the goal. Thus, if a product has a cost estimate based on actual performance (even if it is as low as 60%) and winds up with that performance level, there is no variance and management has deprived itself of information about areas needing remedial action.

The whole purpose of the variance technique (management by exception) is to focus management's attention to exploit the favorable variances, and to remedy the unfavorable ones.

Estimating on the Computer

Cost estimates, performance reports, variance reports (as well as other profit-planning data) can be handled by computer. Minicomputers can handle a broad range of this work and are also modularized to provide additional capacity and capability.

Cost estimating can be computerized in several ways.

Exhibit 13–3
Cost Estimate and Price Evaluation: Example of Estimating on the Computer

THIS IS A DIE CUT LABEL USING DIE NO 11

# OF COLORS	1	PERFORATIONS	NO
# OF TEETH	51	LINEAL SCORES	0
# ACROSS	2	LAMINATION	NO
# AROUND	3	COLOR MATCHES	0
$/M IMPRESS	125	VARNISH	NO
TOTAL WASTE o/o	15	FLOOD COAT	NO
		PLATE CHANGES	0
		COLOR CHANGES	0

LABEL SIZE 1.5000 INCHES BY 1.5000

MATERIAL SUPERMARK PERM   4.3750 INCHES WI .2800 /MSI
THE PRESS MHR IS 22.93   THE SLITTER MHR IS 23.21

ORDER QUANTITY	25000.00	50000.00	75000.00	100000.00
PLANNED QUANTITY	27500.00	55000.00	82500.00	110000.00
EST RUN QTY	30250.00	60500.00	90750.00	121000.00
PRESS MR HRS	1.00	1.00	1.00	1.00
SLITTER MR HRS	.25	.25	.25	.25
PRESS RUN HRS	.50	1.00	1.00	1.25
SLITTER RUN HRS	.50	1.00	1.00	1.25
TOTAL PRESS HRS	1.50	2.00	2.00	2.25
TOTAL RUN FEET	2103.60	4207.21	6310.81	8414.42
OOP COST PRESS MR	22.93	22.93	22.93	22.93
OOP COST SLITTER MR	5.80	5.80	5.80	5.80
OOP COST PRESS RUN	11.47	22.93	22.93	28.66
OOP COST SLITTER RUN	11.61	23.21	23.21	29.01
TOTAL OOP CONV COST	51.80	74.87	74.87	86.41
TOTAL SQ IN MAT	115.46	230.92	346.38	461.84
TOTAL MAT COST	32.33	64.66	96.99	129.31
INK COST	2.55	3.40	3.40	3.83
DIE W/T	.63	1.26	1.89	2.52
CORE COST	.42	.85	1.27	1.66
CARTON COST	.50	1.00	1.50	2.00
FREIGHT	0.00	0.00	0.00	0.00
OTHER	25.00	25.00	25.00	25.00
TOTAL DOCS	29.10	31.51	33.06	35.00
SUBTOTAL OOP	113.23	171.04	204.92	250.73
SALES COMMISSION	20.32	30.36	34.49	41.58
TOTAL OOP COST	133.56	201.40	239.40	292.31
OOP COST/M	4.86	3.66	2.90	2.66
TSP CONV	118.11	170.71	170.71	197.01
TSP MATERIAL	35.56	71.12	106.68	142.25
TSP DOCS	49.43	61.87	67.54	76.58
TOTAL SELLING PRICE	203.23	303.60	344.85	415.80
PRICE/M	7.39	5.52	4.18	3.78
CONTRIBUTION	69.67	102.20	105.45	123.49
PV	.34	.34	.31	.30
BOOKING CONTR	51.19	74.60	74.10	85.69
CONTR./HR.	46.45	51.10	52.72	54.89
PRESS RUN SPEED	5250.00	5250.00	6750.00	6750.00

MATERIAL M/U = 1.1   CONVERSION M/U 2.28

1. A program can be established to do only the computations. All data are entered manually for each estimate. The estimator selects the production centers, the sequence of operations, the current PS and MHR, and the computer does the rest.
2. The PS and MHR are in the computer's file and then the program identifies and applies the correct PS and MHR when the estimator enters the parameters.

In the first case, the estimator would have to look up or calculate the PS, of say, 5.00 standard minutes per thousand. In the second case, the computer would be programmed to select the PS based on parameters. The estimator might enter such items as quantity, color, material type, and type of item being processed on the machine. The computer would search its files for the matching base information and then multiply or divide by certain factors retrieved from its files.

Once the formulas and factors are entered, and the computer is programmed, the correct answer is assured providing the computer operator has entered the proper parameters. Computer estimating is no panacea because the output information is solely a function of the quality of the input data. It does save much of the cost of estimating and produces estimates at a quicker rate. This is vital when the company is handling a large number of small transactions.

It also makes it far easier to have, for example, optional methods and quantities measured. If these must be done manually, they tend to be rushed or avoided, resulting in an incomplete information base on which to make decisions.

If the company has a complete profit-planning system, a proper data base will enable an effective interface between cost estimates (standard direct costs) and measurement of: performance variances, spending variances, material control, contribution logging, and so forth.

Exhibit 13–3 is an example of a printout produced by computer estimating.

14

Application of PS in Productivity and Performance Measurements

Standard time and cost are used in the estimating process and in the development of expected contribution measurements (as discussed in the previous chapter) which, of course, is the basis for pricing and price evaluation. Since the standard time is usually calculated in advance of the actual manufacturing process it can be useful as a guide for the production department. The standard time for all estimates (even if they must be made after the order is manufactured) become very useful to determine just how the operators performed—and the extent to which the estimated (expected) contribution was achieved. In the initial stages of the profit planning program, this type of measurement is needed to identify the subsidy that must be included in the MHR.

Direct production hours and costs are required to measure the effectiveness of individual workers, production centers, departments, and plant totals. This applies to both manual- and machine-controlled operations.

The direct costs are derived from hourly rates at direct production centers (MHRs) and the number of hours (PS) estimated to be used at each center.

If the quantity to be run through an operation is 10,000 units and the operation has a production standard of 5,000 per hour, or 0.200 standard hours per thousand, then the number of hours required at that operation is 10,000/5,000, or 2. Alternatively, 10,000 × 0.200 standard hours per M equals 2. The 2 standard hours are then multiplied by the MHR, of say $42 to give a *standard* direct production cost of $84. This is the standard direct cost *expected* to be incurred in the processing of the 10,000 units through that work station, center, or machine, and that cost is considered to be *predetermined*.

The terms productivity, performance, and efficiency are used somewhat interchangeably, but the authors are using only the first two as defined in the following sections.

Productivity The term productivity is used to describe or measure actual time against standard time. In a manually controlled operation, this means that worker effort is compared to a standard task. "One hundred percent productivity" is the effort (pace) at which the worker is fully earning his base hourly pay rate. Productivity deals with time (not cost), the measurement is calculated on the basis of production achieved; e.g., actual output versus standard output. Thus, if the standard for an operation is 500 pieces per hour and the worker produces 400 pieces per hour, productivity is the actual divided by the standards, or 400/500 = 80%. If a worker receives $8 base rate per hour and produces work at an 80% productivity level, he is said to be earning 4/5th of his pay, or $6.40 per hour. Since no deduction is made (in the payroll department) to lower his base hourly pay rate, the difference between his *earned* pay and base rate (i.e., $1.60), is termed *makeup pay* or *subsidy* cost.

Productivity and subsidy also apply to other segments of the MHR. In a machine-controlled operation, for example, the operator must run the equipment at 100% in order to earn the actual hourly rate, but the concept is still the same as above stated.

Exhibit 14–1 illustrates how one worker's productivity is measured for a specific day.

Exhibits 14–2 shows productivity measurements for a department during one week. Exhibit 14–3 reports productivity for all departments in the plant for the week, and separates clock hours into chargeable and nonchargeable time for other managerial control. This breakdown is also essential information for the construction of the MHRs in order to apply a productivity estimate to the chargeable segment and develop the subsidies. The subsidy cost is an economic (nonpayroll) cost and must be included in each MHR. These data are also useful in the collective bargaining process and provide, in a measured daywork environment, historical information for planning, and later, as a guide for an incentive program.

Performance The authors use the term Performance in a cost sense. Productivity and Performance percentages are the same in any production center when the same MHR is used as illustrated in Exhibit 14–4. However, both terms are

**Exhibit 14–1
Worker's Productivity
Report: Hand Work
(For the Day)**

Name of employee: John Jones   Date: February 4, 198X

Job Number	Actual Pieces Produced	Actual Clock Hours	Standard Pieces per Hour	Standard Earned Hours
1,043	3,200	3	1,000	3.2
1,897	800	2	500	1.6
2,180	3,000	3	1,200	2.5
Totals		8		7.3

Worker Productivity = 7.3/8 = 91.25%

Exhibit 14–2
Departmental
Productivity Report
(For the Week)

Department: <u>ABC</u>   WEEK ENDING: <u>February 9, 198X</u>

Production Center	Clock Hours	Earned Standard Hours	Productivity
121	40	32	80%
122	40	36	90%
123	40	44	110%
124	40	40	100%
Totals	160	152	

Departmental Productivity = 152/160 = 95%

Exhibit 14–3
Plant Productivity Report (For the Week)

WEEK ENDING: <u>February 8, 198X</u>

Department	Clock Hours	Nonchargeable Hours	Chargeable Hours	Earned Standard Hours	Productivity, Percent
ABC	160	20	140	133	95
DEF	160	10	150	164	109
GHI	160	40	120	106	88
JKL	160	0	160	154	96
MNO	160	60	100	75	15
Totals	800	130	674	632	94

Plant Productivity = 632/674 = 94%

Exhibit 14–4
Production Center
Performance Report
(For the Week)

Production Center: <u>A31</u>   O.O.P. MHR: <u>$41.47</u>
Machine Unit: <u>#3</u>   Week Ended: <u>5/20/8X</u>

Job Number	Actual Clock Hours	Earned Standard	Variance Hours	Contribution Gain (Loss)
4,707	8	6	(2)	$(82.94)
4,819	8	7	(1)	(41.47)
4,961	8	9	1	41.47
4,984	8	8	0	0
5,011	8	5	(3)	(124.41)
Totals	40	35	(5)	$(207.35)

Productivity = Earned Standard Hours/Actual Clock Hours
    = 35/40
    = 87.5%

Performance = Standard Cost/Actual Cost
    = $1,451.45/$1,658.8
    = 87.5%

Exhibit 14–5
Relationship between Productivity and Performance Measurements

Production Center	Standard MHR	Standard Pieces per Hour	Actual Production	Earned Hours	Actual Hours	Productivity, Percent	Standard Cost	Actual Cost	Performance, Percent
A	$10	500	5,000	10	12	83	$100	$120	83
B	60	5,000	10,000	2	2	100	120	120	100
C	50	4,000	16,000	4	3	133	200	150	133
Totals				16	17		420	390	
Weighted Averages						97			108

used in this text because they can have different meanings if the measured production centers have different MHRs. Refer to Exhibit 14–5.

Productivity and Performance variances in each production center are the same, and are both caused by differences between earned and actual hours (or standard and actual production) because it is assumed that no variance exists in the MHR (the latter is treated as a ''spending'' variance).

The weighted average Productivity and Performance are not similar however, because the weighting factors are different in each case. The Productivity is affected by the relative number of hours in each production center; whereas the Performance is affected by the relative costs. Production center A has only 83% productivity, but because it has the largest number of hours, it tends to keep the weighted average down. The Performance measurement however, is influenced more by center C, which has the greatest cost. Since center C has the highest Performance, the weighted average Performance is higher than the weighted average Productivity.

Since Performance is related to cost, it is also related to contribution. It is worth repeating one of our profit-planning principles, to wit: a change in direct cost is equal but opposite to a change in contribution. This principle is illustrated by using three conditions of productivity for an order of 10,000 pieces:

Condition	Work Center	MHR	PS/Hour	Standard Cost	Actual Production	Actual Run Cost	Contribution Gain or Loss
1.	K	$42	5,000	$84	5,000	$84	$0
2.	K	$42	5,000	$84	4,000	$105	($21)
3.	K	$42	5,000	$84	6,000	$70	$14

The actual cost for the 10,000 pieces is calculated by dividing the actual rate of production by 10,000 to obtain actual hours used and multiplying these by the MHR. In condition 2, this is 10,000/4,000 = 2.5 hours × $42 = $105 and in condition 3, 10,000/6,000 × $42 = $70. However, the *plantwide* effects of productivity changes must be measured through the calculation of *performance* as shown in Exhibit 14–5.

If a company's sales were $500 and the standard o.o.p. costs were $400, the contribution would be $100 if Performance was 100%. If Performance is 90%, the actual o.o.p. costs would be $400/.90 = $444 and the contribution would be only $56, a drop of 44%. This simple example shows the direct impact that Productivity and Performance have on a company's profit!

15 Application of PS in Make-or-Buy Decisions

Manufacturing companies consider make-buy decisions constantly. Sometimes present methods of operation reflect make-buy decisions of the past, yet few people are aware of this fact. As such, they are hidden but are constantly repeated. For example, an outside trade service has been regularly used on certain types of work and this practice continues without being questioned. In other instances, the make-buy decision is thrust upon management and therefore stands out distinctly.

Before discussing the concept in detail, a distinction should be made between a make-buy decision and a proposal to justify the acquisition of additional equipment. In the former case, the company owns the machinery and is capable of producing the product if it elects to do so. In the latter case, the additional machinery does not exist at the company and this requires a different set of considerations as will be demonstrated in the next chapter.

Reasons for Considering Buying

The reasons for a company to farm out some of their work even though they have the capability of making it are

1. Use of vendors' available skills that may be in short supply at the company;
2. Benefits from using vendors' research skills without having to acquire permanent talent to keep up with the times;
3. If the company buys from one or more suppliers, it is more flexible and avoids problems in the ''make'' process;
4. To meet sudden emergencies when the company's facility is fully loaded;
5. When the company cannot add additional shifts or overtime;
6. Use of the company's facilities on more contributing work;
7. Minimization of variable capital employed in making the product.

Reasons for Considering Making

The reasons for not farming out work are (assuming equal quality with buying):

1. Being able to make the product for less cost;
2. Being able to produce the work without buying delays;
3. Maximizing the contribution-per-hour (CPH) on the facilities used.

Cost Considerations

Direct costs of making the product are essential in the make-buy decision. Including a unitized figure for internal fixed costs will result in the wrong decision, since it does not matter whether the make or the buy is selected, *the annual fixed costs* will not change. Exhibit 15–1 demonstrates this point.

To arrive at the correct decision, the comparative direct "make" costs and direct "buy" costs must be prepared. The latter is simple, as this is the invoiced price from a supplier. On the other hand, the internal direct make costs must be estimated for materials and direct conversion costs.

To obtain the production costs, both the MHR and PS must be used. If, as shown in Exhibit 15–1, the company can use its facility to produce the required 1 million units per month, we have to estimate the direct production

Exhibit 15–1
Make or Buy?

1,000,000 Sheets/Month	Make		Buy	
	per M	Monthly Total	per M	Monthly Total
Direct material cost	$10.00	$ 10,000	$20.00	$ 20,000
Print				
O.o.p. conversion cost	7.00	7,000		
Period[a] conversion cost	5.00	5,000		
Total O.o.p. costs	17.00	17,000	20.00	20,000
"Full" costs	22.00	22,000	20.00	20,000
Annual variable capital employed:				
(Current Assets)				
Cash and accounts receivable		$ 73,000		$ 79,000
Inventory		410,000		260,000
Total variable capital employed		$483,000		$339,000

Return on Variable Capital Employed:

$$= \frac{\text{Increase in Annual Contribution}}{\text{Increase in Variable Capital}}$$

$$= \frac{(\$20,000 - \$17,000) \times 12}{\$483,000 - \$339,000}$$

$$= 25\%$$

[a]arbitrarily allocated to printing press; annual period cost does not change with decision to make or buy.

costs in the same number of units as they could buy it from the outside, namely, buy cost per M.

Assume that this work is to be processed through one facility at a MHR of $28 and a PS of 4,000/hour = 0.25 standard hours per M. The direct production cost would therefore be $28 × 0.25 standard hours per M = $7 per M. Adding direct materials cost of $10 per M gives an internal direct cost to make of $17 per M.

If the company bought this work from the outside, it would have to pay $20 per M, or an additional direct cash cost of $3 per M. By "making," the company would save $3 per M, which is the same as obtaining an additional contribution of $3 per M. If production is expected to be 1 million units per month, the monthly additional contribution would be 1,000 × $3 per M or $3,000, amounting to an annual increase in contribution of $36,000.

It is obvious that the company has to give up something in order to capture this additional contribution. If the company makes the units, it has to incur the specific identifiable variable capital associated with making; viz, direct labor, raw materials, and so on. If the company's variable capital increased by $144,000 as a result of the make, we can now determine the true economic benefit of the "make." In this instance, $36,000 of additional annual contribution is available from an additional $144,000 of variable capital thus, providing the company with a pretax 25% return on incremental capital. This now gives the company further depth in making the ultimate decision.

Again, this type of decision is impossible without the use of costs directly identified, traceable to and related to the specific project. Since a major element of this cost is the production costs, the use of proper PS are indispensable.

The Critical Link

The production standard of 4,000 per hour is the critical link in this decision. Sound engineering standards are needed since an error in PS could cause an incorrect and expensive decision or could dissuade the company from making an attractive economic move. Suppose that there is a high probability that the standard could be off by 20%, either way, the conversion direct cost could be off by ± 20%, either high or low. This would make the incremental contribution to be off by the same amount, and could change the entire decision with respect to the return on the capital.

In other words, with poor PS, what should be a "go" could wind up being a "no-go" and vice versa.

16 Using PS in Scheduling and Machine Loading

Maximum plant utilization and maximum performance are a winning combination. To plan and control these factors management needs first class standards. They must be credible and be a part of the working environment in the plant.

Effective scheduling depends on the company's ability to project (or anticipate) demand and translate this into facility requirements. Then, strategies must be developed to work around any limiting factors and to exploit underutilized facilities.

The key ingredient for this entire scenario is the production standard. The company must know the standard time required to process or manufacture each product and the information must be available for each production center. Anticipated *performance* must obviously also be known.

Suppose a plant is operating a 5-day week on two shifts. In effect, 80 hours are available for each production center. An order is received and is promised for a one-week delivery (a rush) but it is not completed for almost 3 weeks. The customer is very dissatisfied and may take future business elsewhere; not an uncommon picture.

Scheduling A simple scheduling and shop loading system would have prevented the surprise. It would have projected the fact that the order would not be finished in one week, thereby giving management a chance to work on some alternate strategy.

Scheduling and shop loading must always be done on the basis of *expected*, not 100%, performance. The scheduling cannot be done or provided by the sales department on an optimistic view of the plant's capability and without due regard for the existing state of loading. Engineered standards, with sufficient factors to recognize the differences between various types of work, are the only tools that will provide good utilization and reliable customer service.

Suppose (for the sake of simplicity), that there is only one production center and the standard is 2,000 units per hour. If a backlog (work ahead) of 400,000 units exists, it will take 400,000/2,000 = 200 hours to process it and an additional 20 hours for make ready if the machine can work at 100%. This represents 2.75 weeks of work. However realistically, the performance may be about 85% for both run and MR. Therefore, the production center produces only 2000 × 0.85 = 1,700 units per hour and the MR will take 20/0.85 = 24 hours. Now this translates the work ahead into 259 hours (almost 3.25 weeks).

When the next order is received (unless priorities are rearranged), it cannot be started for $3\frac{1}{4}$ weeks. These concepts seem basic, but many otherwise well-run companies exist on a day-to-day and week-to-week basis, constantly changing promised dates, struggling to juggle schedules, and explaining why delivery dates are not being met. The reason is the lack of a simple scheduling and shop loading system or that they *do not have reliable standards*, or both. Interestingly, we sometimes find that standards are being used for estimating (and the company is using this data for pricing and marketing) but no one in the shop considers them to be reliable enough for scheduling. What sort of quality can they have in their profit-planning function? When a schedule is set up it must be maintained, that is, it must be updated frequently enough to reflect changes that have been made in priorities, new orders, equipment availability, and so forth, including a "ventilation" concept (gaps in the scheduling) to provide for contingencies.

Loading *Full* shop loading probably causes more scheduling systems to fail than any other factor. If all available production center hours are scheduled with known orders, any emergency orders will require an entire restructuring of the schedule, or it will make the schedule meaningless. In the previous example, we discovered that there were about 259 hours of work ahead for the center and if fully loaded, it would take almost $3\frac{1}{4}$ weeks to complete it. To be practical, it should be anticipated that emergency work will show up which, for whatever good business reason, the company will want to promise in less than 3 weeks delivery. Some experimentation may be needed, but as a starter they should schedule only 80% of the hours. Thereby, the known work should be scheduled over the next 4.1 weeks, because only 80% of the 80 hours each week will be available for scheduling normal work.

With this arrangement, the emergency orders can be slotted in the schedule until the 20% free time is used up. Obviously, this situation must be controlled by this realistic technique to minimize schedule changes and the resulting chaos and confusion. Again, none of this planning and structuring can be done realistically without the use of sound PS.

17 Application of PS in Justifying Capital Expenditures

Machinery acquisition proposals require the use of direct costs and/or changes in direct costs. In turn, this analysis results in prospective additions or changes in contribution levels, from which incremental profit can be determined. When these profit measurements are compared to the amount of incremental capital to be employed, the return on this capital can be computed; management then has the basis for a go no-go decision.

One-half of the direct cost calculations are the production standards that apply to the operation(s) for which the machine(s) is being considered. To the extent that the PS are wrong, so will be the quality of the decision.

Reasons for Acquisition

Management often considers the purchase of additional equipment to:

1. replace an old piece of machinery
2. automate a hand operation
3. produce parts at lower direct cost than that paid to outside vendors.

In each case, the reduction in direct cost and related increase in contribution, together with the incremental period (fixed) costs, must be the basis for the decision. Both accurate MHRs and credible standards are required to make this measurement.

Replacing a Manual Operation

Assume that a machine is being considered to replace a manual operation, and the following data are estimated.

	Hand Operation	*Proposed Machine*
MHR	$16	$43
PS	60 units/hour	300 units/hour
Direct cost	$26.67/100	$14.33/100

The proposed machine represents a 46% reduction in direct production cost, or an increase in contribution of $12.34 per hundred units. This appears to be an attractive contribution increase.

The incremental capital to purchase the proposed machine, the annual volume of unit production, and the incremental fixed expenses related to the purchase, will allow the measurement of the capital return from this seemingly attractive project:

Purchase Cost of the Machine   = $150,000
Expected Annual Unit Volume =   300,000
Annual Incremental Fixed Costs =   20,000

The Annual Incremental Profit

Incremental Contribution − Incremental Fixed Costs
= (300,000 × $12.34/C) − $20,000
= $17,020

The Pretax Return on Annual Incremental Capital

Incremental Profit/Incremental Capital
= $17,020/$150,000
= 11.3%

These capital justification decisions should be made based on the alternative uses the company may have for the same amount of its capital. If, for example, the company policy states that at least a 30% pretax return on incremental capital has to be generated, what annual volume is required to produce this return? The approach is:

Pretax Return Required

30% × $150,000 = $45,000

Annual Incremental Contribution Required

Incremental Profit + Incremental Annual Fixed Expenses
= $45,000 + $20,000 = $65,000

Annual Volume of Units Required

Annual Incremental Contribution/Unit Contribution per C
= $65,000/$12.34 per C = 526,742 units

This indicates that unless the company can raise its volume to this larger number of units, the company policy will not be satisfied and the capital funds should be reserved or assigned to competing projects.

Can the company count on the production standards used in the proposal? If the speed of 300 units per hour is based on the manufacturer's data and does not reflect the realities of this product in this plant, the production rate may be 25% lower because of delays, layout, material handling methods, machine interference, and so on. Suppose a more realistic PS of 225 units per hour is used? Then, a direct cost of $19.11 per C and an increase in contribution of only $7.56 per hundred units would result. This would produce the following data:

Annual Incremental Profit = $2,680
Pretax Return = 1.8%

As is easily seen, the return on capital is very sensitive to a change in standards; viz, a 25% decrease in hourly production causes a 84% decrease in the capital return.

Replacing the Need for a Supplier

It is usual for a company to use parts made for them by others without considering the possibility of buying a piece of equipment to make the parts themselves. A proper analysis requires the same kind of data, namely, an estimated MHR, PS, purchase capital, and annual fixed costs. If the annual volume purchased from a supplier is high enough, the savings may well justify buying equipment to make the part in-house.

Case 1. The company now buys and uses 100,000 parts per year at a cost of $1.00 each. This amounts to $100,000 per year. The company estimates that if they had equipment to manufacture the part, it would cost $.20 each. They arrive at that figure by estimating that the MHR would be $20 and the PS would be 100 units per hour. The increase in contribution if they owned and operated the machine would be the difference between the direct cost of purchasing parts and making parts, or $0.80 each. If the incremental fixed costs of the machinery purchase is $60,000, the break-even quantity would be $60,000/$0.80, or 75,000 pieces. Thus, the company would generate profit between the annual expected volume of 100,000 units and the break-even volume of 75,000. Profit would be 25,000 × $0.80, or $20,000. If the machine cost $90,000, the return would be $20,000/$90,000 or 22.2%.

Case 2. A flexible packaging converter is considering the acquisition of a "free-blown" extruder to extrude their own plastic sheeting instead of continuing to buy the sheeting from outside suppliers. The facts are:

Direct costs to make	= $0.29 per pound
Direct costs to buy	= $0.33 per pound
Annual period costs to own	= $42,000
Acquisition cost	= $320,000
Annual consumption	= 1 million pounds

The break-even unit quantity is the annual fixed expenses divided by the increase in unit contribution or $42,000/$0.04 = 1,050,000 pounds per year. Therefore, the company will be short 50,000 pounds of the break-even quantity, and the 1 million pound volume will generate contribution of 1 million × $0.04, or $40,000. Thus, if the company made this acquisition, they would sustain a loss of $2,000 annually and would generate a negative return on the capital investment. Again, the estimated direct costs to make are based on a calculated MHR and a realistic production standard. Therefore, if the PS is wrong and the direct costs to make are overstated by "loose" standards, the company could be deprived of an attractive investment opportunity. For example, if the make costs are really $0.21 per pound, the increase in contribution is $0.12 per pound, the break-even quantity is 350,000 pounds, the profit is $650,000 \times \$0.12$ or $78,000, and the return on capital 24.4%.

18 Using PS for Alternate Facility Selection

The same product can be manufactured in several different ways in the same plant, depending on the extent of the facilities available. The alternate methods can use machines with different speeds, capabilities, and setup or makeready times. Assuming that the facilities are available, each capable of producing the same quality, the decision as to which method to use is a function of hourly direct cost (MHR), the processing times (PS), and the quantity of the run.

Thus, if a hole-drilling operation is to be performed on a small quantity of products, a single-spindle drill press may be the choice. It would require an inexpensive setup, but would have a long cycle time per piece. On the other hand, if the quantity is large, it may be more economical to accept the higher setup cost of a multiple-spindle drill in return for a shorter cycle time per piece.

	Single-Spindle Drill	Multiple-Spindle Drill	Difference
MHR	$12	$37	
Standard setup hours	0.10	0.80	
Standard setup cost	$ 1.20	$29.60	+$28.40
Standard run hours per cycle	0.030	0.024	
Pieces per cycle	1	6	
Standard run hours per piece	0.030	0.004	
Standard run cost per piece	$ .360	$ .148	−$ .212

Different quantities run will have different costs depending on the method. To illustrate this point:

	Costs		
Run Quantities	**Single**		**Multiple**
1 piece	$1.20 + $ .36 = $ 1.56		$29.60 + $ .148 = $ 29.75
10 pieces	$1.20 + $ 3.60 = $ 4.80		$29.60 + $ 1.48 = $ 31.08
50 pieces	$1.20 + $ 18 = $ 19.20		$29.60 + $ 7.40 = $ 37.00
100 pieces	$1.20 + $ 36 = $ 37.20		$29.60 + $ 14.80 = $ 44.40
150 pieces	$1.20 + $ 54 = $ 55.20		$29.60 + $ 22.20 = $ 51.80
500 pieces	$1.20 + $180 = $181.20		$29.60 + $ 74 = $103.60
1,000 pieces	$1.20 + $360 = $361.20		$29.60 + $148 = $177.60

It is clear that at the low quantities, the single method is cheaper and vice versa at the high quantities. With short runs, the multiple method suffers from a high first cost, and with long runs, the single method is penalized for its higher unit run cost.

Up to 100-piece runs, the single method is cheaper. At the 150-piece runs, the multiple method is cheaper. Obviously, there must be a quantity run between these two quantities that will equalize the cost for both methods. When this quantity is found, it can be used as a production and estimating policy in order to yield the least direct production cost. This quantity is found by the break-even approach, namely,

Break-Even Quantity in Units = Constant Costs/Unit Contribution

OR

Break-Even Quantity = Increase in Constant Costs/Increase in
Contribution
= $28.40/$0.212
= 133.96 pieces

Basically,

Break-Even Quantity = ΔConstant Costs/ΔUnit Contribution

OR

Break-Even Quantity = ΔConstant Costs/ΔUnit O.o.p. Costs

In effect, this approach states that the additional setup cost of $28.40 ($29.60 − $1.20) will be paid for by an additional unit contribution of $.212 ($0.360 − $0.148) for "x" number of units. When the quantity run is 134 pieces, the total contribution for this quantity will equal the additional setup cost and this increment will then be fully paid for. Thus, if an order for a quantity of 80 pieces is to be run, the single method will produce the lower unit direct production cost. And, if an order of 300 pieces is to be run, the multiple method will be cheaper.

It should be kept in mind that both the MHR and the quality of the production standards are determined by the respective setup and run costs. If the PS are wrong, the break-even or equalizing quantity point will shift and contribution on either side of this figure will be wrong. Good PS are essential to this determination.

Another Example of This Technique

Alternate facility selection is a technique for *increasing* the contribution over and above the contribution already booked at the price acceptance point. In other words, if the booked contribution on an order shows $1,000 for a given sequence of production centers listed on the estimate, it may still be possible to increase this amount to $1,200 by the way the order is ultimately run in the plant.

Unfortunately, there is a prevalence of rules-of-thumb used to operate companies. Selecting a production method from existing alternatives is one of the areas in which this is practiced. In plants that have both high- and low-

Exhibit 18–1
Finding the Lowest Cost Method to Run the Order

Data for Alternate Methods

Press	Speed	MR Time	MR O.o.p. MHR	Run O.o.p. MHR	Number of Passes
2-color	1,800 IPH	4 hours/pass	$23	$23	2
4-color	3,600 IPH	11 hours	$51	$58	1

$$\text{Cross-Over (B-E) Quantity Point} = \frac{\text{Increase in MR Costs}}{\text{Decrease in Running Costs/M}}$$

$$= \frac{\$377}{\$9.46/\text{M}}$$

$$= 39,850 \text{ impressions}$$

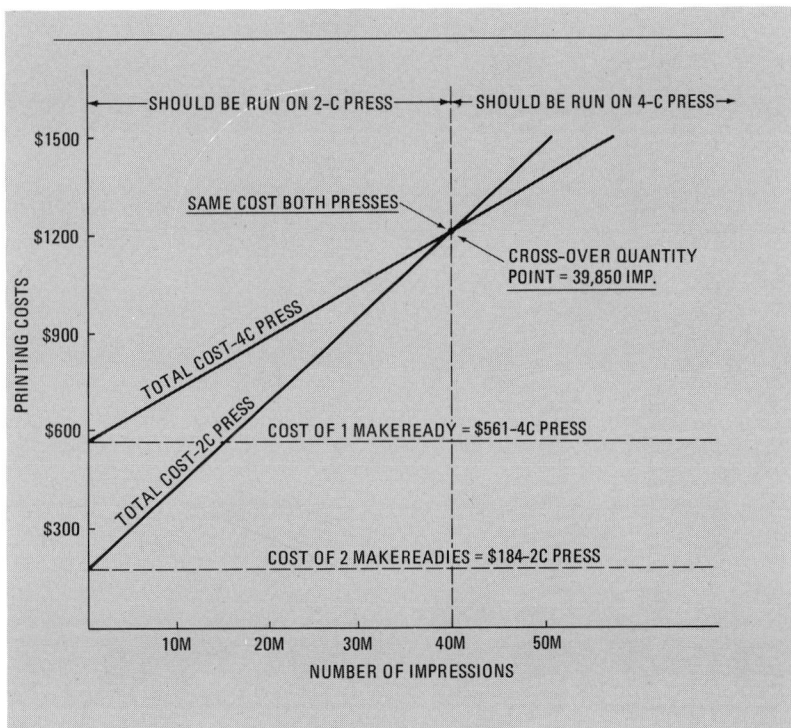

speed machinery, one hears, "Well if the run is over 2,000 pieces, we should use method x" and "if the quantity is over one-half million, we should use this machine," and so forth. Often, these rules-of-thumb are set up arbitrarily and generally reflect the thinking of a previous supervisor or the practice used at a supervisor's previous employer. These were found to be contribution-draining because they all lack the rational, objective approach.

For example, in two different printing plants there are 2-color and 4-color presses available. For purposes of this illustration, assume that the MHRs and PS are the same for both companies. Company A states that for their 4-color work, if the quantity of the run is at least 20,000 sheets they will run it on the 4-color press. Company B says it requires at least a run of 60,000 before placing it on the 4-color press. If the run quantity is under 20,000 and 60,000 respectively, they will print the 4-color work by running the sheets twice through the 2-color press. Who is correct?

Exhibit 18–1 shows the data for both presses; both the formula and curves show that the equalizing quantity point is approximately 40,000 sheets. Without knowing this number, Company A incurs a loss of contribution (increase in direct production costs) between 20,000 and 40,000 sheets (which should have been run on the 2-color press), and Company B loses contribution by using the 2-color presses between 40,000 and 60,000 sheets. Once the equalizing quantity concept is in place as estimating policy, each company will be able to maximize their "internal" contribution.

Again, and finally, proper PS are critical in establishing this policy.

Appendix

Allowances for Time Standards

The duration of the timestudy is usually relatively short, and even the accumulation of a number of studies will not fully show all delays and factors that affect the operator's production. Several factors are well defined for work measurement purposes: Personal, Fatigue, and Delays. Since these are usually beyond the control of the operator, they must be accounted for in the final time standard.

Personal

This includes time for personal needs during the day. These can be allowed as percentages of standard time or as definite periods of time for the day. When these are determined, they can be integrated into a combined allowance with those below.

Fatigue

There has been much study of fatigue in industry, conducted by researchers in the fields of engineering, medicine, physiology, and psychology, and although no definitive conclusions have been reached certain guideline quantitative measures have been identified and used with measured daywork and incentive systems in many plants.

The human machine is a very complex mechanism with many interreactions involving the body functions, age of the worker, emotional stresses, plus many external factors such as temperature, humidity, extremes of exertion, duration of exertion, frequency and duration of rest periods between exertion, and many other complex interrelationships.

In any given plant, it is possible to establish fatigue allowances that will work satisfactorily for that plant, if the figures used are consistent with the demands of the various operations. A general agreement can usually be reached between the workers and the company that the allowances permit the establishment of fair and equitable standards.

It is important to recognize that fatigue allowances (covering both physical and mental conditions) are not designed to fully refresh a worker during or at the end of a work day—rather, the allowance is designed to permit him or her to continue working until the end of the shift. It is expected that most employees will be appropriately tired at the end of a day's work.

Delays

Depending upon how well production is organized, there will be varied short delays during the day that occur at random intervals, including short waits for materials, supervision, minor machine delays, defective materials, equipment, and numerous other similar occurrences. Such delays can be determined through work sampling, by long timestudies (interruption studies), historical production records, and so on.

Application Techniques

Allowances to cover the above conditions can be applied individually. Or in many cases, they are combined. For instance, fatigue allowance can be considered to a certain extent during time that is allowed for personal needs. Also, since work breaks are permitted in many work environments, they may cover both personal and fatigue requirements.

The following examples are illustrations of various techniques used in different situations. Each company must evaluate its own conditions in order to establish equitable allowances.

Allowances can be included in production standards in several ways, and the choice is usually related to the way in which the conditions (which require the allowances) behave.

Fatigue, for instance, generally varies directly with the amount of work done. Therefore, the allowance can logically be added (as a percentage) to the basic time standard. In this manner, more allowance will be provided as more work is performed.

Time for personal needs tends to relate to the amount of actual time a person is on the job rather than to the amount of work performed. Therefore, it may be convenient to provide a daily allowance. These daily allowances can also be converted into percentages applied to the standard time for ease of application.

Delays of certain types may vary inversely with the amount of work performed. Thus, the required allowance may decrease as the standard or earned time increases during a day. Part of the reason that more work is accomplished is that fewer delays are encountered. Advanced techniques (not covered in this book) are available for special situations requiring this type of application.

P and F Allowance per Shift

A combined allowance for fatigue and personal may be 5% for certain types of work. This would amount to 23 minutes during a 480 minute shift if the allowance was added to the normal or base time for doing the work:

Normal Time $\times 1.05 = 480$ minutes
therefore, Normal Time $= 480 \div 1.05 = 457$ minutes
and the Allowance $= 480 - 457 = 23$ minutes

Combining P, F, and D with Shift Allowance

Assume a situation in which certain time allowances are provided on each shif. and fat' ie and delay allowances have also been determined:

Shift Allowances

Start Up	15 minutes per 8 hour shift
Area Clean Up	30 minutes per 8 hour shift
Total	45 minutes per 8 hour shift
Personal and Fatigue Allowance	11% of base time
Delay Allowance	2% of base time

These allowances can be combined (to facilitate the calculation of the standards) as one percentage to be applied to the base time. Use the following formula for *manual* work.

$$\text{Total Allowance \%} = \frac{480 \times \text{\% Allowances} + \text{Shift Allowance}}{480 - \text{Shift Allowance}}$$

If we substitute the given values we get the following:

$$\text{Total Allowance \%} = \frac{480 (.11 + .02) + 45}{480 - 45} = \frac{62.4 + 45}{435} = 24.7\%$$

If the 24.7% is applied to the base time, it will provide a 13% allowance for fatigue and delays, as well as 45 minutes per shift. The 45 minutes will actually vary somewhat if the shift performance is above or below 100%. This will be discussed later.

When an operation contains machine-controlled elements, the total allowance calculation is modified somewhat because these elements do not require an allowance for fatigue. The shift allowance may also be different; but assume, for purposes of illustration, that it is again 45 minutes per shift.

If we substitute the given values in the formula:

$$\text{Total Allowance} = \frac{(480 \times .02) + 45}{480 - 45} = 12.5\%$$

Internal and External Work

The required allowances on manual elements depend on whether the work is internal or external (to the machine cycle), and how large these components are. For instance, if relatively little external work was done in relation to the amount of internal nonworking time, there would be no need to add a fatigue allowance to the external elements. Assume the following:

Machine Time = 1.00 minute
Internal Work = 0.20 minute (base time)
Internal-Nonwork = 0.80 minute
External Work = 0.50 minute (base time)

The fatigue for the internal and external work would be (if we use 11%):

0.11 × (0.20 + 0.50) = 0.11 (0.70) = 0.077

This is smaller than the 0.80 nonwork time and therefore, no fatigue allowance is needed on the external work. Fatigue allowance on the internal work has no effect on the cycle or the standard.

A Consistent Basis

If allowances are combined, they must apply to a consistent base. For instance, if the shift allowance (in the above example) was taken as a percentage of the full 480 minutes, it could not be added to the fatigue and delay allowance (because the latter two are expressed as percentages of the base time).

Shift Allowance = 45/480 = 9.4% of the total shift time
Personal and Fatigue = 11.0% of the base time
Delay = 2.0% of the base time

These three allowances cannot be added together because they do not apply to (and cannot be multiplied by) the same quantity.

If the shift allowance (45 minutes) is expressed as a percentage of the base time, it *can* be added to the personal fatigue and delay allowance. The base time can be determined as follows.

When the 13% (personal fatigue and delay) allowance is added to the base time, the resulting standard time is equal to 480 − 45 = 435 minutes for the shift. Therefore, the standard time is:

Base × 1.13 = 435 minutes

and

Base Time = 435/1.13 = 385 minutes

The shift allowance is 11.7% of this base time

45/385 = 11.7%

Now all three percentages can be added because they are expressed in terms of the same quantity (base time).

Shift Allowance = 11.7% of base time
Personal Fatigue = 11.0% of base time
Delay = 2.0% of base time
Total = 24.7% of base time

(Notice that this is identical to the answer we obtained previously with the formula for manual work.)

Standards for Incentives

Incentives are used to provide an opportunity for workers to earn extra money for performance above a fair day's work or a measured daywork pace.

The calculations are handled in one of several ways. A pay scale can be established to identify the pay (as a percentage of the base wage) with each performance level. For manually controlled operations, it might be as follows:

Performance	Pay
80%	100%
100%	100%
120%	120%
130%	130%

For machine-controlled operations, the scale would be different because there is no opportunity to beat the machine time. Thus, performance cannot be higher than 100%. An example might be:

Performance	Pay
80%	100%
100%	130%

With mixtures of manual- and machine-controlled elements on a single standard, a common scale must be used. In this case, the machine-controlled elements are usually increased to include the incentive earnings expected at 100% performance. For instance, assume the machine cycle is 1.0 minute and the pay for achieving this cycle time is to be 130%. If the 30% is added to the 100% base time, the calculated performance will indicate the pay performance.

1.0 minute $\times$ 1.30 = 1.30 minutes incentive base

The necessary allowances are, of course, added to this incentive base. If the allowance (as calculated in the previous section) was 12.5%, the total incentive standard (which is sometimes called "high task") would be:

1.30 $\times$ 1.125 = 1.462 allowed incentive minutes.

If the operator succeeds in achieving a 1.125 cycle time on the average, performance and pay will be 130%.

If the average cycle is 1.35 minutes, the performance (and pay) would be:

$$\frac{1.462}{1.35} = 108\%$$

Incentive earnings begin at a cycle time of 1.462 minutes.

Comparison of Measured Day Work (MDW) and Incentives

Assume that the following data pertains to an operation with both manual- and machine–controlled elements.

Total Manual Time (external)   = 0.50 minute
Total Machine Time   = 1.00 minute

Appendix

Total Allowances (derived earlier):

Manual	= 24.7% of base time
Machine	= 12.5% of base time
Incentive Potential (machine)	= 30.0% of base time

	Incentive Allowed Time	*MDW Standard*
Allowed manual time	$0.50 \times 1.247 = 0.623$ minutes	$0.50 \times 1.247 = 0.623$ minutes
Allowed machine incentive time	$1.0 \times 1.3 \times 1.125 = \underline{1.462}$ minutes	$1.0 \times 1.125 = \underline{1.125}$ minutes
Total allowed time	2.085 minutes	1.748 minutes
Cycles/hour	28.78	34.32

To evaluate the difference in results that may be obtained by incentives as compared to MDW, it is obvious that the higher the ratio of machine-controlled work to manual work, the *less* attractive incentives are likely to be from a direct labor point of view. If management can maintain "good" machine performance, MDW might yield lower direct labor costs than incentives. The key determinant is the extent to which management can obtain a high level of machine performance without incentives.

Suppose, for instance that under incentive conditions the company expected 130% against the allowed incentive time. Thus, the manual work would be accomplished at 130%, and the machine time would be the machine cycle.

Suppose also, that under MDW conditions, the company expected 80% against the 100% production standards.

The results of these projections would appear as follows:

	Incentive	*MDW*
Expected actual time		
Manual	$0.623/1.30 = 0.479$ minutes	$0.623/0.80 = 0.779$ minutes
Machine	$\underline{1.125}$ minutes	$1.125/0.80 = \underline{1.406}$ minutes
Total	1.604 minutes	2.185 minutes
Cycles per hour	37.41	27.46
Pay percent	130%	100%
$\dfrac{\text{Cost}}{\text{100 Cycles}}$ @ \$10/hour	$1.30 \times 10 \times \dfrac{1.604}{60} = \dfrac{\$34.75}{100 \text{ cycles}}$	$1.00 \times 10 \times \dfrac{1.185}{60} = \dfrac{\$36.42}{100 \text{ cycles}}$

This projection indicates that the direct cost would be $1.67 less with incentives ($36.42 − $34.75 = $1.67). But, for other performance levels, the MDW cost could be less than the incentive cost, or the incentive cost could be even more attractive than the above example suggests.

The contribution per hour is also a factor that must be considered, particularly if the number of machine hours is limited.

The pay formula may also be modified for the incentive plan. For instance, 120% rather than 130% might be paid for achieving the minimum machine time. This would tend to make the above incentive plan more attractive if the same cycle time could be achieved; or it would require a lower performance level to make the incentive plan less costly than the MDW plan.

Notice that the Incentive Allowed Time and the MDW Standard are expressed in terms of the same performance and pay level. Both the manual and machine time indicates the performance level at which 100% of the base wage will be paid. If, on the incentive plan, the actual cycle time is 2.085

minutes, the operator would be paid the same base wage as for achieving a 1.748 cycle time on the MDW plan. This is not as inequitable as it might look however, because the plan is providing a motivation and opportunity to earn more money; the real comparison is between the *expected* performances under the two plans. If the performances projected above can be achieved, the cost to the company will be $34.75 versus $36.42 per cycle for the incentive and MDW, respectively. The operator will be achieving more cycles per hour and therefore earning more pay per hour. Assuming that the base wage is $5.00 per hour, the earnings will be as follows:

Cycle Time (minutes)	Incentive Plan	MDW Plan
Actual Minutes Per Cycle	1.604	2.185
Cycles/Hour (previously developed)	37.41	27.46
Pay Per Hour	$6.50	$5.00

Determining the Base Time

Allowances are added to base (normal) time to compensate for the factors that reduce the total available work time. For example, the preceding calculation of the manual PFD (24.7%) accounts for nonwork time of 95 minutes during an average shift:

Base time $\times$ 1.247 = 480 total minutes

then

Base Time = 480/1.247 = 385 minutes

therefore,

Nonwork Time = 480 − 385 = 95 minutes per shift

Before the PFD allowances can be added, the base (normal) time must be determined. The following data apply to a die cutting operation.

	Actual Minutes Observed	$\times$ Level Factor	= Base (Normal) Minutes
Manual (external elements)			
Load sheets on table and square	0.25	1.10	0.275
Open clamps and remove die cut blanks	0.35	1.15	0.402
Remove die cut waste	0.12	1.25	0.150
Total			0.827
Machine time	1.35		

For an incentive plan in which 130% will be paid for achieving the minimum machine time, the latter will be increased by 30% to provide the base incentive time. This will be:

1.35 $\times$ 1.30 = 1.755 minutes

For a MDW plan this factor is not applied.

Calculation of Cycles and Allowance Time per Shift

Incentives

The combined allowances (calculated above) are added to the base times, as follows:

	Base ×	*Combined Allowance* =	*Allowed at 100%*
Manual	0.827	1.247	1.031 minutes/cycle
Machine	1.755	1.125	1.974
Total	2.582		3.005

The difference between the total base time and the total allowed time is the total allowance:

$$3.005 - 2.582 = .423 \text{ minutes/cycle}$$

This allowance can be determined for an hour or for a shift. If the operation is performed at 100% (that is, in 3.005 minutes per cycle) the cycles and PFD are as follows:

Cycles ×	*PFD Per Cycle* =	*PFD*
60/3.005 = 19.97/hour	0.423	8.45 minutes/hour
480/3.005 = 159.73/shift	0.423	67.57 minutes/8 hour shift

Another way of identifying the same PFD is to determine the total base time and subtract from 60 minutes/hour (or 480 minutes/shift)

PFD per Hour = 60 − Base Time
               = 60 − [19.97 cycles/hour × 2.582 minutes/cycle]
               = 60 − 51.55
               = 8.45 minutes
PFD per Shift = 480 − Base Time
               = 480 − [159.73 × 2.582]
               = 480 − 412.43
               = 67.57 minutes

In the above two illustrations, we have assumed that the operation was being performed at 100% (that is, in 3.005 minutes including PFD, or 2.582 minutes without PFD). We could also identify the total PFD if the operation was performed at 130%. In this case the elapsed time without PFD would be:

Manual   0.827/1.30 = 0.636 minutes/cycle
Machine   = 1.350
Total   = 1.986

With the PFD allowance the time would be:

Manual   0.636 × 1.247 = 0.793 minutes/cycle
Machine   1.350 × 1.125 = 1.519
Total   = 2.312

The PFD per cycle is now 2.312 − 1.986 = 0.326 minutes. This is less than it was at 100% performance (.423 minutes per cycle). The total PFD per hour or per shift is the same, however, because a greater number of cycles is being performed at 130%. This can be shown as follows:

$$60/2.312 = 25.99 \text{ cycles/hour} \times 0.326 \text{ minutes/cycle}$$
$$= 8.45 \text{ minutes/hour}$$
$$480/2.312 = 207.81 \text{ cycles/shift} \times 0.326 \text{ minutes/cycle}$$
$$= 67.57 \text{ minutes/shift}$$

These allowances are identical to those shown above for 100% performance.

Measured Day Work (MDW)

The PFD allowances, when added to the MDW base times, produce the following standards:

	Base	×	*PFD*	=	*Standard*
Manual	0.827		1.247		1.031 minutes/cycle
Machine	1.350		1.125		1.519
Total	2.177				2.550

The difference between the base time and the total allowed (standard) time is the amount of PFD allowance.

$$2.550 - 2.177 = 0.373 \text{ minutes/cycle}$$

On an hourly and daily basis the PFD allowance is as follows:

$$60/2.550 = 23.53 \text{ cycles/hour} \times 0.373 = 8.78 \text{ minutes/hour}$$
$$480/2.550 = 188.24 \text{ cycles/shift} \times 0.373 = 70.24 \text{ minutes/shift}$$

This assumes that the performance is 100%. If the performance was 85%, the PFD per cycle would be determined as follows:

	Base				*PFD*		*Total Times*
Manual	0.827/0.85	=	0.973	×	1.247	=	1.213
Machine	1.350/0.85	=	1.588		1.125	=	1.787
			2.561				3.000

$$3.000 - 2.561 = 0.439 \text{ minutes/cycle}$$

Fewer cycles per hour and per day, will be accomplished, but the PFD allowance for the time period (as shown for the incentive standard) will be the same at any performance level.

At 85% performance the PFD allowance is

$$60/3.00 = 20 \text{ cycles/hour} \times .439 \text{ minutes/cycle}$$
$$= 8.78 \text{ minutes/hour}$$
$$480/3.000 = 160 \text{ cycles/shift} \times .439 \text{ minutes/cycle}$$
$$= 70.34 \text{ minutes/shift}$$

Note that these values are identical to those developed above at 100% performance on MDW standards.

Cycle Time versus Incentive Pay

The employee must perform the work cycle in the time required to earn the desired performance and pay. Assuming that a 30% incentive allowance has been built into the standard and he or she wishes to earn 30%, the manual work must be performed in 1.0/1.3 of the base time.

The base time for the manual work (in the example we have been using) is .827 minutes without PFD, or 1.031 minutes with PFD. The required cycle time to earn 130% can be determined with or without PFD. The same is true for the machine element.

	Without PFD		With PFD	
	Base	*130% Time*	*Standard*	*130% Time*
Manual	0.827	0.636	1.031	0.793
Machine	1.755	1.350	1.974	1.519
	2.582	1.986	3.005	2.312

Note that these values are the same as those previously calculated in the discussion of the addition of allowances.

Performance Levels: Manual and Machine Elements

For incentive plans the machine and manual time values must be set at the same pay performance level. In previous examples, the machine time was increased by 30% to reflect a 100% pay performance level (which could then be added to the manual standard time so that the total would reflect a 100% pay performance level).

The purpose of this conversion is to establish a single time value for the entire operation that can be divided by the actual time in order to calculate the pay performance:

$$\frac{\text{Allowed Hours}}{\text{Actual Hours}} = \text{Pay Performance}$$

If the desired earnings opportunity is something other than 130% (such as 120%), the "allowed" machine time would reflect 120% pay performance—and if the manual work was performed at 130%, the resulting composite pay performance would be somewhere between 120% and 130%.

For MDW plans the machine elements are not factored because the intent is to measure actual performance rather than identify pay performance.

Allowance for Infrequent (Nonrun) Elements

Infrequent elements such as machine adjustment, tool care and adjustment, are often expressed (and then added to the time standard) as a percentage of the time spent on the regular elements. Suppose a number of studies are taken, and the sum of these elements is:

Total Machine Adjustment	=	46.2 minutes
Total Attachment Adjustment	=	93.9 minutes
Total Nonrun Time	=	140.1 minutes
Total Observed Time	=	1652.8 minutes
Total Run Time: 1652.8 − 140.1	=	1512.7 minutes

Each allowance can be expressed as a percent of the work time:

Machine Adjustment $\quad \dfrac{46.2}{1512.7} = 3.05\%$

Attachment Adjustment $\quad \dfrac{93.9}{1512.7} = 6.21\%$

Total Nonrun Allowance $\qquad\qquad = 9.26\%$

Each nonrun allowance should be shown separately, at least in the work papers, with the derivation of the allowance, but the total can be used to calculate the total base time ($1512.7 \times 1.0926 = 1652.8$)

In setting time standards, these allowances must be included as part of the base time when the PFD allowances are added. Using the following example:

Element Base (run) Time $\;= 2.00$ minutes
PFD $\qquad\qquad\qquad\quad\; = 24.7\%$
Nonrun allowance $\qquad\; = \;\; 9.26\%$

The two allowances must be multiplied (rather than added) in order to include a PFD allowance for the nonrun as well as the element base (run) time. Thus, the total standard should be:

$2.00 \times 1.096 \times 1.247 = 2.725$ standard minutes

If the PFD and nonrun allowances were added, the calculation would be:

$2.00 \times (1.00 + 0.0926 + 0.247) = 2.679$

The difference ($2.725 - 2.679$) is 0.046, which is the PFD allowance for the nonrun time ($2.00 \times 0.0926 \times 0.247$) = 0.046

It is often useful to indicate the size of the nonrun time by showing its value separately:

Element Base (run) Time $\;= 2.000$ minutes
Nonrun Allowance 9.26% $= 0.185$ minutes
_____
Total Base Time $\qquad\quad = 2.185$ minutes
PFD Allowance of 24.7% $= 0.540$ minutes
_____
Total Standard Time $\quad\; = 2.725$ minutes

Performance Rating

It is essential for sound work measurement administration to establish performance criteria and definitions that apply to the plant and are agreed upon by the employees and management.

Normal is an agreed upon level for a particular plant and it becomes the plant's Acceptable Productivity Level (APL). It is not necessarily applicable to all plants or for all parts of the country.

Other levels of performance, for instance, those achieved by financially motivated incentive workers, are sometimes more uniformly recognized.

For machine-paced elements (which account for a substantial part of production cost in many industries), the applied leveling or performance rating is 100% for measured daywork shops. For a wage incentive program, an allowance (such as 20%, 30%, and so forth) is added to provide the incentive-earning opportunity.

For hand-paced operations, the rating can vary substantially. It is not unusual, for example, to find performance ratings of 60 or less for setup or makeready operations, especially if the operator believes the backlog is low. On the other hand, some workers will perform at a consistently high rate whether or not they are being observed. The reasons vary from plant to plant and there is no simple explanation for this phenomenon.

Equitable performance rating requires a substantial amount of training and experience. Even then, it is difficult to rate in increments of less than 5%. The process of rating is usually accomplished mentally by comparison to what is recognized as normal.

Developing Elemental Time Standards

Timestudy is a process of sampling what occurs on the operation being studied. Timestudy techniques should be governed by the same principles that apply to statistical quality control, work sampling and so forth.

When a timestudy of 20 cycles is taken and a standard is set based on this study, these 20 cycles, in effect, should be representative of the operation and fully reflect all the delays that will be encountered at the operation in the next umpteen thousand cycles. If it is not fully representative, more studies are required.

There are various methods for developing standard elemental values from timestudy data.

1. An average performance rating can be applied to the average observed time.
2. Each observed time can be converted to normal. Then, an average of these values can be developed.
3. Selected values (observed times and ratings) can be used.

For purposes of the following discussion, assume that method 1 is being used to illustrate the complete development of a standard. The following are definitions of terms used in the illustrative example.

Observed Average Element Time: Mathematical average of the elapsed times in the timestudy.

Base Time (Normal): Observed average element time × leveling factor.

Leveling or Performance Rating: The process of modifying the observed average element time by a factor in relation to the mental concept of normal. All examples cited use 100% as normal (and 130% as high task performance where incentives are involved).

Standard Time

$$\frac{\text{Base Time} \times (100\% + \text{Allowance \%'s})}{100}$$

Calculating Cycles   **Measured Daywork**

Assume the following operation in which an operator loads and unloads a lift into and from a machine externally. The cycle consists of manual and machine elements:

	Observed Average Time	Leveled at
1. Load sheets on table and square	0.25 minutes	110%
2. Machine (fully automatic)	1.35 minutes	
3. Open clamps, remove die cut blanks	0.35 minutes	115%
4. Remove die cut waste	0.12 minutes	125%
	2.07 minutes	

Assume that the same PFD allowances, previously developed, are to be used here:

Manual PFD = 24.7%
Machine PFD = 12.7%

The base time and allowed times are determined as follows:

	Actual Minutes	$\times$ Leveling Factor	$=$ Base Minutes	$\times$ PFD	$=$ Allowed Minutes/Cycle
Manual time (external)					
Load sheets, etc.	0.25	1.10	0.275		
Open clamps, etc.	0.35	1.15	0.402		
Remove, etc.	0.12	1.25	0.150		
Subtotal			0.827	1.247	1.030
Machine Time	1.35	—	1.35	1.125	1.517
Total					2.547

This can be expressed as hours per 100 cycles and cycles per hour:

1. (2.547 × 100)/60 minutes = 4.245 standard hours per 100 cycles
2. 60 minutes/2.547 = 23.56 cycles per standard hour

It should be noted that we are reflecting, in these calculations, a 100% performance in a MDW environment. In actual practice, it is usually lower—in the 80–95% range.

Incentive

In order to show the difference between a MDW and Incentive Application, we will use the same basic data. It is repeated below and the reader can refer back to the preceding sections to see how it applied to a MDW situation.

Manual PFD = 24.7%
Machine PFD = 12.5%

	Actual Minutes $\times$	Leveling Factor $\times$	Basic Minutes $\times$	PFD $\times$	Allowed Minutes/Cycle
Manual Time (external)					
Load sheets, etc.	0.25	1.10	0.275		
Open clamps, etc.	0.35	1.15	0.402		
Remove, etc.	0.12	1.25	0.150		
Subtotal			0.827	1.247	1.030
Machine Time	1.35	1.30[a]	1.755	1.125	1.974
Total					3.004

[a]Incentive allowance of 30 (bonus-earning opportunity)

Note that the total allowed minutes per cycle for the measured daywork plan (MDW) was 2.547. To express the Incentive Allowance as hours per 100 cycles or cycles per hour, the *expected* performance should be used. In this case it is 130%, therefore the expected cycle time is:

3.004/1.30 = 2.311 minutes
(2.311 × 100)/60 minutes = 3.852 hours per 100 cycles
60 minutes/2.311 = 25.96 cycles per hour

The calculations and definitions are the same as for MDW. Of course, productivity is expected to be higher. In the above data, the standard is 3.004 minutes per cycle and at 130%, 25.96 cycles per hour or 207.72 cycles per day, are expected.

207.72 cycles × 3.004 min/cycle = 624 earned minutes per day

Then,

624 earned minutes/480 actual minutes = 130% Pay Performance

Alternate Shift Allowance   The nonrunning time during the day is the total of the 45 minutes shift allowance plus the 13% personal and fatigue allowance. Note that this is not 13% of the total day, but rather 13% of the base running time. As an illustration, assume a cycle of 2.00 minutes (all manual; no machine time), then

Allowed Time = 2.00 × 1.247 PFD = 2.494 standard minutes.

The cycles per day at standard performance would be

480/2.494 = 192.46 cycles per day.

The total running time during the shift = 480/1.247 = 385 minutes. Therefore, the nonrunning time is 480 − 385 = 95 minutes. This nonrunning time is composed of the 45 minutes plus 13% of run time:

45 + (0.13 × 385) = 45 + 50 = 95 total nonrun minutes.

Another way of indicating the running time is to multiply the known number of cycles per day by the 2.00 minutes run time per cycle:

192.46 × 2.00 = 385 run minutes.

Of course, if the 45 minutes per day was not included in the total allowance, only 13% would be added to the 2.00 minute base time.

2.00 × 1.13 = 2.26 allowed minutes.

This would be an alternate method of expressing the standard. But, since the 45 minutes are not included in the allowance, they cannot be considered as time available for work. Therefore, only 480 − 45 = 435 can be used to determine the number of cycles:

$$\frac{435 \text{ minutes per day}}{2.26 \text{ minutes per cycle}} = 192.46 \text{ cycles per day}$$

Note that this agrees with the answer developed previously, and the running time is 435/1.13 = 385 minutes, as calculated previously.

Productivity is defined as the ratio of output to input or, earned time to actual time. Suppose a worker produced exactly 192.46 cycles during the day as shown above. We can use the 2.26 minute standard and then add the 45 minute allowance:

192.46 cycles × 2.26 minutes/cycle = 435.0 earned minutes per shift
Added Daily Allowance   =   45.0 earned minutes per shift
Total   = 480.0 earned minutes per shift

Then, this would be divided by the actual time (elapsed or clock time) of 480 minutes to calculate the productivity:

480 earned minutes/480 actual minutes = 100% productivity

If the cycle standard, which includes the 45 minutes, was used, we will get the same answer:

192.46 cycles × 2.494 minutes per cycle = 480 earned minutes

Dividing by 480 actual minutes gives 100% productivity again.

Both forms of the standard result in the same productivity, if it is 100%; however, if the productivity is above or below 100%, the answers will not be the same. For example, assume that the worker produced 220 cycles. Using the 2.26 allowance, we get the following:

220 × 2.26   = 497.2 earned minutes
Daily Allowance   =   45.0 earned minutes

Total   = 542.2 earned minutes
Percent Productivity = 542.2/480 = 112.96%

On the other hand, using the 2.494 minute allowance, we get:

220 × 2.494   = 548.7 earned minutes
Percent Productivity = 548.7/480 = 114.31%

The reason for the difference is that when the 45-minute daily allowance is included with the total PFD, it increases or decreases with the number of cycles produced. In the above example, the difference of 6.5 earned minutes (548.7 − 542.2) occurs because the 45 minute allowance was raised by the percentage increase in cycles; viz,

$$220.00/192.46 = 1.143$$

Thus, there has been a 14.3% increase in production above the 100% productivity level (see prior calculation) and the 45 minute daily allowance has also been increased by 14.3%:

$$45 \times 0.143 = 6.5 \text{ minutes}$$

As we can see, this is the difference in the earned minutes between the two forms of standards. When the 2.20 minute standard is used, the daily allowance remains at 45 minutes. But, when the 2.494 minute standard is used, the daily allowance becomes:

$$45.0 + 6.5 = 51.5 \text{ earned minutes}$$

Note that when the standard including the total PFD is used, the change in productivity (14.3%) is exactly equal to the change in production from the 100% level.

In effect, one method treats the 45 minute allowance as a variable, which increases or decreases with production, and the other treats it as a daily constant regardless of volume. Either method can be used, depending on the specifics of the individual situation.

An Alternate. If the 45 minutes were considered as a percentage of the remainder of the day, it would be: $45/(480 - 45) = 10.35\%$. If this was then added to the basic 13% allowance, the total PFD would be 23.35%. This would result in a productivity somewhere between those of the two methods described above.

If, on the other hand, it was multiplied by the 13%, the resulting PFD is 24.7%; viz, $(1.13 \times 1.1035) - 1.00$ as it was previously.

Reported Nonproductive Time

Certain nonproductive time is not included in the standards, either because it is considered avoidable or should be separately measured and controlled.

In measuring productivity if this time is reported separately as noncharge-able, it is not reflected in the basic productivity percentage. It is controlled by measuring and analyzing it as a separate exercise.

As an illustration, assume a standard cycle time of 2.60 minutes including a PFD of 18%. On a particular day, production is 140 cycles with a machine breakdown of 30 minutes, reported separately as nonchargeable and not included in PFD). The calculation is as follows:

$$\text{Basic Productivity} = \frac{\text{Earned Minutes}}{\text{Actual Minutes}} = \frac{140 \times 2.60}{480 - 30} = 81\%$$

$$\text{Overall Efficiency} = \frac{\text{Earned Minutes}}{\text{Elapsed Minutes}} = \frac{140 \times 2.60}{480} = 76\%$$

The 30 minutes of reported downtime represents 30/480 = 6 of the total paid time. Management's attention must be focused separately on this in order to control it.

Machine Assignment

The number of machines that can be assigned to an operator depends on the machine cycle and the amount of work the operator must perform. This depends on whether the work is internal or external, and the expected performance.

To illustrate a simple case, assume that the machine time is 2.00 minutes and the work per cycle is 1.00 minute. This work could be internal or external and so we will consider both situations:

The total cycle will be:

1. 2.00 minutes, if the work is internal = 30 per hour
2. 2.00 + 1.00 = 3.00 minutes, if the work is external = 20 per hour

If the operator runs only one machine, his workload will be:

1. Internal: 30 cycles/hour × 1.00 = 30 minutes/hour [50% workload]
2. External: 20 cycles/hour × 1.00 = 20 minutes/hour [33% workload]

If the operator runs 2 machines (in staggered fashion), his workload will be:

1. Internal: 60 cycles/hour × 1.00 = 60 minutes/hour [100% workload]
2. External: 40 cycles/hour × 1.00 = 40 minutes/hour [67% workload]

Obviously, if the work is internal, the operator can run only 2 machines. If the work is external, 3 machines can be run.

A simple formula that applies is

Total Cycle Time/Work Time = Number of Machines That Can Be Run.

Of course, the *performance* will affect this machine assignment. Suppose, that (if the work is external) the operator under incentive conditions works at 133% productivity. The work time will be therefore reduced to 1.00/1.33 = .75 minutes. The formula gives the machine assignment:

$$\frac{\text{Total Cycle Time}}{\text{Work Time}} = \frac{2.00 + 0.75}{0.75} = \frac{2.75}{0.75} = 3.7 \text{ machines}$$

In actual practice, the assignment must be a whole number of machines, unless some arrangement can be made to combine jobs (or use some other strategy) in order to make optimum use of this potential. If there were 37 machines in the department, the assignment of 10 operators would be optimum.

Suppose in the above example, that the work was internal instead of external. The work per cycle will not change but the number of machines that can be assigned will change, viz,

$$\frac{\text{Total Cycle Time}}{\text{Work Time}} = \frac{2.00}{0.75} = 2.7 \text{ machines}$$

Here again, some schedule must be developed to provide this opportunity, if at all possible.

In the above examples, we have not mentioned PFD allowances. In actual practice, these allowances must be considered selectively. Any daily allowance (such as the 45 minutes used in previous examples) should be excluded because it does not affect the cycle time. It will however, affect the daily capacity.

As an example, assume that the delay allowance for the machine is 2% and the personal fatigue and delay allowances for the manual work is 13%. If we apply this to the situation of external work and performance is 100%, then,

$$\frac{\text{Total Cycle Time}}{\text{Work Time}} = \frac{2.00\,(1.02) + 1.00\,(1.13)}{1.00(1.13)}$$
$$= \frac{3.17}{1.13} = 2.8 \text{ machines}$$

If the operator has less than a full workload, the cycle time may be shorter because some of the fatigue allowance (part of the 13%) can be absorbed during the machine time when no work is required. Therefore, in the above case, it may be practical to assign 3 machines. The pattern of the delays (or interference) will determine what a practical assignment should be. For maximum manpower utilization, the higher assignment is used, but for maximum equipment utilization, the lower assignment is used. The choice is critically important in a sound profit plan. The company goals and the economic factors must be evaluated in order to make these decisions. The PS as well as the MHRs and sales forecasts are the tools needed for these measurements.

Combined Allowance Formula

When Personal, Fatigue and Delay allowances are comprised of percentages and minutes, the formula to combine these into one overall figure is arrived at as follows:

T = Total length of shift (paid minutes)

m = Shift allowance (time not run) in minutes

a = PFD applied to base time (as decimal)

A = Combined (total) allowance (as percentage)

Formula

$$A = \frac{T - (T - m)/(1.0 + a)}{(T - m)/(1.0 + a)}$$

Simplified

$$A = (aT + m)/(T - m)$$

Comments and Analysis

$$T - m = \text{Time available as running time.}$$

$$1.0 + a = \text{Factor to reduce ``time available as running time'' for time that is unproductive because of PFD.}$$

$$(T - m)/(1.0 + a) = \text{Net productive time after accounting for any constant shift allowance and PFD.}$$

$$T - (T - m)/(1.0 + a) = \text{The total time not productive (for all reasons).}$$

Subsidy   Production Standards are developed to reflect 100% productivity; the pace at which the worker is fully earning his or her hourly base pay rate. However, the present productivity may be something less than 100% (usually 85–95% in MDW companies). For example, a PS is 1,000 units per hour and the worker's base rate is $8.00 per hour. If the present output from the worker is 800 per hour, he or she is earning only 800/1,000 or 80% of the base rate of $8.00, or $6.40. Since the company still must pay the entire hourly rate of $8.00, it is in effect, *subsidizing* or *making up* this difference of $1.60 per hour (the remaining 20% of the base rate). This is known as *subsidy* cost and must be included in the MHR.

Chargeable/ Nonchargeable Costs   When a worker is paid for 40 hours per week, he or she is paid for both time worked and time not worked. At $8.00 per hour, the gross pay (not including fringes and other costs) is $320. However, if 32 of those hours are considered productive work (charged to products or jobs) and the balance of 8 hours are considered unproductive, then the true cost of the productive hour is $320/32 or $10 per hour. The difference between that $10 and $8 is considered *nonchargeable hourly cost* and the additional $2 per hour must be included in the MHR. Besides the need to normalize the MHR, the nonchargeable cost if controllable, should be highlighted for management's remedial action. As with the subsidy, this nonchargeable cost can be expressed as a percent, viz, $2.00/$8.00 = 25%.

Both subsidy and nonchargeable costs are characteristic values. These terms and costs can never be used as generalized or averaged information since they refer respectively, to workers and machines in specific production centers. Using an *average* 20% subsidy figure plantwide (meaning 80% productivity) is to deny performance differences among workers. Using a 25% nonchargeable cost figure *factorywide* implies that the chargeable time for all production centers is 75%. Such averages distort the o.o.p. production costs and the accuracy of contribution measurements.

Exhibit A–1 is a partial list of chargeable and nonchargeable operations, by department, in a large commercial printer. This list reflects this particular company's recognition of these two categories and is not intended to be a pattern for other printing companies.

However, for purposes of sound PS and MHRs, these separations should remain consistent and to the extent that these change in the future, so must the PS and MHRs be changed.

Exhibit A–1
Typical List of Chargeable versus Nonchargeable Costs (Partial List)

Markup Department

Chargeable	*Nonchargeable*
Original copy	No work
Printer's corrections	Research
AA's printouts	Learning
Column makeup	Union duties
Ads	Supervising
Printer's CX ads	Lunch
AA's on galleys	
Pagination	
Tabular	
Printer's CX tab	
AA's tabular	
Special setting	
AA's pages	
AA's after blues	

Proofroom

Chargeable	*Nonchargeable*
Printout reading	No work
AA's on printouts	Desk work
Ads	Learning
AA's on ads	Union duties
Tabular	Supervision
AA's on tab	Lunch
Pages	
AA's on pages	
Form blues	
Plates and press sheets	

Keypunch Department

Chargeable	*Nonchargeable*
Original copy	No work
Printer's correction	Repairs to machine
AA's printouts	Oiling and cleaning
Ads	Learning
Printer's ads	Union duties
AA's ads	Supervising
AA's on galleys	Lunch
Tabular	
Printer's tab	
AA's tabular	
Special setting	
AA's pages	
Justified original copy	
Justified printer's corrections	
Justified ads	
Justified ads printer's corrections	

(continued)

Exhibit A–1
Typical List of Chargeable versus Nonchargeable Costs (Partial List) *(continued)*

Keypunch Department

Chargeable	Nonchargeable
Justified AA's on ads	
Justified AA's on galleys	
Justified tabular	
Justified PE's on tab	
Justified AA's on tab	
Justified special setting	
Justified AA's on pages	
AA's after blues	

Pasteup Department

Chargeable	Nonchargeable
Pasteup all editorial pages	No work
Pasteup combination text and ads	Clean up
Pasteup all ad pages	Research
Pasteup individual ad	Learning
AA's on ads	Operate copying machines
Taping halftones	Supervision
Rule master page layouts	Correct computer error
Cut overlays and silhouettes	Correct pasteup error
Collate ads	Film storage
Collate and organize job	Lunch
Author's alterations	
Handle overmatter	
Our corrections	
Operating headliner	
Ruling	
Repair customer-supplied material	
AA after blues	

Camera Department

Chargeable	Nonchargeable
Prepare for camera	No work
Line shot	Repairs to equipment
Halftone (HT)	Cleaning
HT with silhouette mask	Research
HT drop out	Union duties
Drop out line combine	Correct internal problem
Special shots	Faulty processing
Duotone	Mixing chemicals
Duotone double dot black	Helping on camera
Duotone with silhouette mask	Making screen tints and tabs
Rescreen halftone	Inventory duties
Make screen prints	Lunch
Two step enlarge-reduce	
Repair faulty copy	
Author's alterations	

(continued)

Exhibit A–1
Typical List of Chargeable versus Nonchargeable Costs (Partial List) *(continued)*

<hr>

Camera Department

Chargeable	*Nonchargeable*
Our corrections	
Opaque and touch up	
Pan film shot	
Dot etching	
AA after blueprints	

<hr>

Contact Department

Chargeable	*Nonchargeable*
Contact tints	No work
Spreads and chokes	Repairs to equipment
Inspect pasteups	Cleaning
Contact	Research
Contact pasteups	Union duties
Contact duplicate negs	Correct internal problem
Contact to sharpen dots	Faulty processing
Contact conversions	Mixing chemicals
Contact combines	Making screen tints
Contact for film storage	Lunch
Contact for nyloprint	
Drop out	
Screen prints	
Two step enlarge-reduce	
Repair faulty copy	
Authors alterations	
Our corrections	
Opaque and touch up	
AA after blueprints	

<hr>

Stripping Department

Chargeable	*Nonchargeable*
Spotting and opaquing	No work
Rule up master layout	Desk work
Color separating or combining film	Pull negatives from flats
Repairing customer-supplied materials	Research
Stripping black forms only	Lunch
Stripping 2-color forms only	Learning
Stripping 4-color forms only	Supervision
Strip nyloprint forms	Punching flats
Collating and organizing job	
Author's alterations	
Our corrections	
Line up, trim and fold proofs	
Inspect proofs	
Restripping due to our error	
Prepare layouts and impositions	
AA's after blueprints	

(continued)

Exhibit A–1
Typical List of Chargeable versus Nonchargeable Costs (Partial List) *(continued)*

Proofing Department

Chargeable	*Nonchargeable*
Warren prints (1 side only)	No work
Warren prints (2 sides)	Repairs to equipment
2-color kwikotes	Cleaning equipment
3 and 4-color kwikotes	Research
Color keys	Learning
Transfer keys	Mixing chemicals
Waterkotes	Remake due to proofing error
Individual blueprints of material for customer	Lunch
Reproof requested by customer-author's alterations	
Plant proof—no billing	
Reproof due to our error	
Dylux proofs	
AA after blueprints	

Pressroom Department

Chargeable	*Nonchargeable*
Makeready	No work
Running (show quantity)	Breakdown—machinist or electrician on press
Waiting for plates on new form	Desk work
Customer corrections or change in form	Lunch
Waiting for remake plate due to error in preparation or platemaking	Weekend gearup
Web break	Sweeping
Change blankets, dampeners, or rollers during run only	Waste control
	Extra people
Batter or crackout (including waiting for new or repaired plate)	Learning
	Utility man
Incomplete information	Non running due to incomplete crew
Clean grater rollers, angle bars, chill rollers, formers, etc. during run only	Inspecting
	Supervision
Cocking plates for register	Trucking
Folder change by machinist	Union duties
Defective paper	
Delay due to wrong paper	
Wash blankets during run only	
Washup press during run only	
End of job washup	
Missed paster	

Bindery Department

Chargeable	*Nonchargeable*
All Machines	*All Machines*
Setting	No work
Running (show quantity)	Repairs to machine
Waiting for mailer	Oiling and cleaning machine
Waiting for stock	Cutting waste books
Running rebinds	Lunch

(continued)

Exhibit A–1
Typical List of Chargeable versus Nonchargeable Costs (Partial List) *(continued)*

Bindery Department

Chargeable	Nonchargeable
Hand Section 101	*Hand Section 101*
Hand gathering, inserting, or tipping	No work
Trucking charged to a job	Desk work
Tear apart web signatures	General cleanup
Helping on laws on drill (Machine 25)	Trucking (no specific job)
Repairs to bad books	Union duties
Inspecting	Supervision
Feeding pockets on a machine	Lunch

Mailing Department

Chargeable	Nonchargeable
Hand Section 102	*Hand Section 102*
Machine bagging	No work
Hand polybagging	Desk work
Packing cartons and packages on table	General cleanup
Prepare newsdealer orders	Trucking not charged to a job
Hand inserting and tipping	Union duties
Strapping skids	Supervision
Trucking charged to a job	Sorting sack labels
Packing cartons on machine	Repair tying machines
Hand wrapping single copies	Shipper
Sorting (not on machine)	All work done in storage
Bundling and tying (not on machine)	Lunch
Town marking	
Stamping postage	
Hand labeling	
Preparing subscribers labels	
Shrinking skids	

Formula Consistency

Developers of MHR and PS treat certain cost elements in different ways. Rest period and end-of-shift clean-up costs may be entered into the MHR or into the PS. Mathematically, the same cost estimate can be obtained with either method, but since these activities consume time, it is more rational to add them to the PS rather than to inflate the MHR. In addition, it permits measurement of overall performance, including the rest periods, washups, and so on.

However, it is essential to be consistent in the development and application of the PS and MHR. If, for example, rest periods are added to the base PS in the form of a fatigue allowance, then to measure performance and variances, the rest periods should be charged against the earned hours. That is, the rest periods must be in both the numerator and denominator of the performance ratio:

$$\text{Performance} = \frac{\text{Earned Hours (including Standard Rest Time)}}{\text{Actual Hours (including Actual Rest Periods)}}$$

If washup standards are developed or allowances are included in the run standards, the actual time would be chargeable. If not, the washup is considered nonchargeable, and the MHR will be raised accordingly. When measuring performance, this time should not be charged and will, therefore be, in neither the numerator nor denominator of the performance ratio.

MR Standards   All PS reflect the time to perform the necessary work (person and/or machine) at 100% performance, but they can be applied in different ways depending on the need.

For purposes of cost "estimating," the PS obviously must be applied before the work is actually done. Therefore, the nature of the work must be projected. However, for changeovers (also referred to as "makeready" or "setup") it is often impossible to do this very precisely because the sequence of the jobs cannot be defined in advance.

For example, if two jobs with the same characteristics can be run one after the other, the changeover from one job to another can be very short or even nonexistent. Some companies refer to this as "ganging" the work.

For estimating purposes, however, it may not be possible to project this type of detailed shop loading. Even if a series of similar jobs are estimated at the same time, the estimator might not be safe in predicting that the jobs will be scheduled to run in sequence (ganged) to minimize the setup time. Therefore, for estimating purposes it is often necessary to use some type of average "changeover" time. This type of PS may very well relate to the type of job. For instance, if the characteristics of a job are relatively unusual (rare), it is less likely that similar jobs will be on the schedule and therefore, the probability is greater that the changeover will take longer. Conversely, if the job is a common type there will be (on the average) many other similar jobs on the schedule and the opportunity for ganging, greater. Therefore, the average PS will be lower.

Obviously, the time required to perform the work elements must be considered and is also a factor. Adjustments on some machines take more time than on others. Therefore, although ganging will reduce the average time, the basic setup may be very difficult and the lengthy adjustments may have to be included in the average PS.

For purposes of measuring and monitoring performance in the factory, the exact nature of the changeover is usually known. Therefore, a specific (rather than average) PS can be applied.

The standard hours, which are applied for "estimating" and "performance measurement" during a time period, should be reconciled to assure that there are no serious variances.

Identifying Parameters and Constructing PS   The task of identifying parameters from raw observation data requires skill, experience, knowledge of the industry operations, and a systematic, analytical approach. Generally, when making the studies the observer should record all data on possible parameters so that testing can be done later.

The time values may be affected by only one parameter or a whole family of parameters. Sometimes the effect of the individual parameters can be identified separately—sometimes combined effects must be considered to-

**Exhibit A–2
Timestudy Data for
"RUN" Folder-Gluer**

Study Number	Run Hours	Cartons Produced	Cartons Per Hour	Caliper (in Inches)	Feed Length (in Inches)	Style
1	1.39	28,116	20,200	.023	13	Rev. tuck
2	4.80	160,320	33,400	.027	5	Str. tuck
3	2.00	16,800	8,400	.032	22	Sleeve
4	.75	24,638	32,850	.016	8	Seal end
5	1.10	9,592	8,720	.020	25	Str. tuck
6	3.00	48,540	16,180	.026	11	Glued in cell
7	.48	4,896	10,200	.036	18	Double wall
8	2.15	75,680	35,200	.021	6	Tray
9	6.13	69,759	11,380	.025	20	Rev. tuck
10	1.04	17,316	16,650	.030	14	Display
11	.92	12,519	13,637	.018	16	Auto. tray
12	3.20	48,832	15,260	.032	10	Glued in cell
13	1.48	39,664	26,800	.034	7	Str. tuck
14	1.05	42,210	40,200	.016	5	Seal end
15	2.20	14,058	6,390	.038	24	Sleeve
16	.79	8,220	10,465	.028	18	5-panel
17	2.02	14,706	7,280	.024	26	Str. tuck
18	1.81	40,200	22,210	.022	8	Auto. tray
19	3.07	86,881	28,300	.014	11	Double wall
20	1.32	38,412	29,100	.028	7	Str. tuck
21	4.10	90,199	22,000	.020	10	Auto. tray
22	2.40	15,700	6,540	.034	22	5-panel

**Exhibit A–3
Speed versus Feed Length**

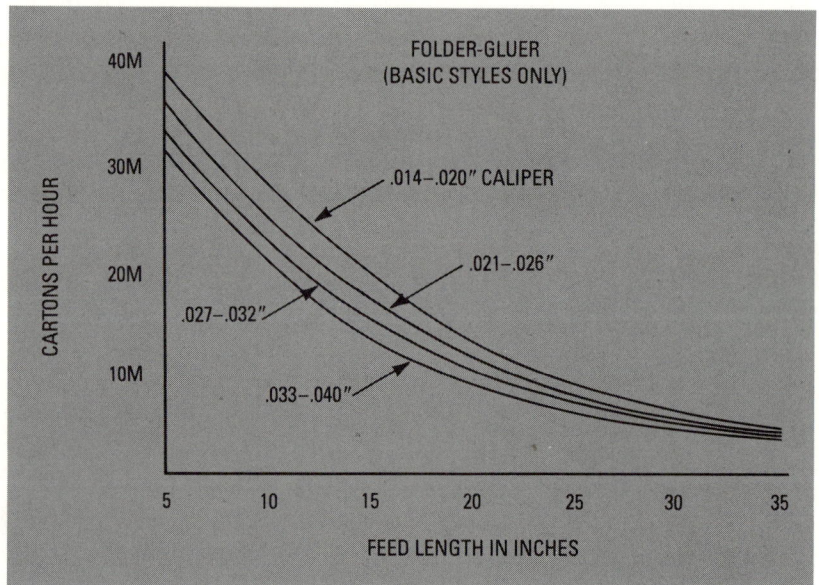

FOLDER-GLUER
(BASIC STYLES ONLY)

.014–.020" CALIPER
.021–.026"
.027–.032"
.033–.040"

CARTONS PER HOUR

FEED LENGTH IN INCHES

gether. Initially some judgment must be made as to which of the parameters might be the most significant (have the greatest effect on the standard time). Then graphical analysis, testing with formulas, etc. can usually identify a straight or curved line relationship with the major parameter. However, there will often be a dispersion of values above and below these lines because of other parameters. These variances can then be analyzed in relation to the secondary (next important) parameter—this may be another linear (or curvilinear) relationship or may be handled as a factor (allowance to be added or subtracted).

The computer can be utilized in these analyses as more software, such as

Exhibit A–4
Effect of Carton Style on Time

Feed Length in Inches	Cartons Per Standard Hour (Basic Styles Only)			
	Caliper			
	.014"–.020"	.021"–.026"	.027"–.032"	.033"–.040"
4	41,667	40,000	37,037	34,483
5	40,000	37,037	33,333	31,250
6	37,037	33,333	31,250	28,571
7	34,483	31,250	28,571	26,316
8	32,258	28,571	26,316	23,810
9	30,303	27,027	24,390	22,222
10	28,571	25,000	22,727	20,833
11	27,027	23,253	20,833	18,868
12	25,000	21,739	19,231	17,544
13	22,727	20,000	17,857	15,873
14	21,277	18,868	16,667	14,493
15	20,000	17,241	15,385	13,158
16	18,182	15,873	13,889	12,048
17	16,667	14,706	12,821	10,989
18	15,385	13,514	11,628	10,204
19	14,286	12,500	10,870	9,434
20	13,158	11,494	10,000	8,696
21	12,195	10,638	9,259	8,065
22	11,364	9,804	8,547	7,519
23	10,417	9,091	7,937	6,993
24	9,524	8,403	7,407	6,494
25	8,850	7,813	6,944	6,098
26	8,197	7,299	6,536	5,747
27	7,576	6,849	6,098	5,405
28	6,993	6,410	5,714	5,102
29	6,536	6,024	5,348	4,831
30	6,135	5,650	5,025	4,587
31	5,747	5,319	4,762	4,367
32	5,405	5,025	4,525	4,167
33	5,076	4,739	4,763	3,968
34	4,785	4,484	4,077	3,788
35	4,505	4,238	3,891	3,610

NOTE: These standards apply to the following "basic" carton styles: reverse tuck; straight tuck; seal end; sleeves; double wall; displays; trays.

For "special" carton styles apply the appropriate Standard Factor.

the least squares, a multiple regression, etc., becomes available to identify and test the interrelationships between various types of data.

Let's consider one set of "run" data obtained through time study on a machine that folds and glues paperboard cartons. This machine runs up to about 40,000 cartons per hour. Twenty-two studies were taken, and the observer tried to get a cross section of sizes and types. The time study data are shown in Exhibit A–2.

This is somewhat condensed—without some of the earliest studies that were discarded because the style was not recorded. Also there were some studies omitted because the operator was new and tentative about running the machine at maximum speed.

Through discussions with the supervisor, and by learning how the machine functioned the Industrial Engineer determined that the caliper of the board and the feed length were the most important parameters that had continuous values, that is, they existed on each study. Some styles could also have a substantial effect but they were treated as exceptions after the basic correlations were developed.

The first step was to plot the speed versus the feed length for all 22 studies. This showed some relationship, but there was a great dispersion of points due to some other factor. This was cleared up by considering the differences in caliper—four categories were sufficient as shown on Exhibit A–3.

The graph reflects two parameters. Most of the 22 points fell fairly close to those lines, but a few were off the mark; therefore, the next step was to see how the carton style affected the time. Three styles seemed to have the greatest variances—an analysis is shown on Exhibit A–4.

The speed based on the graph values, which should be correct for a "basic" style, is compared to the actual speed for that study. The resulting ratio can be used as a factor. For the "automatic tray" style for instance, study number 11 showed that the actual speed was .75 (75%) of the speed obtained from the graph for a basic style carton. Studies numbers 18 and 21 showed .78 and .77 factors, respectively; therefore, an average factor of .77 was established to apply to the basic standard (cartons per standard hour) for this style.

Exhibit A–5
Development of Factors
for Special Carton
Styles—Folder Gluer

Special Style	Study Number	Speed for Basic Style[a]	Actual Speed Observed	Actual ÷ Basic	Standard Factors
Auto. tray	11	18,182	13,637	.75	
	18	28,571	22,210	.78	.77
	21	28,571	22,000	.77	
Glued in cell	6	23,253	16,180	.70	
	12	22,727	15,260	.67	.68
5-panel	16	11,628	10,465	.90	
	22	7,519	6,540	.87	.88

[a] Determined from graph, Exhibit A–2.

Factors were established for the other two special styles also as shown (.68 and .88, respectively). As a result, standards can be applied for any feed length, caliper, or style.

The basic running standard was translated from the graph form to the table form shown in Exhibit A–5.

In the case of this PS the run quantity was not a factor in the final time because (to keep this illustration as simple as possible) only the runs long enough for the machine to reach cruising speed were used in the analysis. To cover short runs, however, additional allowances have to be developed, for many such production centers, to reflect slower average speeds.

Glossary

Allowances are additional time values that may or may not be added to the base (normal) time for various conditions.

Avoidable delays are those that are considered to be within the control of the operating departments, and should therefore be eliminated—and not reflected in PS. Examples are rework, late starts, etc.

Unavoidable delays are those that are considered to be beyond the control of the operating departments and are therefore included in PS. They may occur with regular and/or irregular frequency. Examples are jamups, job interruptions, searching for material, etc.

Personal allowances are included in the PS to permit the operating personnel to take care of their personal needs. In addition, relief people may be employed to keep machines running during these periods.

Fatigue allowances are included in all labor standards to compensate for the wearing effect of the physical and mental demands of the job—thereby permitting the operating personnel to maintain, on the average, a normal pace (when working) through an entire day.

Base time is the actual (observed) time adjusted by a speed rating (or leveling factor) to reflect the time to perform a task or job at a normal pace. It is also called "Normal" time. It does not include personal or fatigue allowances.

Bonus earning opportunity is the potential (in an incentive plan) for earning premium pay. For machine controlled operations a corresponding factor may be added to the standard time.

Cycle is a series of work elements in a production process. Each time the series is repeated another cycle has been completed. Sometimes, within a single overall cycle, there may be repetitions of some elements.

The word "cycle" is generic and can apply to impressions, pounds, rolls, etc. For instance, on a web (roll-fed) press that prints and cuts off 16 pages of a book (called a "signature") at a time, each signature, or each 500 signatures, may be considered a cycle—or the printing of an entire roll could be considered an overall cycle.

Earned standard hour is one hour of work produced at the standard rate (performance). For example, if a production standard calls for 4,000 pieces per hour (.250 standard hours per thousand) and the worker produces 4,000 in an elapsed sixty minutes, he has earned one standard hour. If, in an eight-hour period, he produces 36,000 pieces, he has earned $36 \times .250 = 9$ standard hours. (As every 1,000 pieces has earned him .250 hours.)

Element is a subdivision of an operation. A "regular" element occurs with consistent frequency and usually once in each cycle. An "infrequent" element may occur with varied frequency and usually not in each cycle—the content may not be the same each time it occurs.

For example, the loading of pieces into a feed magazine will occur each x number of cycles, and the number of pieces may vary on each occurrence.

Elemental times are actual, normal, and standard times for all elements. Usually they are determined in one of two ways:

1. Each observed time is leveled, and an average of the normal values is selected as representative. Allowances are then added to develop the standard time.
2. An average of the observed times is selected and an average leveling factor applied. Allowances are then added to develop standard times.

In either method abnormally high or low values may be eliminated if they are not representative.

Elapsed time is the actual time from the start to the end of an element, operation, or study.

Hand-(manual) paced operation is one in which the operator controls the speed and output; i.e., the operator's pace, rather than the machine time, determines the cycle time.

Leveling is the process of judging the pace at which an operator is performing (when observed) relative to "normal" pace, which is considered 100%. The pace is a combination of effort and effectiveness.

Leveling factor is determined through the leveling process and is applied to adjust the actual observed time to the "normal" time. If the operator's pace is judged to be above or below normal, the leveling factor is higher or lower than 1.00. This results in a normal time higher or lower than that observed.

Machine-paced operation is one in which the standard machine speed controls the rate of output; i.e., the standard machine time, rather than the operator's pace, determines the cycle time.

Material standards reflect the quantity of material in the product sold to the customer, plus a standard amount of waste. The waste is composed of set up and run portions.

Method is a specified way of performing an operation. The standard method is the best way of doing the job, under current plant conditions, and it is incumbent on the timestudy engineer to study the job with methods in mind before proceeding to set the time standard.

Normal time is the same as "base" time.

Operation is a term usually used to describe a part of the manufacturing process, as such, it normally contains a number of elements and refers to the product or what is done to the product. The operation can be synonomous with a department or can be generic. Set up, make ready, run, pack, rework, transport material, etc. are examples of "operations."

Parameters are any variables that cause the unit time to vary. The PS are developed and applied to reflect the parameters of the particular operation.

Production standard (PS) is the time to perform a defined amount of work, or a task, at a performance level of 100%. It can be expressed as Standard Hours per unit or as Number of Units per Standard Hour.

The standard time is composed of the normal time plus allowances.

Performance is the ratio of Standard Cost/Unit to Actual Cost/Unit. In an area where all MHRs are the same the Performance is identical to the Productivity because the respective costs are Earned Standard Hours and Actual Hours times the MHR.

Productivity is the ratio of Actual Production/Hour to Standard Production/Hour or the ratio of Earned Standard Time/Unit to Actual Time/Unit. For instance, if the standard calls for 4,000 pieces per hour and 4,000 pieces are actually produced, the rate of productivity is 4,000/4,000 = 100%. If 36,000 pieces are produced in eight clock hours, 9 standard hours are earned and the productivity is 9/8 = 112.5%.

Standard (100%) productivity is considered a normal target for a Measured Daywork plant. This is sometimes referred to as a "Fair Day's Work" level.

Raw speed is the unadjusted machine speed obtained from surface or shaft tachometers.

Selected time (see Elemental times)

Speed rating (same as Leveling)

Timestudy is a technique for developing PS through continuous observation and speed rating by a trained person.

Unit (or unit of measurement) refers to how the work is measured for a particular operation. For "set up" it can be colors, rolls, stations, etc., and for "running" it can be pieces, lbs, feet, impressions, etc. The PS are usually expressed in relation to these units so that they can be multiplied by the number of units when a cost estimate is made.

Variance is the difference between the earned standard and the actual hours. If in an eight-hour day nine standard hours are earned, there is a favorable variance of one hour. Variances can also be expressed in dollar values when extended by the appropriate machine hour rates.

Wage incentives is a system for providing extra pay for extra effort.

Work sampling is a technique for obtaining data about delays, determining frequences of certain elements, setting PS, etc. by making a series of observations at specific predetermined times.

Index

Index

Cost estimate. (Continued)
    sheet, 69
    varying of, 6–7
Cost estimating. *See also* Cost estimate; Production
       cost
    by computer, 134, *135,* 136
    defined, 4
    impact of PS on, 4–6
    for lowest cost, *153*
    for price evaluation, 4–5
Costs
    chargeable, 173, *174–178*
    nonchargeable, 173, *174–178*
Crew size
    analysis, 66
    determining, from timestudy data, 66–67
    effect of price increase on, 67–68
    effect of selling price on, 66
    effect of speed on, 66
    effect on contribution, 64, 65–68
    effect on o.o.p. conversion costs, 66–67
Cycles. *See* Job cycles

Delay
    and absenteeism, 59
    allowances, 58–60, 72, *96,* 156
    avoidable vs. unavoidable, 53, 58–59
    classification of, 58–59
    frequency of, 59
    machine interference, 59
    and PS, 53, 58–59
Direct conversion cost. *See* Production cost
Direct cost, 1, 2, 4, 5. *See also* Machine-hour rate;
       Material cost; Order cost; Production cost
    and capital expenditure, 147
    components of, 128–129
    derivation of, 137
    effect of PS on, 129
    in make-or-buy decision, 143–144
    relation to contribution, 141
Direct hourly cost. *See* Machine-hour cost
Direct material cost. *See* Material cost
Direct observation, methods of, 23–31
Direct-Order Charge (DOC), 30–31
Direct order cost. *See* Order cost
Direct product cost. *See* Order cost
Direct production cost. *See* Production cost
Downtime, 25, 59

Economic crew size. *See* Crew size
Effectiveness, 50
Elemental breakdown
    description of, 45
    reasons for, 45
    steps involved in, 48
Elemental time standards, developing, 166
Elements. *See also* Elemental breakdown
    constant, 48
    division of operation into, 45
    duration of, 48

    frequency of, 51
    infrequent (nonrun), allowances for, 164–165,
       168–170
    and time values, 51
    variable, 48
Equalizing quantity. *See* Break-even quantity
External work, 63, 64, 157–158

Facility selection. *See* Alternate facility selection
Fair day's work level, 21–22
Fatigue (rest) allowance, 58, 155–156, 157
Fein, Mitchell, 12
Frequency of elements, identification of, 51
Full absorption costing. *See* Whole ("full") absorp-
      tion costing

Gilbreth, Frank, 11
Gilbreth, Lillian, 11
"Good" production, 124
Graph, bar, 28

Historical data
    allowances in, 57
    in development of PS, 31–32, 124

Incentive plans, 22
    calculation of standard for, 159
    compared to MDW, 159–160
    cycle calculation for, 162–163, 167–168
    and fatigue allowance, 58
    output achieved by people on, 58
Incremental contribution, 148
Incremental fixed costs, 147–148
Incremental period costs. *See* Incremental fixed costs
Incremental profit, 148
Infrequent (nonrun) elements, allowances for,
      164–165, 168–170
Internal work, 63, 64, 157–158

Job cycles, 64
    calculation of, 162–163, 167–168
    number to be timed, 49
    time, vs. incentive pay, 164

Ladder study, 29–30, *31*
Leveling. *See* Performance rating
Loading, 146

Machine assignment, 171–172
    multiple, 61–63. *See also* Multimachine assignment
      analysis
Machine-hour-rate (MHR), 1, 4, 5
    and accept/reject decision, 131
    and actual time, 134
    and alternate facility selection, 151
    in capital expense decision, 147
    development of, 9–10
    in make-or-buy decision, 143–144
    procedure for developing, 133
    and standard time, 133